A2
Revise
PE
for
OCR

A2 UNIT 3 G453
Principles and concepts across different areas of Physical Education

by

Dennis Roscoe
Bob Davis
Jan Roscoe

A2 Revise PE for OCR
by
Dennis Roscoe
Bob Davis
Jan Roscoe

Jan Roscoe Publications

Text copyright to Dennis Roscoe, Jan Roscoe, Bob Davis.

Graphics copyright to Jan Roscoe Publications, Bob Davis.

Published as 978-1-901424-53-9 in 2009 by Jan Roscoe Publications.

'Holyrood'
23 Stockswell Road
Widnes
Cheshire
WA8 4PJ
United Kingdom

tel: +44(0)151 420 4446
fax: +44(0)151 495 2622
e-mail: sales@jroscoe.co.uk

A Catalogue record for this book is available from the British Library

ISBN   Published as 978-1-901424-53-9

Cover designs by Helen Roscoe.

Published via Adobe InDesign, Adobe Illustrator 9.0, Smartdraw 6.0

Printed and bound by

Poplar Services
Poplar House
Jackson Street
St Helens
WA9 3AP

tel: 01744 23363
fax: 01744 451242

www.poplarservices.com

INTRODUCTION

Examination courses in Physical Education have now become established within the post-16 curriculum and are a very popular and successful part of school, college or higher education.

This new edition has been written to address the change in content and style of the OCR A2 Physical Education syllabus which commenced in September 2009 (first examination 2010).

This Physical Education course is multidisciplinary in nature, and the A2 course requires you to make three choices from the areas of historical studies, comparative studies, sports psychology, biomechanics, and exercise and sport physiology. These subject areas have generated a substantial quantity of specialist literature each with its own specific language. At times you may be overwhelmed by the amount of material covered in such a one year examination course. 'A2 Revise PE for OCR' addresses the problem of dealing with copious notes by summarising the content of the subject matter and attempting to explain in simple language what are sometimes complicated concepts or issues. Practice questions are provided at the end of each chapter, with answers provided on a CD ROM. The answers will amplify the subject matter and provide clues as to how the exam itself should be approached. A new feature this time is the requirement that the final exam questions on each section of the syllabus shall include an essay type answer. This allows students to express their ability and knowledge in the context of properly written language (prose) with attention to grammar and punctuation.

Materials are presented in a concise and visual approach for effective and efficient revision. Modern terminology, nomenclature and units have been used wherever possible. At the end of the book there is a comprehensive index available for easy reference.

Note that the AS course provides the foundation for study of the A2 programme, so students need to refer to 'AS Revise PE for OCR' ISBN: 978 1 9014242 52 2 for background support.

HOW TO USE THIS REVISION GUIDE

The ideal use of this Revision Guide would be to purchase it at the start of the course and relate each of the summary pages to the specific areas of the syllabus as an aide memoire. The inclusion of specific questions and full answers (see below) provide a means of self-testing. Don't be tempted to find out the answers before attempting a question.

In reality, whole examination questions contain a much broader content than those given in this guide. Examiners will attempt to examine more than one small area of the syllabus within the context of one full question and therefore it is important that you revise all aspects of your selected options.

The main use of the Revision Guide should be during the final revision period leading up to your examinations, as it should help you to understand and apply concepts i.e. link summary content with examination question.

The aim of this book is to provide an aid that enhances syllabus analysis, and to raise your level of success in examinations.

ANSWERS TO QUESTIONS

The CD-ROM enclosed with this book includes answers to all the questions in the text by chapter. You will have noticed that the AS version of this book included the answers in the main text. Feedback from teachers tells us that students have a habit of looking at the answers before actually attempting to derive their own answers as part of the revision process. Hence, people will now have the option of removing or delaying the answers provided by us - to give students a chance to undertake the revision process properly. Note also that although our answers are presented in bullet format, some questions will require to be answered in prose format as mentioned above.

To access the information on the CD-ROM, if it does not autorun to bring up a list of chapters, then the main CD directory should be accessed from 'my computer' and the programme 'run.bat' double clicked. This will bring up the list of chapters. Each answer chapter is in pdf format.

THE QUALITY OF AUTHOR

We are an expert team of writers, who have considerable experience in teaching 'A' Level Physical Education, who have written past and current examination syllabuses, who have set and marked examination questions within this subject area and taught at revision workshops throughout the UK. Much of the material within this book has been thoroughly student tested.

We hope that this Revision Guide will prove useful to staff and students. Jan Roscoe Publications will welcome any comments you would wish to make about the book's utility or layout. Thank you for using our work.

Dennis Roscoe
Jan Roscoe

CREDITS

ACKNOWLEDGMENTS

We would like to thank Bob Davis for his co-operation and adherence to our demanding deadlines. We thank Pete Rich for his painstaking proofing of the text. We thank Poplar Services for their patience in linking our work to their computers, and JRP staff member Linda Underwood for working hard in the background while I put this book together. We thank Helen Roscoe for her contribution as cover designer and photographer and Lois Cresswell for her patience as photographic model. We thank members of the Belgian Olympic Athletics Squad for permission to use their images.

Dennis Roscoe
Editor

ACKNOWLEDGMENTS FOR GRAPHICS
Figure

3.7	Wikimedia Commons/GNU free documentation/Ian Thorpe
4.8	Wikimedia Creative Commons/Kelseye
4.7	Shutterstock/Albo
4.14	Shutterstock.com/Hanzrussell
4.17	Aldenham School
4.21	LTA Wimbledon
5.8	istockphoto.com/Toby Creamer
5.9	PGL
5.10	istockphoto.com/Purdue9394
7.4	Wikimedia Commons/Johnmaxmena (talk) John Mena
7.5	Wikimedia Commons/Joshua Massel
7.6	Wikimedia Commons/Nrbelex
7.8	Wikimedia Commons/Mathew Ingram
7.9	GNU free documentation/Einer Einarsson
7.11	GNU free documentation/Kvaran
8.7	Wikimedia Commons/GNU free documentation/User.MatthiasKabel
8.11	Wikimedia Commons/Bob Sandberg/ LOOK magazine
8.12	Wikimedia Commons/GNU free documentation
8.15	Wikimedia Commons/creative commons attribution/Share Alike3.0
9.1	Physical Education and the Study of Sport 5e, ISBN: 978 0 7234 3375 0
9.4	Wikimedia Commons/http://www.australianhistory.org/sport-ach.php
9.5	Wikimedia Commons/flickr user nellistc
11.2	Wikimedia Creative Commons/John the scone
12.5	Wikimedia Commons/Yann Caradec/Flickr
13.2	Getty Images/AFP/Stringer
13.4	Shutterstock/Vladmir Wrangel
13.6	Getty Images/David Rogers
13.9	Shutterstock/Albo
13.10	LTA Wimbledon
15.7	GNU free documentation/Richard Giles
17.2	Wikimedia Creative Commons 3.0/Jim Lamberson
17.9	Physical Education and the Study of Sport 5e, ISBN: 978 0 7234 3375 0
23.7	istockphoto/nikada
23.8	istockphoto/Ron Summers Damir Spanic
24.6	the stretching institute
24.12	istockphoto/Ed Hidden
25.3	istockphoto/Birgitte Magnus

Helen Roscoe is the author of the following graphics:
The front cover/4.3/11.9/13.11/19.2/19.13/21.1/23.2/23.4/23.5/24.2/24.3/24.4/24.5/26.10
All other graphics are by Helen Roscoe, Jan Roscoe, Bob Davis and Dennis Roscoe.

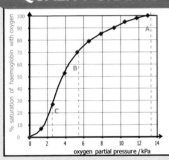

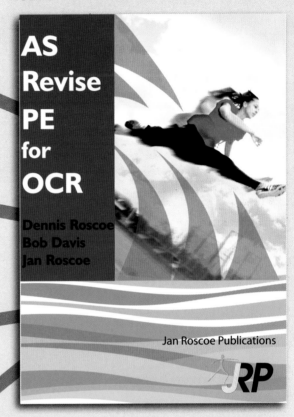

CONTENTS

A2 Revise PE for OCR
A2 UNIT 3 G453: Principles and concepts across different areas of Physical Education

SECTION A: SOCIOCULTURAL OPTIONS

UNIT 3 – OPTION A1

HISTORICAL STUDIES

UNIT 3 – OPTION A2

COMPARATIVE STUDIES

SECTION B: SCIENTIFIC OPTIONS

UNIT 3 –OPTION B1

SPORTS PSYCHOLOGY

UNIT 3 – OPTION B2

BIOMECHANICS

CONTENTS

SECTION A: SOCIO-CULTURAL OPTIONS

OPTION A1: HISTORICAL STUDIES

CHAPTER 1 – POPULAR and RATIONAL RECREATION

Popular recreation

It is important to understand the structure and function of popular recreation as it existed in pre-industrial Britain. Some of these recreations continued in rural society well after industrialisation, and others have been revived today as ethnic festival occasions.

The emergence of rational recreation was very much triggered by pupils and staff at upper middle class schools as they converted **mob** schoolboy sports into a controlled format. This controlled **athleticism** was seen to be a vehicle for desirable values and a way of life for respectable society.

Sport in pre-industrial England

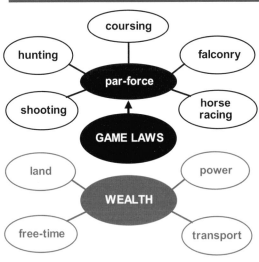

figure 1.1 – rural upper class pursuits

The rise of **aristocratic and popular sports in England** reflected the influence of the Roman conquest on the existing Ancient British Celts and subsequent waves of invaders including the Anglo-Saxons and Vikings. By the time of the Norman Conquest, many folk activities existed, but the Norman aristocracy imposed their own activities, which divided sporting pastimes into **aristocratic pursuits** and **folk games**. Aristocrats indulged in such pastimes as '**par force**' hunting, which combined most of the attributes of the killing of 'game', while the **folk games** emerged as religious festivals. These festivals were imposed on older pagan customs and became **holy day** celebrations and **wakes**. At this time, **violent annual mob games** existed in many towns and blood sports remained part of a cruel public ritual.

Many such activities continued until the end of the 19th century. In feudal times, **popular** sports were only possible with the sanction of the **clergy** and often the involvement of the landowners.

Rural upper class pursuits

The rural upper class (figure 1.1) had **power, land ownership** and **wealth** which allowed them to engage in activities (figures 1.2 and 1.3) controlled by the game laws as and when they liked without interference from the public. Gradually, aristocratic constraints were relaxed to include an emerging county gentry.

figure 1.2 – hunting as a sport?

figure 1.3 – falconry as an upper class pursuit

Popular recreations

The culture of the English lower classes before the late 19th century was linked with social conditions and formed the characteristics of their recreation and pastimes (figure 1.4) – in so far as there were any!

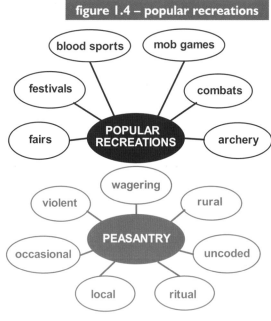

figure 1.4 – popular recreations

blood sports · mob games · festivals · combats · fairs · **POPULAR RECREATIONS** · archery

wagering · violent · rural · **PEASANTRY** · occasional · uncoded · local · ritual

- They were **occasional** because there was limited free time.
- They were **local** because there was limited transport.
- They were **uncoded** (figure 1.5) because the peasantry was often illiterate.
- They were **ritualised** because of the influence of older pagan and existing church influences.
- Any recreations of a sporting nature were often in the context of village fêtes or **fairs** held on holydays.
- The activities were often **violent and cruel** (figure 1.6), because life was hard and harsh at that time.
- **Wagering** was a primary feature of life at this time, and wagers would be made on the outcome of any contest.

Many of these activities have survived both at an aristocratic and popular level, but many have been either curtailed or reformed. Nor is there the clean separation between the two groups (upper and lower classes) within our present democracy.

Among the **upper class sports**, coursing is pretty-well banned in this country, hunting is now legally restricted and shooting is strictly controlled.
- Popular recreations like **baiting** have long since been made illegal.
- **Festivals** are more respectable.

figure 1.5 – mob football as a lower class pursuit

figure 1.6 – bull baiting, brutal but exciting

figure 1.7 – archery as preparation for war?

- **Archery** (figure 1.7) has changed from military combat practice to a codified target sport.
- And **mob football** has only survived in rural areas which escaped the impact of reform.

The **socio-cultural influences** which brought about the evolution of the various pastimes of the middle ages are summarised in figure 1.8.

The changes which led to modern versions of existing sports will be explained later with the focus on the mid 19th century development of **public school athleticism** and **rational sport**.

Emergence of rational sport as a product of the industrial revolution

Changes in society

The development of **physical education** and **sport** reflected changes in British society. Hence we place **social and cultural** changes in the context of elitist **institutions** like the **English public schools**.

The major changes which occurred in society influenced participation in sport today. We will now discuss how society changed during the period over which the industrial revolution occurred, as it influenced **development and change** in English institutions.

The early 19th century marked the beginnings of **three social revolutions** in England:

- The **agrarian revolution** (figure 1.9) which involved the gradual movement of workers from the countryside to the larger towns, caused by:
  - The emergence of a **gentry** class.
  - The **enclosure** of much of the countryside.
  - The growth of the **Methodist** movement.
  - The gradual increased significance of **respectability** in early Victorian society.
  - The **poor wages** of the rural working class.
  - The gradual **mechanisation** of tenant farms.

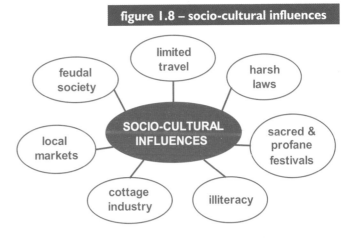

figure 1.8 – socio-cultural influences

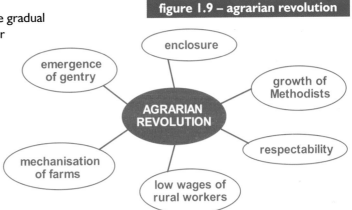

figure 1.9 – agrarian revolution

- This latter point was also a reflection of the **industrial revolution**, which gave increased power to the middle classes, better wages for the industrial working class and greater prosperity for the country at large.
- The **urban revolution**, which marked a massive rise in the population, as industrial and commercially well-placed towns grew in size and national significance.

Popular and rational recreation

These two strands of development towards modern sport had the characteristics identified in figures 1.10 and 1.11.

Popular and rational recreation are not totally different. They both involve **physical activity**, they are both **competitive** and they are both **enjoyable** and **fulfilling**. They both have features of **ritual** and **festival** and both have elements to be seen in modern sport.

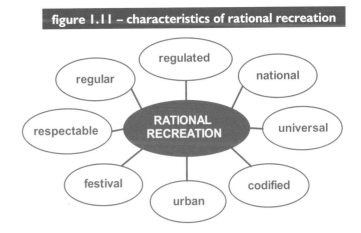

figure 1.10 – characteristics of popular recreation

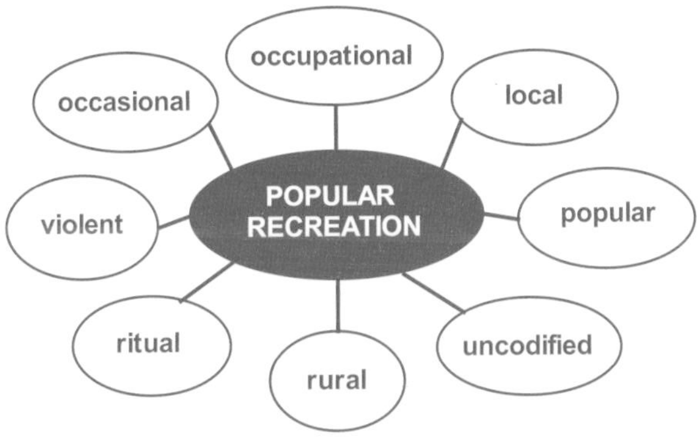

figure 1.11 – characteristics of rational recreation

Table 1.1 – **the cultural factors which influenced the conversion of popular sports into rational sports**

popular	rational
agrarian	industrial and urban
feudal	emergent middle class
limited travel	railways
illiterate	elementary education
cottage industry	factories
payment in kind	wages
limited free-time	regular free-time and the Saturday half day
markets	shopping centres
harsh laws	law and policing
church festivals	muscular Christianity - athleticism
fields and rivers	parks and baths

The effects of industrialisation on the development of rational recreation

Industrialisation had the effect of improving three major **developmental** factors in society, these were:

*   **Communication**, the sporting press (rather than just current affairs) was established, receiving results quickly kept spectators interested in their favourite sport, and newspapers were transported by rail.

figure 1.12 – 1859 - excursion to Brighton for 3s 6d

*   **Transport**, better transport meant fixtures could be played in different towns thus leagues and competitions became more developed. Factory owners would arrange excursions to the coast (figure 1.12), hence workers' morale was maintained. Rail travel was vastly improved with the arrival of steam power, hence spectators and racehorses could be transported to different events. Also, as cycling grew more popular, road improvements were demanded.

*   **Technology**, clothing was made by machines in the mills, and sport specific clothing and footwear became available. More sophisticated timing devices (stop watches) and other sport equipment (balls, racquets, athletic equipment) made sport more fair and more competitive. Printing presses were used to produce the popular press as literacy amongst the working class improved. The electric telegraph meant results of games could be distributed faster, to more places.

Negative effects on sport of urbanisation and industrialisation

*   There was less open land-space for pre-industrial games to take place.
*   Transport from towns to the country was poor which deterred country based people from travelling in order to participate.
*   Long working hours in factories decreased leisure time.
*   Low wages meant that there was little disposable income available for participation in sport.
*   Women and children were used as cheap labour.
*   Workers were too tired for leisure activities.
*   The 12 hour working day meant that it was dark before and after work in the winter months.

The development of professional sport

Popular recreation is normally centred on the **lower classes**, with **aristocratic** or **gentry** sports co-existing alongside peasant sports. Normally, **patronage** by the gentry not only determined whether the popular activities and **festivals** flourished in a community, but it was also why they were allowed to continue well after levels of industrialisation and urbanisation had increased.

The key factors were:
- The significance of **wagering and possible corruption**.
- The **limited free time** available to the urban lower class and agricultural labourers.
- The **minimal pay** for workers who were on the bread-line.
- The **lack of transport** except for the wealthiest classes.

As a result, the **occasional festival** and fair offered the chance to **earn money prizes** through sporting competition to young people with talent and bravery. If they were good enough, they could increase their income by travelling to different fairs and wakes to compete in combat sports like single stick play and wrestling or running events. In addition to prize money, there was always **wagering** where you could risk money on backing yourself to win or lose!

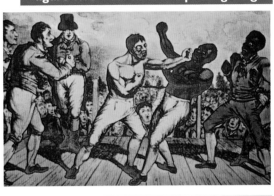

figure 1.13 – bareknuckle prizefighting

The prize fighter

Prize fighting is chosen as an example because it involved **professional** performers by the end of the 18th century. The sport gave the opportunity to win large sums of money, and even more through wagering. This involved the upper class and the peasantry in a partnership in which high standards were achieved. Pedestrianism followed similar lines, see page 25 below.

figure 1.14 – Figg and Broughton

Prize fighting

Prize fighting (figure 1.13) dates back to the 13th century when there were gladiatorial schools, relics of the Roman Conquest, where individuals were prepared to defend themselves and compete in 'sword and buckle' contests. When **Jack Broughton** (figure 1.14) became champion, he changed the rules of the prize ring to establish **pugilism**, limiting the contest to **bare-knuckle** punching and throws. The tradition of teaching the gentry resulted in '**sparring**' being developed and '**mufflers**' (the precursor of modern boxing gloves) for protection.

This is the context within which the notions of amateurism became an issue which looked at the intrinsic worth of a sporting activity following developments in the 19th century public schools.

Amateurism and professionalism in the 19th century

- The distinction between amateurs and professionals in so far as sport is concerned was mainly on a class basis.
- In cricket, the 'gentlemen' were the amateurs who played for the fun, the 'players' were professionals - usually employed by the gentlemen.
- 'Players' started as the employed groundsmen who prepared the pitches, but also played for the teams.
- This was deemed the correct way of paying professional players in what was essentially an amateur sport.

- In rugby, it was expected that players would not be paid and were therefore amateur.
- This changed in 1895 when the Rugby League was formed, but Rugby Union remained amateur until 1995.
- Soccer became a professional sport in 1885, because players were mostly working class.
- Athletics, swimming and rowing remained strictly amateur until the 1980s.
- Tennis had both amateur and professional factions until the 1950s, when the Lawn Tennis Association (LTA) and Wimbledon began to pay winning players, and the sport was unified.

Female sport in the 19th century

- Historically, sport was a male pastime. Sport had evolved from violent activities undertaken by males in connection with the need to prepare for war (fencing, jousting, stave fighting, archery, wrestling and fist fighting), and since hunting and horse riding were gentry pastimes, women tended not to be involved until later.

Female sport

- The middle classes did not expect their wives to work, but increasingly they were allowed to play as long as the activities were private and genteel. As a result croquet, lawn tennis and golf were acceptable.
- Working class women did not generally have the time, money or provision for sport until the end of the 19th century.

Victorian attitudes to women led to females being excluded from rational sport on the grounds that:

- It was too manly.
- It could endanger childbirth.
- Victorian fashion, among upper and middle classes (restrictive clothing), prevented freedom of movement and so discouraged women from vigorous activity.
- It was not expected that Victorian women should display their bodies.
- Or be competitive and sweat!

Practice questions

1) Describe the link between the local festivals and the Church in popular recreation and explain how church attitudes changed during the 19th century.   4 marks

2) Making use of the illustrations in figures 1.15 and 1.16, explain why you would expect popular recreations in the early 19th century to be harsh and cruel and suggest how this was gradually reduced.   5 marks

figure 1.15 – mob football as a lower class pursuit

figure 1.16 – bull baiting, brutal but exciting

3) Outline the main differences between popular and rational recreation in the 19th century and give some reasons why rational recreation largely replaced the older approach.   6 marks

4) What were the main characteristics of popular recreations in England before the development of rational sport? Give examples of activities where you can.   4 marks

5) a)   Describe the characteristics of popular recreation and discuss the socio-cultural factors which determined them.
                                                                                                                   8 marks

   b)   Discuss the changes which occurred in 19th century British society and the effect these had on the most popular sports and games by 1900.   10 marks

6) Describe and explain the effect that the Industrial Revolution had on sport after 1800.   5 marks

7) Some popular recreation festivals have survived into the 21st century alongside modern sporting occasions. Discuss the possible socio-cultural reasons for their survival and reform, highlighting what these rural festivals still have to offer today.
                                                                                                                  20 marks

8) Select an activity to describe the influence of a railway network on the development of regular sport in 19th century rational recreation.   4 marks

9) What were the main effects on sport of an emergent urban middle class in the mid-19th century?   5 marks

10) Rational recreation reflected changes in social class and gender opportunities in the 19th century. Discuss this and explain how the Sport for All policy is an extension of this today.   20 marks

CHAPTER 2 – The IMPACT of NINETEENTH CENTURY PUBLIC SCHOOLS

Nineteenth century public schools and athleticism

figure 2.1 – public schools

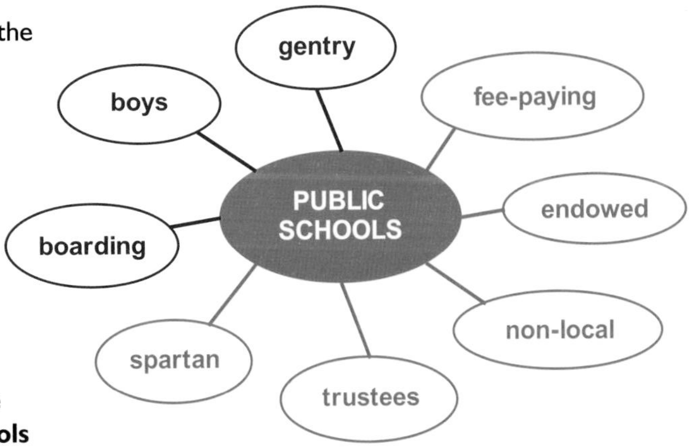

The **characteristics** of the 19th century public schools included the facts that they were for the **sons of the gentry** and they were **boarding**, **fee paying**, and **non-local** establishments (figure 2.1).

- The non-local feature of these schools was very important in that the developments that occurred in the schools became spread across the nation.
- There were also scholars from poorer families and by the 1870s the number of schools had increased to accommodate an emergent middle class.

Nine of these schools increased in size and were identified in the **Clarendon Report** (1864) and later called the **Barbarian Schools** by Matthew Arnold. These **Clarendon Schools** are Eton, Harrow, Charterhouse, Westminster, Winchester, Rugby, Shrewsbury, St. Paul's and Merchant Taylors. The first **seven** of these were boarding schools (known as EHCWWRS) and were at the centre of a later expansion of boarding schools as middle class copies appeared throughout the country.

- There was a delay before similar selective high schools emerged for **upper and middle class girls**.
- By the end of the nineteenth century, there was public or grammar school access for wealthy and bright boys and girls. The schools had an active policy of **athleticism** (**goodness**, **manliness**, **restraint** and **discipline**). Other reforms also occurred such as a broader curriculum, reduced flogging, and control of school sport by the Sixth Form.

Public school definition

- A definition of such a school is '**an endowed place of old standing to which the sons of gentlemen resort in considerable numbers and where they reside for eight or nine years to eighteen years of age**'.
- The characteristics of these schools are identified in the model (in figure 2.1), where each component had a positive effect on the growth of athleticism.

Athleticism

Athleticism was originally defined as '**a muscular Christian view of manliness reflecting physical endeavour and moral integrity**'. By the end of the 19th century, athleticism had become so popular that some authorities felt that it was undermining other educational values. Hence a second critical definition was given as '**the exultation and disproportionate regard for games, which often resulted in the denigration of academic work and in anti-intellectualism**'.

The growth of this movement is best broken up into **three stages**.

figure 2.2 – cricket in an early girls' academy

Stage one – schoolboys' recreations

- There is a link between developments in the schools and changes in society. At the beginning of the 19th century, communications were limited to carts, stage coaches and wagons. Only the **very wealthy** had the **time, money** and **transport** to travel any distance.
- As a result they were the only people with the tradition of sending their sons to boarding schools. It is important to mention that at this time the daughters of the very wealthy either had governesses or went to **academies** near to home (figure 2.2).
- **Recreations** within this first stage followed local folk customs and practices.
- With game laws in place, hunting and shooting were controlled by the upper classes, and traditional festivals were held in the towns and villages on occasional **holy days** and chartered fair days.
- The upper class played a courtly role and the lower classes made the most of a festival day, which of course was a day off from the grind of work.

Stage one

The **boys** therefore took local **folk activities to school**, so that there were regular fights, mob games (figure 2.3), cricket (of course), swimming in the river or open pools, and boating. Very few schools had hounds, so the young boys became the **hares** and the seniors chased them labelled as **hounds**. This was the basis of the '**boy culture**' within which these schools flourished.

figure 2.3 – mob games

Stage two – Arnold and Christian gentlemen

By 1830, a **new breed of headmasters** were **reforming** their schools and starting to link Christianity with the Ancient Greek model of **Mind, Body and Spirit**. They chose to link the energy identifiable in the games and sports with education. The Headmaster would have led the revised programmes, with prefects and junior members of staff establishing basic rules. House matches allowed healthy, social competition.

Social control (figure 2.4) was an important objective of this process. It was an attempt to reduce the bullying and lawlessness in the schools and the effect of the boy culture outlined above. Dr Thomas Arnold is known to have led this reform, but much of his reputation comes from the book Tom Brown's Schooldays, rather than research evidence. In the eyes of Arnold and others, the **desire to produce Christian gentlemen** was central and the moral code of **fair play** was introduced at this level.

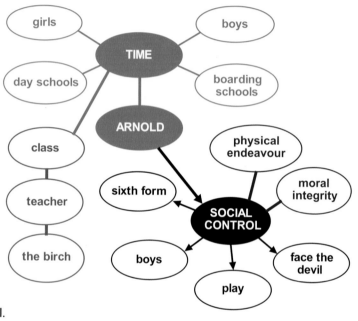
figure 2.4 – Arnold and social control

Stage three – Corinthian athleticism and the emergence of rational recreation

With more regular play of games and sports, **written rules** were established. But because this was an internal programme, each school devised its own version of rules depending on the facilities available. Only the game of **cricket** had a set of **universal rules** across several different schools throughout the country at this time. **Football** and **fives** rules were different in each school. **Swimming** was popular wherever there were lakes, ponds or rivers available, as in the Duck Puddle bathing pool at Harrow (figure 2.5).

At Eton, **boating** was encouraged instead of swimming in the Thames, but Shrewsbury and Eton established safety rules that only those boys who could swim, could row.

As the schools and society changed to meet the energy and reforming zeal of Victorian England, so the lesser gentry and **industrial middle class** presumed the right to public boarding school education. They were not allowed into the Clarendon Schools and so they built new ones. These new schools had extensive sports facilities, were built in attractive spa towns and other wealthy areas, and were linked by the new **railway** system.

Middle class developments

*   The middle classes were not only wealthy and industrious, they wanted the status previously reserved for the gentry and they felt that the **public schools** would at least give that to their sons.
*   Meanwhile, with some upper class women gaining access to Oxbridge, these women opened boarding schools for their daughters (figure 2.6).
*   This was eventually taken up by the middle class with a **girls' high school** opening in every major town.

figure 2.5 – the Harrow School Duck Puddle

Sport in public schools

Sport in public schools was now **widespread**, as teachers moved schools to obtain headships and took the notion of sport as part of a school with them. But certain idiosyncrasies remained, such as soccer and rugby having separate codes and fives having several versions. **Regular play** and **written codes** evolved as senior boys continued with sport at the **universities** and, as **old boys**, they continued to encourage athleticism in their old school and in amateur sport.

- For example, a group of **university graduates** discussed the rules of football. They accepted the divide between the two codes of association and rugby, and established the **governing bodies** of the Football Association (FA) in 1863, and the Rugby Football Union (RFU) in 1870.

- The notion of the **gentleman amateur** continued, while several games had acknowledged the place of the **professional** performer.

- In **cricket** and **association football**, the professional player and club were controlled by middle class administrators, who accepted the code of **physical endeavour and moral integrity** as the basis of all modern games and sports. Hence the nineteenth century public schools had a major part to play in the development of most modern day sports and games.

Some cultural changes, such as working class free time, elementary education and the emancipation of the lower class female, took more time. But the cultural changes were under way, and perhaps sport led the way.

Girls' schools started with callisthenics and girls also played organised games based on similar principles to the boys. Established men's games were generally avoided. The girls played **hockey** and **lacrosse** (figure 2.6) in the winter and **lawn tennis** in the summer, but cricket was often limited to junior girls.

Spreading the message

With the lead coming from university graduates, there was a focus on the things men had learnt at school and university. These men were experienced **all-round** sportsmen, often getting 'blues' in several sports at university. They formed **elite clubs** (for example, Leander for rowing and the Corinthians for cricket and soccer), setting a high standard of sportsmanship. This process was the basis of early **amateur governing bodies** and the birth of **rational recreation**.
See figure 2.7 for an outline of the factors affecting the birth of rational recreation via the public schools.

The next step

In turn, young men drawn from the middle classes went back to their factories, commercial businesses and schools. There, they set up clubs for children, friends and salaried workers. This expansion led to benevolent businessmen forming **social and sports clubs** for their **workforce**. With this impact **physical education** was carried into grammar schools and later into primary and secondary comprehensive schools.

All this development reflected the improved wage structure for working men and the **provision** of town sports facilities. Specialist teacher training colleges were set up where physical educationists were trained.

The code set by the governing bodies held true to the amateur ethic until the last 30 years, when they reluctantly allowed amateur rules on financial aid to be revoked. Today, **professionalism** has taken over the status of most sports.

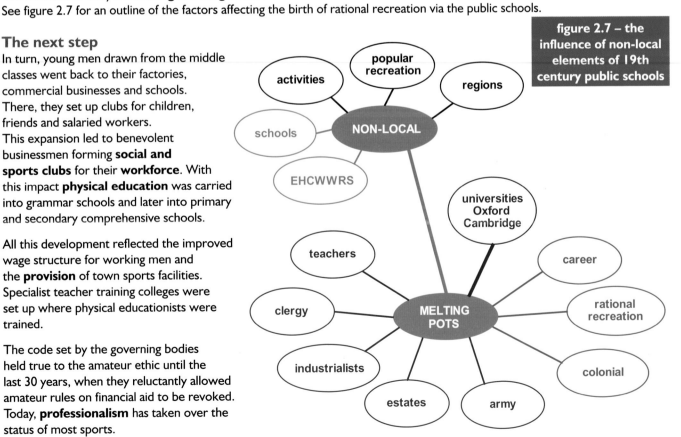

Fair play, sportsmanship, gamesmanship and cheating

Nevertheless, governing bodies continue to also represent grass roots development which has remained amateur. However, with media coverage showing regular examples of **gamesmanship and cheating**, it is increasingly difficult to maintain the importance of **sportsmanship** in sport. In spite of this trend in society, the teaching of **fair play** is still a basic principle underlying the role of sport in society.

The role of ex-public schoolboys in the development of rational sport

Activity development

We can use examples of different activities to **explain** how development occurred. The main popular example is of **mob football** which tended to differ in each school:

- Eton played a field game and a wall game.
- Rugby School played a handling game.
- Harrow and Charterhouse played a so-called dribbling game.
- Local conditions (the availability of large grassy areas or pitches, and whether or not the areas were bounded by fences or walls) at each school largely determined these differences.

When the boys left school for **Oxford or Cambridge** Universities, they had already established an acceptable combination of the rules in public schools to produce a **set of rules** which allowed them to play at their university college. From there it was necessary to produce unified rules and a stringent organisation for competitions **between** university colleges, and finally a set of rules for **inter-varsity** games and contests, with the reward of **blues** for representation.

A large number of these boys returned to teach in the public schools after graduation, and spread the new rules to the next generation of schoolboys. Hence inter-school matches (figure 2.8) and competitions were held according to the new unified rules, and the word was spread.

The gentleman amateur

- The university college competition structure and the inter-varsity structures remained an elite development and represented the foundation of the **gentleman amateur**. When graduates left university, they entered various careers including industry, the church and the army, and they took their amateur sport with them throughout Britain and the Empire.

figure 2.8 – inter-school cricket by 1851

- Hence **cricket** was the first sport to be taken by former **Oxbridge** students into the British Empire.

- They initially promoted it amongst themselves, **expanded** to take in the middle classes in their community, and finally took amateurism to the working classes as a **reforming vehicle**. Hence it became **respectable** for the middle and working classes to participate in the new games and sports, since it was what the upper classes spent their time doing!

- As the schools and society changed to meet the energy and reforming zeal of Victorian England, so the lesser gentry and **industrial middle class** presumed the right to public boarding school education.

The notion of the **gentleman amateur** continued throughout the nineteenth century in some sports, but **governing bodies** gradually reformed their rules to change the class and gender **definition of amateurism** to a regulation based on **no financial gain**.

Meanwhile, towards the end of the 19th century, several games had acknowledged the place of the lower class **professional performer**, especially in cricket and association football.

STUDENT NOTE

The crucial point concerning this 'amateur' period was the element of purity of the morality of competition with others on an equal basis. This was to be unsullied by payment, wagering or corruption. Therefore participation had to be only by those who could afford to perform without payment, and who were the wealthy members of an upper or middle class in society.

Practice questions

1) How was the 19th century class system in the UK reflected in the development of cricket?   5 marks

2) What do you understand by the terms codified, regulated, and respectable in relation to rational recreation?   6 marks

3) Discuss the changing attitude to sport in the elite 19th century public schools and its effect on the emergence of amateur sport in the UK.   14 marks

4) What influence did 'non-local' admission to the public schools and universities have on the development of rational sport?   6 marks

5) Discuss the term 'athleticism' as interpreted in 19th century Britain, and its influence on modern day sports.   4 marks

6) Why were Oxford and Cambridge Universities able to make such an impressive contribution to elite sport in the late 19th century?   6 marks

7) a)   Explain why the social changes during the industrial revolution of the 19th century led to the formation of National Governing Bodies.   3 marks

   b)   Describe the role that National Governing Bodies play in the organisation of sport.   4 marks

8) Participation in sports and games was a key feature of 19th century public schools.
Describe three factors which lead to increased participation in physical activity by young people in public schools in Stage three of development (the 'cult' of athleticism). How do these factors continue to impact upon participation and performance in physical activity in schools today?   9 marks

9) Explain the developmental changes which took place in rational recreation during the second half of the 19th century.   6 marks

10) Briefly explain the introduction of popular recreations into gentry public school play time, using one activity as an example.   4 marks

11) What were the effects on 'boy culture' when Heads developed a level of social control of physical activities?   5 marks

12) What is meant by the term 'melting pot' in connection with 19th century public school athleticism?   6 marks

13) Explain the emergence of physical endeavour and moral integrity in 19th century public school athleticism and discuss the issues which threaten it in today's sport.   20 marks

CHAPTER 3 – CASE STUDIES – BATHING/SWIMMING and ATHLETICS

> **STUDENT NOTE**
>
> For each case study you should be able to analyse the activity as popular recreation, and assess the influence of nineteenth century public schools on the development of the activity. You should be able to demonstrate knowledge and understanding of the activity as rational recreation, and of both participation and barriers to participation in the modern day activity.

Bathing and swimming

figure 3.1 – bathing as recreation?

Bathing and swimming as popular recreation

Historically, many towns were situated at **river crossings** or large meandering rivers, because the river provided necessary living requirements for defence against intruders, sanitation (for washing and bathing), communication (boats and bridges), and recreation facilities (figure 3.1).

This was how bathing as a part of **popular recreation** developed. Young people (mostly) played and learned how to swim in rivers and pools, kept cool on long hot summer days and raced one another through the water.

Evolution of bathing

It had been the fashion to 'take the waters' since Roman times (the Romans were very keen on their baths), and towns were built around hot springs. Bathing in spa towns (figure 3.2) became a recreation for the middle and upper classes from Tudor times onward, and during the industrial revolution factory owners would escape to these facilities for recreation.

Seaside bathing in the 19th century (figure 3.3) became possible as travel (particularly by rail) became easier. Note the all-covering swimsuits worn, especially by the women.

| figure 3.2 – Bath as a spa town | figure 3.3 – seaside bathing |

Bathing and swimming in the 19th century public schools

Alongside other recreational and 'sporting' activities, bathing and swimming became a feature of those public schools which had access to lakes, ponds or rivers, for example, the Harrow School duck puddle (see figure 2.5 above on page 18 above).

Some schools (Shrewsbury and Eton for example) would only allow rowing in their nearby river if a pupil could swim, this was an incentive to learn how to swim - for safety reasons.

figure 3.4 – public baths from 1840

Bathing in industrial towns, beginnings of swimming as a sport

In 1734 the first open air swimming pool was built in London. Front crawl was introduced from Native American Indians from South America, first seen by Europeans in 1844. A version of this stroke was first used in races in Britain in 1873. Captain Webb first swam the English Channel in 1875.

There were increases in public baths (figure 3.4) following on from the **Public Baths and Washhouses Act** in 1840, which was aimed at improving the cleanliness of the smelly lower classes!

From 1850, prizes began to be awarded at local galas for swimming races usually won by professionals. These were usually swimming teachers who were employed to teach in the new baths.

figure 3.5 – women's fashion on the beach

Seaside bathing continued to be a popular pastime of this period. Women's clothing for swimming became very restrictive in the Victorian era, since respectability was essential even on the beach. Hence bathing costumes (figure 3.5) covered the body from head to toe.

Rationalisation of swimming

- In 1885, water polo was developed in public baths and then codified.
- In 1886, the Amateur Swimming Association (ASA) was formed and specifically excluded professional teachers of swimming. This was an example of the imposition of '**gentleman amateur ideals**' by the middle and upper class administrators of the period.
- In 1886 also, FINA (Federation Internationale de Natation Amateur) was formed as the international governing body. The first modern Olympic Games (Athens 1996) had 100m, 500m, 1200m freestyle races - for men only!
- In 1901, the Amateur Diving Association was formed.
- In 1912, the first swimming events for women were introduced in the Olympic Games. The image from 1912 (figure 3.6) shows how women's swimwear had become more streamlined. Note that the women swimmers at the games had to be accompanied by a female chaperone at all times (she is hiding on the right hand side of figure 3.6!).

figure 3.6 – women at the Olympics 1912

Swimming as a modern sport

Swimming has expanded enormously from 1912, with evolution of records, and gradual equalisation of numbers of events between men and women. Standards have become amazing as athletes have begun to train full time (figure 3.7). The opportunities for reward in 2010 are substantial, with sponsorship and full time professionalism being the norm for the top swimmers.

figure 3.7 – modern swimmers in shark suits

Further developments in the international arena are **open water races**, an increase in **triathlon** participation, and **synchronised swimming**.

The UK also has had substantial success with double gold medallists Rebecca Adlington, and Eleanor Symmonds at Olympic and Paralympic levels.

Recent developments of the technology of the sport

The **shark suit** dilemma developed in 2009. At the 2009 World swimming championships, almost every race produced a World record swim (from 50m fly to 1500m freestyle). The suits being used (figure 3.7) were essentially wetsuits with characteristics which reduced drag when swimming. The suits have been banned from the end of the 2009 season - will World performances fall?

Pool development includes deck level pools with anti-splash channels, variable depth floors, flumes for training and fun, wave machines in leisure pools, and hydrotherapy jetting and jacuzzis. All this is aimed at increasing participation.

Increase in participation in the UK

The 2009 UK government policy to reduce obesity and increase participation included **free access** to public baths for under 16s and over 60s on an optional basis for the councils who own the baths.

There has also been a big increase in the **private club provision** of baths for swimming and leisure. Most big hotels have a reasonably sized pool, and there are a number of private fitness centres, for example, Total Fitness, LA Fitness, Fitness First, JJB/DW Fitness Club, some of which have flumes, jacuzzis and pools.

Clean beaches (the blue flag award) are also aimed at increasing participation and safety on our coastline.

Role models (such as Rebecca Adlington, Eleanor Symmonds and Tom Daley, figure 3.8) have a big effect on participation.

Barriers to participation in swimming

*   **Obesity** acts as a self-fulfilling barrier to people's self-esteem, and some local councils have introduced special sessions for women, whose aim is to overcome this barrier.
*   There are also **ethnic issues** (Moslem women for example) in which body exposure would act as a barrier.
*   **Lack of provision** of pools in some small towns reduces opportunity for participation and therefore acts as a barrier.

figure 3.8 – Tom Daley, Beijing Olympian at 14 years of age

Athletics

The sport of athletics (track and field) encompasses a range of events which include running, jumping and throwing activities. These activities had differing origins, based on differing cultural developments within human society.

Popular recreation

Running became a part of human recreation as the time to indulge in such activities became available. The ancient Olympic Games, for example, included both the sprints (the diaulos, a once round the stadium race of about 400m depending on the size of the stadium), and endurance running (the dolichos, a race of about 1500 metres). Awards of recognition and status were given to the winners, but not usually cash prizes (see page 118 of 'AS Revise PE for OCR' ISBN: 978 1 901424 52 2).

The javelin was based on spear throwing which evolved alongside archery as a combat pastime. The discus evolved from the ancient Greek pastime found within the ancient Olympic Games.

English festivals of the 16th, 17th and 18th centuries organised to celebrate something or other (often religious, hence the days on which this happened were called **holy days**) included the following rural activities:
*   Wrestling, other combat pastimes such as stave fighting and archery, and pole climbing.
*   Tug-o-war.
*   Throwing the stone (brick/boot/haggis/hammer).
*   Ditch or wall jumping.
*   Foot racing (sprinting and endurance) and horse racing.
*   Smock races (figure 3.9) for the women.

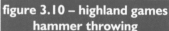

figure 3.9 – smock races for the women?

Jumping as sport began with the wall or ditch jumping mentioned above at holy day festivals or wakes. The pole vault was a part of some ancient Greek Games, and began in Britain as a way of clearing higher walls or wider ditches. There are still competitions held in Brittany for clearing ditches using a pole, which are part of an occasional festival popular activity.

Stone **throwing** evolved from the highland games activity. The use of metal shot instead of stones was presumably because of the availability of shot from military usage.

Hammer throwing evolved from medieval pastimes (Henry VIII was known to throw a sledge hammer for fun) through highland games (figure 3.10), to an Olympic event (steel ball with wire) by 1904.

Some of these activities became the basis for future athletics festivals.

The more formal beginnings of running as sport occurred when prizes started to be given to the pedestrians of the 18th and 19th centuries in England.

figure 3.10 – highland games hammer throwing

Pedestrianism

The term **pedestrianism** referred to a group of mainly lower class individuals who earned part of their living by competing in certain sports **for money**. It was a forerunner of the term **professional**. One of the earliest examples of this was racing 'wager boats'. The most famous example was the Doggett Coat and Badge event involving Thames watermen coming out of apprenticeship (an early winner of which was Jack Broughton, pugilist).

figure 3.11 – gentleman v pedestrian

Members of the upper class used **footmen** on their coaches and these footmen took part in **wager foot races**. These races eventually developed into **challenge events** over **long distances**, with **wagers** being made on the result or on the 'walker' completing a self-imposed task successfully.

Wagering

In 1800, **Captain Barclay** completed 1000 miles in 1000 hours. There was so much money to be won that wealthier athletic young men took up these challenges, although many events had a circus element and were open to **corruption**.

figure 3.12 – hare and hounds

Even though amateur sport was emerging, these professional contests continued well into the 1870s with an American athlete, **Edward Payson Weston**, coming to England and completing 2,000 miles in 2,000 hours.

- As with the prize ring, pedestrianism **attracted huge crowds**.
- There was a great deal of **wagering** at each stage of the race.
- The gentry were only too prepared to bet on men as well as horses at this time.
- The professional walkers and runners were managed by businessmen and considerable **commercialism** was involved.
- The **gentry** were also willing to test themselves by **competing against a pedestrian** in public arenas (figure 3.11).
- This marked the age of the **Corinthian gentlemen**, prior to the emergence of public school athleticism.

The public schools

Running and racing games were developed in the public schools during this period, for example:

- Hare and hounds (from Tom Brown's Schooldays 1850, figure 3.12).
- The steeplechase (cross country races over barriers, figure 3.13).

figure 3.13 – steeplechase 1850

Both these activities simulated equestrian sports which the young men at the schools would be familiar with. They took place in the school grounds and so were confined to the facilities available (similar to the evolution of football discussed on page 20 above).

Codification and 19th century public school developments

School sports days began to be held which included running, jumping and some throwing activities. Parents were invited and school governors were there to present the prizes. These were occasions at which a school could be presented at its best. The competitions were organised on a house basis with teams from each house, and each house had to furnish participants for each event (volunteers were required for the less popular events!).

Athletics as rational recreation

From the **Oxford and Cambridge** Universities **melting pot** of ex-public schoolboys, competitions began to be held at the universities and rules began to be established as to:

- Distances to be run and height of barriers (hurdles and steeplechase).
- Track sizes and shapes.
- Jumping events (originally included standing high jump and long jump).
- Throwing implements' shapes and weights, and size of throwing area (from which implements would be thrown).
- Conditions of events (heats and finals in the track events, how many rounds in the field events).

Athletics as rational recreation

- **Exeter College, Oxford** held the first recognised 'Athletics' meeting in 1850.
- The Amateur Athletic Club (AAC) was formed in 1866 but excluded the working class.
- AAC championships were held for example at Stamford Bridge (figure 3.14) in about 1870.
- The **Amateur Athletic Association** (AAA) was formed in 1880 and became the National Governing Body and held National Championships.
- 1896 saw the inception of the modern Olympic games, and the international appeal of track and field athletics.
- The AAA redefined amateurism as 'not for financial gain'.
- **Women's** Amateur Athletics Association (WAAA) formed in 1922.

figure 3.14 – AAC championships 1870

The change from amateurism to professionalism in athletics

The gentleman amateur ideal was a strict role model for competitors between 1900 and 1950. Athletes would compete for the love of the sport, and few would adhere to a 'win at all costs' attitude.

figure 3.15 – Coe and Ovett in Moscow 1980

Training was seen as something to be done if there was time to do it, but not otherwise. This was until Paavo Nurmi, Emil Zatopek and Vladimir Kuts in the mid-part of the 20th century made it clear that success came from the number of miles run in training and not natural ability alone.

Amateurism was strictly adhered to until around 1975. The rules included the fact that you could not compete if you made a living from sport as a sports journalist, as a professional player in another sport (for example Rugby League), or as a professional coach in athletics or another sport. The rules also banned the receiving of payment for newspaper articles about sport or issues connected with sport.

Athletes were given a lifetime ban from competing if they fell foul of these rules.

From 1981:

- **Amateurism was redefined** to allow payment in the form of trust funds to be held and administered by the BAAB - (the British Amateur Athletic Board, which administered sport for the whole of the UK).
- **Under-the-counter payments** (affectionately known as the brown envelope!) were made to competitors for competing in big continental meetings.
- Athletes were not allowed to portray sponsor logos on clothing while competing.
- But they were allowed to receive 'gifts' of clothing and shoes (a form of sponsorship).
- From 1980 following the Moscow Olympic Games, Sebastian Coe (gold 1500m) and Steve Ovett (gold 800m) were the first British competitors (figure 3.15) who made their living from the international athletics circuit.

figure 3.16 – Loughborough University HIPAC

Opportunities for participation 2010

- **Opportunities** for participation in athletics depends on the availability of facilities.
- **Provision** of track and field facilities (tracks) expanded in two phases. During the 1930s when councils built many cinder tracks in parks and schools, then after 1970 as Local Authorities (Councils) built all-weather (rubber based) tracks in most towns.

- Most schools would have a grass track and basic field event facilities (including a sand landing pit for the high jump!).
- City schools tend to use council tracks.
- Nowadays, this has expanded further with the advent of lottery funding, and the establishment of HIPACs (High Performance Athletic Centres) or HUBs in 12 locations in the UK (figure 3.16).
- **Lottery funding and prize money** now supports elite athletes such as Jessica Ennis (World heptathlon champion 2009) and Dame Kelly Holmes (800m and 1500m champion, Athens Olympics 2004).
- Relatively **cheap access** to nationwide track facilities, free coaching and a traditionally strong club structure, attracts all.
- **Sports Hall Athletics** provides a nationwide opportunity for all primary and secondary pupils to compete indoors in team competitions that involve running, jumping and throwing events.
- Participation levels have improved dramatically as interest, general health needs and sponsorship have created **media-supported** road running events such as the London Marathon and Great North Run.
- **Fell running** (running and racing over upland country where the gradient climbed is a significant component of the difficulty) has also increased in popularity.
- Middle distance running is a key component of sports such as **triathlon** and modern pentathlon.

Barriers to participation
- On the downside, barriers to participation include the effects of high profile **drug scandals** created by Ben Johnson (1988) and Dwain Chambers (2003).
- The pressure of the **short summer term** and conflict with annual examinations reduces the time available in schools for track and field athletics.
- **Poaching young talent into team games** is a major factor. For example, big potential throwers are attracted to team games such as rugby.

Practice questions

1) Tell the story of the development of organised bathing from public schools to urban public baths and compare this with competitive swimming today. 20 marks

2) The development of rational recreation was very much the result of Britain becoming an industrialised society.
   a) Using figure 3.14 opposite, explain the characteristics of an AAC Athletics Meeting. 4 marks

   b) Describe amateurism as it concerned Track and Field Athletics towards the end of the 19th century. 4 marks

3) Explain the transition from folk festivals and pedestrianism to amateur athletic sports, comparing this with athletics today. 20 marks

CHAPTER 4 – CASE STUDIES – FOOTBALL, CRICKET and TENNIS

Football

figure 4.1 – 17th century town mob game

Popular recreation

As mentioned on page 11 onwards and figure 1.5, rural mob games were played during fairs and wakes in and between villages across medieval England. These games were held on holy days like Shrove Tuesday, May Day, and Whitsuntide (and therefore were **not regular** or frequent). Games were played mostly by male members of the lower classes and were **violent** without many rules. Games often led to injury and sometimes death!

Town games (figure 4.1) were played with a similar lack of rules, but were probably even more violent.

Each town or village would have its own unique tradition of unwritten rules, and games were played according to custom. Most of the population could not read or write, so a verbal tradition of how to play the games was used, and there was very little formal publicity about games - word of mouth arranged the games.

figure 4.2 – the Eton wall-game

Developments in the 19th century public schools

- During the first half of the 19th century, boys from all over the country were sent to the Clarendon Schools by wealthy parents, bringing with them the various versions of mob games from their locality.
- These boys would play the games in their free time, then proceeded to develop a tradition within each school for a particular version of a mob game (usually football) which fitted in with the buildings and grounds of the school.
- This tradition led to rules being made from about 1850, as football became established in many schools, and head teachers began to use games as a way of keeping control over pupils.

figure 4.3 – Rugby's game from 1850

- As mentioned above (page 20), schools had different versions of football, for example a kicking and dribbling game at Charterhouse, the wall game at Eton (figure 4.2), and a handling (as well as kicking) game at Rugby School (figure 4.3) which had soft turf in 'The Close' where the game was played.

Rational recreation
- But when the schools needed to play between houses (within the school) or between different schools, rules needed to be agreed and written down.
- This was a process developed by the ex-public schoolboys at Oxford and Cambridge Universities (see page 20 above) as the melting pot within which many sports at that time were codified and transmitted to the population as a whole.

figure 4.4 – old-boys' association football

Codification of two games
- The **Football Association** was created in 1863 (hence association football - soccer), but a number of clubs in the London area withdrew from the association having disagreed with the proposed rules for the handling game.
- Hence two main strands of football emerged, with rugby football being established and fully codified as the **Rugby Football Union** in 1871.

Soccer

figure 4.5 – soccer in a **Northern industrial town**

- Although the rules were established by the sons of gentry (within the Oxbridge melting pot), the game originated as **mob football** as played by peasants and city working classes.
- This led to a separation of clubs in which southern teams were based around old boys from the public schools and Oxbridge, and were strictly amateur (figure 4.4), whereas northern teams were based around the working classes from the industrial towns (figure 4.5), with professionalism (players being actually paid).
- The **Football League** was established in 1885 to organise fixtures between city and southern teams.
- Saturday afternoons off work allowed men's soccer to develop, since the working class element developed a strong spectatorism.
- Inner city teams (Manchester City, Birmingham City, Nottingham Forest, Liverpool, Everton, Chelsea, Arsenal and Bristol City for example) were based around grounds placed within the major conurbations.

- The development of the **railways** meant that spectators could travel to away games.
- Some cities had Wednesday half days in shops and stores, and teams evolved to use this time (Sheffield Wednesday).
- This led to **mass support** of inner city teams, since the grounds were within walking distance of the working class back-to-back terraced housing of the early 1900s.

Lancashire and Yorkshire railway company Newton Heath Football Club

figure 4.6 – the Heathens in about 1880

This soccer club was founded in 1878 and based at Belle-Vue stadium Manchester (figure 4.6, notice the Belle-Vue circus park in the background). 'The Heathens' became a professional football team in 1885 and adopted its present name in 1902, Manchester United FC.

The club came from modest beginnings as a working men's social club - in 1886 the team won its first trophy, Manchester Senior Cup.
http://www.manchester2002-uk.com/sports/footballers5.html

Newton Heath Football Club's early fortunes did not fare well. By 1902 they were declared bankrupt, and only the efforts of full back, Harry Stafford, to raise the money to get them out of trouble saved the club. Stafford's fortunate meeting with local brewery owner, John Davies, resulted in Davies buying the club, paying off their debts, and initiating a fresh start for Manchester United.

Participation in football today
Traditionally, soccer has been a 'lads and dads' pursuit.

Factors that have helped participation are:
- Soccer provides **family entertainment**.
- Soccer provides a pathway from '**rags to riches**' within the UK's highly structured professional leagues.
- Academies have the sole purpose of **developing talent**.
- **Role models**, such as David Beckham, inspire young boys and girls to play.
- On the global stage, there are **prestigious events** such as the World Cup.
- The FA's **Respect** campaign combats issues such as racism and unacceptable behaviour.
- All that's needed is a ball, a space and unlimited players, so anyone can play.

Recent commercial developments
- In 2003, Roman Abramovich, the Russian oil billionaire, spent £200m to buy Chelsea Football Club and fund the biggest sports spending spree seen in Britain.
- There are hundreds of thousands of devoted fans who will spend thousands of pounds following their clubs. For example, a Chelsea season ticket-holder will pay £805 to sit in the Upper East Stand at the club's Stamford Bridge ground.

Rugby

From formation of the Rugby Football Union (RFU) in 1871, it was expected that players would not be paid and were therefore amateur. This changed in 1895 when the Rugby Football League was formed. But Rugby Union remained amateur until 1995.

The rugby split of 1895 - The 'Great Schism'

The Rugby Football Union (RFU) as national governing body refused to allow broken time payments (time away from work during which players would train or play rugby). They insisted on rugby being an amateur game. In 1895, 22 northern clubs got together and formed the Rugby Football League - in which payments would be allowed to players. Hence the formation of a professional game in which working class players could be paid for participating.

This split also led to **different rules** (13-a-side, the play-the-ball rule, scoring), and the formation of leagues. The RFU continued as amateur and so rugby union was played by middle/upper class men. Rugby union players played 'friendlies' (not league games) in which they played for the fun (in spite of the violence!). Friendships were cemented over many pints of beer in the bar after the game.

Rugby Union became professional in 1995, and welcomed Rugby League players into club and international sides. This was the beginning of the full-time player in the code.

Modern opportunities

Modern football with leagues, multi-million pound wages, transfers, nutrition, technological analysis of games, full-time professional coaches and managers in **both football codes**, provide an industry based on the commercialisation of sport. The opportunity for participation is therefore wide and not just dependent on talent at the games.

Alongside this are the provision of facilities or stadia (figure 4.7). The spectators who fund these sports have to be catered for with comfortable seating and clear sight lines to the play, all of which are expensive and add to the total ambience of the game as an industry.

figure 4.7 – the modern soccer stadium

Women's participation

Rugby was traditionally seen as a man's game, but some women decided they wanted some of the fun (figure 4.8), and started to play. The Women's Rugby Football Union (WRFU) was formed in 1983, with 12 founder member clubs. By 1992, 142 clubs were registered and the first national teams played, and by 1993, 2,000 women were playing. However, the north/south, working-class/middle-class orientation of men's rugby league and union respectively, is reflected in the women's game.

figure 4.8 – women's rugby flourishes

The Olympic Games in Rio de Janeiro in 2016 will have both men's and women's sevens Rugby as part of the programme.

In soccer:
*   Women played in the North of England from 1920, and achieved spectatorship of 50,000 in some matches. This was stopped by the FA in 1921 by banning women from playing in men's club grounds.

*   Women's participation in England expanded from 1971 (when the FA reversed their 1921 decision). The women's game is not as professionalised in the UK as in the USA.
*   Women's teams first appeared in the Olympics in Atlanta 1996.

*   Today has seen the massive development of the girls' game, from grass roots school/community level to semi-professional women's leagues and World Cup.

Barriers to participation

- **Less street football** due to increase in road traffic.
- **Smaller gardens** with modern houses means less room to kick a ball around or play touch rugby.
- Some school fields have been sold for housing and commercial developments, thereby reducing available facilities.
- **Parental work commitments** may impinge on time available to take children to clubs.
- **Armchair spectatorship** provides an easy option for people to watch and not perform.

Cricket

figure 4.9 – 18th century village cricket

Popular recreation

- In 1598 there was a written record of a game called 'creckett' or 'crickett' played as an evolution of target games (stoolball and rounders), played in the villages and hamlets of southern England. The first identifiable games were played on the South Downs (figure 4.9).

- By 1611 cricket had become an adult game, which was unfortunately considered illegal and immoral.
- Two men were arrested for playing the game on a Sunday rather than going to church.
- At the end of the English Civil War in 1648, the new government clamped down on recreational cricket that was played on Sundays.
- At this time cricket was played mostly by the working class and Sunday was their only opportunity to play.

Rational recreation and county cricket

Kent and Hampshire were the first counties to have clubs playing regularly in the eighteenth century, with Hambledon club the most famous village team. By the 1840s, the gentry employed **groundsmen as professional players**, county level competitions increased, and more **gentry played as amateurs**. There was a huge growth in gentlemen's county cricket clubs due to the All-England tour (see page 33 overleaf), and there was a large increase in the number of urban middle-class clubs and spectators.

The gentry were able to participate in cricket because it was **non-violent** and therefore posed no physical threat. The way the game was played was gentlemanly with respectable overtones, and it was played in the summer when light was at its best and people could play on long summer evenings (after work).

Women's participation

- Women also played in this pre-Victorian era and there was a thriving county championship for women (1811 Hampshire v Surrey - figure 4.10). The game became accepted in women's public schools (see page 17 above), and there was a famous women's match in 1745 in which Bramley (village) played Hambledon, which was reported in local papers.
- From figure 4.10 note the freedom of female opportunity prior to the Victorian period. Women had bare legs and unrestrictive clothing. Women then had the freedom to run about and get hot and sweaty!
- The first women's club was established in 1887, and the women's cricket association was formed in 1926.

figure 4.10 – 1811 women's cricket

England's women's team won the 2009 World cup, but did not acquire the financial rewards or kudos of their male counterparts. The media do not look favourably on women's sport in general, and give far less exposure to their exploits than relatively low quality men's sport.

Codification and development of the game

- The **first written rules** were drawn up by the Duke of Richmond in 1727 to control country house games on which large sums of money were wagered. Clubs pre-dated this codification - for example the White Conduit Club for gentlemen 1719, which became the MCC (Marylebone Cricket Club) in 1787.
- Cricket remained in the hands of the gentry, with the lower classes acting as 'players'. This led to an annual game between 'gentlemen' and 'players'.
- **County games** were generally played mid-week, making it necessary to give middle class players expenses. The saturdays partiicularly attracted large crowds, and led to the growth of venues like Lord's cricket ground and those in major county towns.
- **Professional leagues** like the Lancashire League, were created for working class players and spectators from the 1880s.

Developments in the 19th century public schools

Headmasters embraced the game of cricket because it was **codified**, **non-violent** and **respectable**. Inter-house and inter-school matches lasted all day, and so kept the boys out of mischief.

The All-England Tour

In 1846, William Clarke formed the All-England Eleven (figure 4.11) as a touring team of leading players to play matches at big city venues throughout the country, and as such spread interest in the game. Clarke's team was a top-class side worthy of its title. Some of these professional players became employed in public schools, and coached cricket to the boys. This spread expertise, and led to a higher level of cricket being played thoughout the country.

Matches were a huge success and very profitable, Clarke kept the surplus profit, and thus became the first cricket entrepreneur - the 19th century equivalent of Kerry Packer! (see below).

figure 4.11 – William Clarke's eleven in 1846

The Ashes

- On the 29th August 1882, an Australian team defeated the English team in a test match at the Oval. A week later a newspaper printed the notice in figure 4.12.
- Since then, when England and Australia play **test matches** at cricket, we say they are playing for the '**Ashes**'.
- The ashes were from the stumps used in the original game - which were ceremonially burnt.
- Afterwards they were stored in a wooden urn which has been kept in the Lord's Museum as a memorial of that occasion (figure 4.13).
- The debate remains as to whether, if Australia win a series, they have the right to hold the urn in their country.
- The argument against is that the urn is a memorial not a trophy.

figure 4.12 – the Ashes announcement

In Affectionate Remembrance
of
ENGLISH CRICKET
on
29th August, 1882
Deeply lamented by a large circle of sorrowing
Friends and Acquaintances
RIP
N.B. The body will be cremated and the Ashes
taken to Australia

figure 4.13 – the Ashes

Into the 20th century

The system of gentlemen and players (amateur and professional) in which amateurs played against paid professionals persisted into the 1960s. This reflected the **rigid social class system** of the time (different dress, changing rooms and entrances) which was gradually relaxed during this period until all the players at the top level became professional.

Cricket became the sporting symbol of the British Empire, and most present-day Commonwealth countries play the game.

- **Kerry Packer** was an Australian businessman who owned Austraila Channel 9 TV. Packer was best known for founding **World Series Cricket** in 1977 in opposition to the World cricketing authorities.
- He promoted players in coloured kit, playing with a white ball under floodlights (figure 4.14). Top players from several countries rushed to join Packer at the expense of their national sides.

- They played a **limited-over game** (started in England in 1963) - which was the forerunner of present one-day and twenty20 formats.
- This was **professionalism at its extreme** - as long as players were paid large amounts, they ignored the then international cricket authorities.
- The International Cricket Council (ICC) eventually had to concede to the new patterns of play, and incorporated them in the World Cup and most match series between nations.
- **Sky Sports** have had a big influence on the earning potential top players. Sky successfully bid for the TV contract for very important matches. For example, England games and the World Cup, which provided a big income stream for World cricket.

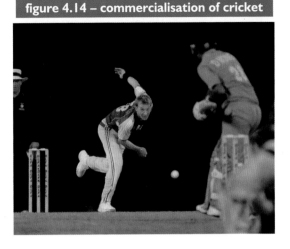
figure 4.14 – commercialisation of cricket

Participation in cricket today

Between 2008 and 2010 there has been a significant **increase in participation** in club cricket, estimated at a 50% annual increase for females and 25% increase for males.

Factors that have helped participation:
- From 2008 the ECB initiated a **£30million investment** in facilities, club development and supporting new initiatives such as '**Get into cricket**'. This investment is paying dividends in increasing the numbers participating in club cricket in England and Wales.
- **Academies** have the sole purpose of developing talent.
- England's Women's cricket team won the 2009 World cup, enhancing the status of the women's game, supported by **role models** such as the captain Charlotte Edwards.

figure 4.15 – jeu de paume, Real Tennis

Barriers to participation
- The pressure of the **short summer term** and conflict with annual **examinations** reduces the time available in schools to play cricket.
- **Public schools** are able to offer more opportunities in terms of facilities, professional coaching and fixtures when compared with state schools.
- At the elite end of the game, **Kolpaks** (cricketers within the EU who can play domestic cricket in England without being classified as an overseas player) provide a cheaper option and short term fix that is undermining the development of the ECB youth programmes.

Tennis

Real tennis (also called Royal tennis - figure 4.15) was a game which originated in France in the 12th century. It was played by royalty within the enclosed courts of the various palaces in which they lived.
The racquet was not introduced until the 16th century, before this the ball was hit by hand.
The Tudor monarchs of the early 16th century popularised the game, and in 1536, acts of parliament were passed to restrict the playing of this game in England to the nobility.

Rackets and fives as popular recreation

Apart from cricket the main striking game which evolved for the lower classes alongside real tennis was **rackets**.

This game involved striking a ball with a hand or racket **against a wall**. Opponents would take it in turns to hit the ball - sometimes there were 4 or 5 people on each side (striking in turn). The game was played in pubs, prisons (figure 4.16), and schools, where any wall could be adapted to play the game.

figure 4.16 – rackets played in 18th century prison

Development of rackets in the public schools

Fives was a variation of rackets in which a ball was struck against a wall normally with the hand. Some versions used gloves, others just bare hands. Courts were different in each place where fives was played, depending on the shape of the buildings. Two versions of this game survive today:

- **Eton fives** (figure 4.17) in an indoor court which looks like the buttressed and stepped courtyard in which the game was developed at the school.
- **Rugby fives** in a plain rectangular court.

figure 4.17 – Eton fives played on a school court

Squash (originally called 'squash rackets') is a development from both fives and rackets in 19th century public schools. It was played with a **squashy** ball with a racquet on a plain indoor court to help younger players enjoy the game.

Lawn tennis as a rational recreation

Lawn tennis was a game developed by the **wealthy middle classes** in the 19th century. It was played on their lawns (figure 4.18) within the privacy of walled gardens. The middle classes wanted a game to occupy increasing leisure time, hence the name 'lawn tennis'.

figure 4.18 – tennis played on 19th century lawns

Tennis as a vehicle for women's emancipation

- The nature of lawn tennis was seen to be particularly suitable for **middle class women**, to be able to play privately away from public gaze. This was a game which could remove some of the stereotypes.
- Women could run around becoming increasingly energetic, and clothing could become less restrictive. This was a stimulus for women's sport development.

The roots of modern lawn tennis

- 1866, Major Gem introduced the game at Leamington, and had written rules by 1870.
- 1873, J.H.Hales introduced Germain Tennis.
- 1873, Major Wingfield patented a game called Sphairistike, which had an hour-glass shaped court and could be purchased in a 'kit' form for playing on people's lawns.
- 1875, the modern rules were codified by the MCC (the Marylebone Cricket Club).
- 1876, the All-England Croquet and Tennis Club were founded at Wimbledon. Early tournaments were run by cricket clubs.
- 1884, public championships were held for women at Wimbledon.

figure 4.19 – Wimbledon 1920

Evolution of tennis

In 1900, the game was played on grass, whites were always worn, racquets were made of laminated wood with catgut strings, and Wimbledon represented the **middle class amateur** nature of the game (figure 4.19).

In 2010, the game is played on a **variety of surfaces** (grass, clay, concrete, indoor carpet) and most tournaments allow players to wear coloured and fashionable kit (figure 4.20).

There are also:
- **Special shoes** (the Rafa style).
- **Carbon fibre racquets** with a larger sweet spot and variation in stringing to give greater spin control.

figure 4.20 – top female players 1953 and 2009

- The Grand Slam, Wimbledon, Roland Garros, Australia, US open.
- The ATP and WTA masters rankings.
- **Rule changes** including the tie-breaker, Hawkeye challenges and instant replay.
- Professional players, physio and conditioning coaches, technical coaches, psychologists and managers.
- **Sponsorship** and substantial **prize money**, via the commercialism of the media, particularly satellite TV.
- Indoor/outdoor stadia, the Wimbledon roof (figure 4.21).

figure 4.21 – the Wimbledon roof 2009

Participation in tennis today

Around 3 million people throughout the UK are involved in tennis, but recent surveys have shown that there has been a substantial drop in the number of 11-19 year-olds who play tennis on a weekly basis.

Factors that have helped participation:
- Inspiration from **role models** such as Laura Robson and Andy Murray.
- Media hype around annual **global events** such as the Wimbledon Grand Slam tournament and excellent coverage of masters tournaments featured on Sky TV.
- **Free access** to local courts in parks.
- **Grass roots** initiatives such as 'Play tennis' and 'RAW tennis' funded by the revenue from the Wimbledon fortnight.
- **Academies** with the sole purpose of developing talent.

Barriers to participation
- Is the LTA ignoring the grass roots?
- Tennis is still considered to be a predominantly **middle class** game, which does not attract the lower class pool of physical talent.
- The **expense** of hiring courts (for example, £16.00 for 1 court for 1 hour in 2010 in the Liverpool Tennis Centre + the cost of coaching, and similar prices in David Lloyd tennis centres).
- Local courts in parks become **vandalised** and often neglected.
- **Restricted free access** to these courts. For example, three years ago there were 33,000 courts but that figure has now dropped to an estimated 10,000.
- Unpredictable British weather.
- The pressure of the short summer term and conflict with annual examinations reduces the time available in schools to play tennis.
- **Public schools** are able to offer more tennis opportunities when compared with state schools.

Practice questions

1) Describe the transition from mob football to the rational game of soccer and discuss the changes which have occurred in the modern game.   20 marks

2) Describe the emergence of cricket and the 19th century influence of the public school followed by a discussion on how the modern game matches contemporary society.   20 marks

3) Discuss factors that led to Lawn tennis increasing women's participation in physical activity in the nineteenth century. Explain which of these factors continue to affect participation in today's contemporary game.   6 marks

4) Describe the origins of the game of tennis and its early development with the modern game.   20 marks

CHAPTER 5 – PT and PE in STATE SCHOOLS 1900 to 1990

The 20th century opened with the **Boer War** in South Africa and the extremely bad publicity which was given to Swedish drill in elementary schools, where blame was placed on the poor standard of physical fitness of young soldiers.

In the larger towns at this time, working class children were really poor, many suffering from malnutrition often without warm clothing and receiving harsh treatment at home.

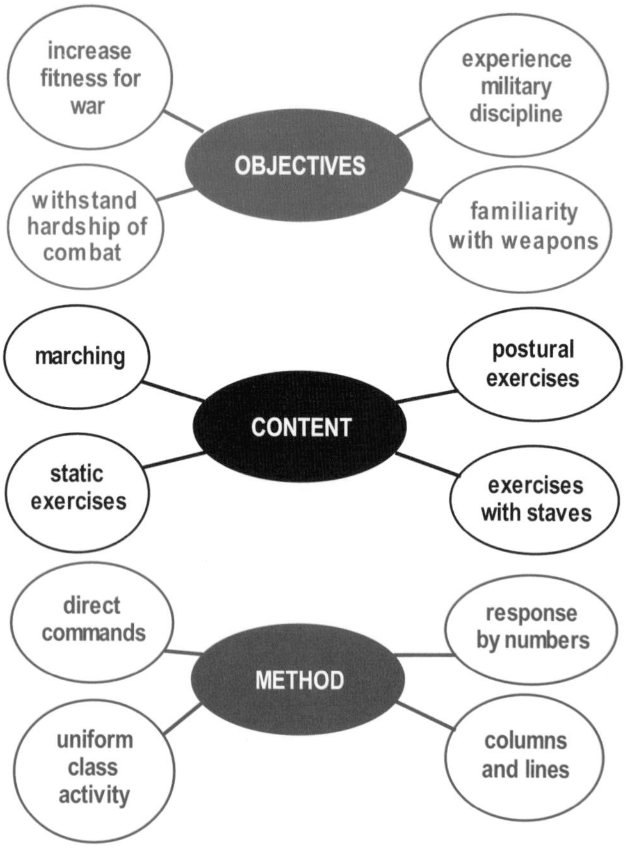

The 1902 Model Course

Colonel Malcolm Fox (ordered by the War Office) set up the **Model Course**, which imposed **military drill** (figures 5.1 and 5.2) as part of education for elementary school children. Regular soldiers went into the schools (the forerunner of our present primary schools), and instructed boys and girls in a set of fixed exercises, originally designed for army recruits. Girls were included even though there was no prospect of them joining the army.

The aims were explicitly:
*   To increase **fitness to fight**.
*   To improve **discipline** at work and war.
*   To help children to **understand hardship**.
*   To teach them to be familiar with military **weapons**.

The content consisted of a series of set exercises by numbers and included marching and drill with staves, which took the place of rifles. The teaching method was direct **instruction**, with the whole class doing the same thing at the same time to numbers, as in the army itself.

Replacement of the 1902 syllabus
The 1902 syllabus was replaced because of:
*   Its **militaristic** nature, and it was delivered by NCO **soldiers**.
*   It had **no educational content.**
*   It had no reference to the **stage of physical and emotional development** of the children, it consisted of adult exercises all done at the same time in unison.

Within two years the 1904 Ministry of Education syllabus (figure 5.3) replaced the 1902 syllabus and reverted to the **Swedish** style of **Physical Training** taught by **teachers**.

*   1904, the teaching method remained direct with the whole class working **in unison**. To some extent this was necessary because of the **large groups**, the small playground space, and little or no apparatus available.
*   1909, an increased number of exercises were used, and an increasing number of teachers were now trained to do this work.
*   1919, the First World War brought a halt to progress and delayed the next syllabus, in which a separate programme was identified for children under seven years old. The main new element was the introduction of **play activities**.

figure 5.1 – structure and function of the model course

increase fitness for war

experience military discipline

OBJECTIVES

withstand hardship of combat

familiarity with weapons

marching

postural exercises

CONTENT

static exercises

exercises with staves

direct commands

response by numbers

METHOD

uniform class activity

columns and lines

figure 5.2 – exercises from the 1902 course

figure 5.3 – exercises on the yard 1904

The 1933 syllabus

The recovery of living standards in the UK continued into the 1930s and sport became popular among all classes. But the government was concerned for the medical and physiological well-being of school-age children.

- Between 1920 and 1930, secondary schools were being built in all towns to support those pupils who did not go to grammar or private schools.
- These were built with good physical education facilities and so it was no surprise when the **1933 syllabus** was published that it contained games.
- This was the last syllabus, but certainly the most detailed and progressive.
- It took the **Swedish scientific principles** and presented them in a 20th century social setting.
- This reflected the emergence of a literate working class and an easier progression into skilled labour and trades.

The concepts still included the notion of health and fitness, but increased the significance of skills. Classes were **decentralised** into group work at the end of each lesson. This was the first step in recognising the importance of the **individual child**, and encouraged the extension of **play activities** for older children. This was now possible because there was normally a playground and at least the use of small equipment. These advances meant that **physical training** was changing into **physical education**.

The **influence** on activities was considerable.

- Systematic exercises were continued, there was a section in the syllabus which involved individual activities like cartwheels together with gymnastic skill which depended on the apparatus available (figure 5.4).
- **Minor games** and **relays** became commonplace, and rotating group activities allowed small numbers to work in a rotating series of gymnastic skills.
- The teaching method in general was direct training, but during the introduction and **group work**, there was individual teaching. In addition, for the first time there was also a competitive fun element in parts of the average lesson.

Figure 5.5 summarises the factors within the social setting in which physical education was able to grow between 1900 and 1950.

Post 1945

The Second World War not only meant that women teachers had to take the place of men (who were in the Forces), but there was considerable bombing which destroyed many of the schools.

The 1933 syllabus was replaced in 1950 because:

- After the war, a major building programme resulted in a large number of new junior and secondary schools being built with **indoor and outdoor sports facilities**.
- This war had been fought in a different way and so commando techniques using assault courses gave educational advisers the idea of **adventurous apparatus**.
- There was a double revolution involving idealistic aims of **freedom of the individual** and **gender equality**.

figure 5.4 – 1933 syllabus included gymnastics

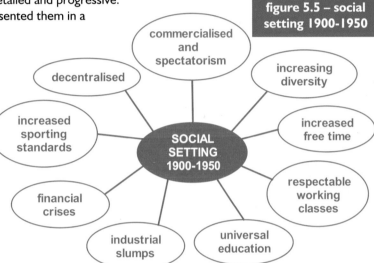

figure 5.5 – social setting 1900-1950

(SOCIAL SETTING 1900-1950: commercialised and spectatorism, increasing diversity, increased free time, respectable working classes, universal education, industrial slumps, financial crises, increased sporting standards, decentralised)

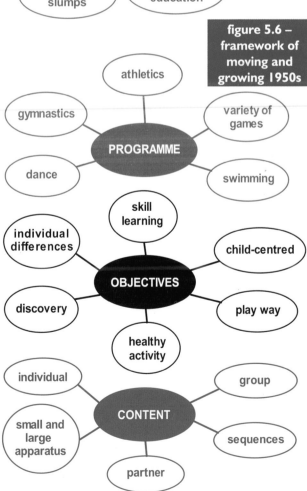

figure 5.6 – framework of moving and growing 1950s

(PROGRAMME: athletics, variety of games, swimming, dance, gymnastics)

(OBJECTIVES: skill learning, child-centred, play way, healthy activity, discovery, individual differences)

(CONTENT: group, sequences, partner, small and large apparatus, individual)

Moving and Growing

The outcome was a Ministry book called '**Moving and Growing**' (see figure 5.6 for an outline of the framework of this programme, and figure 5.7 for an example of the type of activity) and a support text of activities called '**Planning the Programme**'.

- These changed the face of physical education, by putting the well-being of the individual child first.
- This meant that the children had a chance to select the activities they practised and were able to experience two new approaches called **Educational Gymnastics** and **Modern Dance**.
- These programmes were designed to engage children's interest and imagination, with skill sequences produced through guided rather than direct teaching.
- In this way activity and skill learning were seen as an alternative way of achieving health and fitness in a post-war world, during which our Welfare State was established and child poverty was markedly diminished.

figure 5.7 – modern dance theme in action

Over the last twenty years, some of this free expression has been reduced, given the pressure presented by rising standards and competitions in sport. The focus has to some extent changed from guided theme work to specific skills, with particular emphasis on games skills and tactics. Certainly the quality of specialist teacher training has helped this diversity of knowledge and the 'A' Level in PE gives teachers a sound theoretical background in their subject.

1970s and 1980s

Between 1984 and 1986, there was considerable industrial action by teachers whose effect as far as sport and PE was concerned was to more or less eliminate extra-curricular sport and PE in state schools in the UK. PE teachers felt no longer able to commit the extra time at lunch times, after school and at weekends. This was in the face of cuts and re-allocation of the education budget which affected the salary and conditions of service for every teacher.

The effect of this action was to reduce opportunity and provision for most pupils, to shift participation (which was in turn reduced) into community clubs, and to disappoint and frustrate many children and staff.

The national curriculum for physical education

The belief that education in schools was best left to an advisory inspectorate, professional bodies and school staff, was shaken in the 1980s by a drop in standards. The result was the issue of a **National Curriculum** identifying four key stages in the Education Act of 1996. These key stages are coded as **Key Stage 1** (**KS1** – years 1-2, ages 5-7), **Key Stage 2** (**KS2** – years 3-6, ages 7-11), **Key Stage 3** (**KS3** – years 7-9, ages 11-14), and **Key Stage 4** (**KS4** – years 10-11, ages 14-16).

In this Education Act, physical education was recognised as a non-core **foundation subject** which made it compulsory, with a note that **two hours a week** of physical activity, including the National Curriculum for Physical Education and extra-curriculum activities, should exist in all schools. This applied throughout all key stages. The reaction by school staff was that this was less than the best primary schools were already doing, but subsequent trends have been to increase primary PE time to approaching an hour a day.

Figures 5.8, 5.9 and 5.10 show examples of types of activity at KS2 or KS3.

figure 5.8 – KS2 sports day

figure 5.9 – KS2 outdoor activities

figure 5.10 – KS2 swimming

- Today's curriculum offers children of different ages a variety of activities.
- It is a compulsory part of education and is becoming increasingly important as the health of the nation is decreasing due to increases in obesity and heart disease.
- The government currently aims to increase the exposure of physical activity among school age young people to 5 hours per week (called the **5-hour offer**).

Table 5.1 – **principles of the National Curriculum**

KS1 (5-7yrs)	KS2 (7-11yrs)	KS3 (11-14yrs)	KS4 (14-16yrs)
fundamental motor skills	furthering of motor skills	refine motor skills	undertaking different roles – official/player/coach
sequences of movement	co-ordination developed	learn rules/tactics of games	preparing training programmes for specific sports
individual and pair work	more complex movement patterns	learn more complex movements	refining skills and tactical knowledge
understand and recognise effect of exercise on the body	experience, understand and maintain sustained period of exercise	learn how to prepare for and recover from activities	understand theoretical principles on which exercise programmes are based

These were the far-reaching aims, which teachers were obliged to make a basis of their programme, with the expectation that an inspectorate would assess the level achieved through **OFSTED**.

Advantages of the National Curriculum

- A wide and balanced PE curriculum for all.
- It is open enough to allow for some variation between schools (allowing for teacher specialism).
- It enables and develops learning and analytic skills in the context of PE.
- Encourages and develops fair play, integrity and independence.
- It enables students to manage risk and cope with difficulty.
- Content should be broadly the same across the nation, so pupil transfer between schools should be made easier.

Disadvantages of the National Curriculum

- Large amounts of time consumed in record keeping.
- Primary PE will still vary and produce differing quality of experience prior to secondary school.
- Can reduce creativity of the teacher in producing a meaningful and worthwhile PE experience for pupils.
- Schools without the facilities for some activities will be disadvantaged.

Practice questions

1) Describe the changes resulting from the introduction of the 1902 Model Course. 4 marks

2) What were the main objectives of the 1933 syllabus and give two reasons why they were thought necessary? 5 marks

3) How was child-centred teaching identified in 'Moving and Growing' and to what extent were some of the changes due to the experiences in World War II? 6 marks

4) Briefly explain the changes in school physical education since 1950 and suggest ways in which these changes reflect developments in UK physical education and sport today. 20 marks

SECTION A: SOCIO-CULTURAL OPTIONS

OPTION A2: COMPARATIVE STUDIES

This option focuses on the factors that affect participation and improve competence in physical activity as part of a balanced, active and healthy lifestyle in the USA and Australia as compared with the United Kingdom.

Table A2.1 outlines the geographical factors which may determine the opportunity for participation in sport and physical activity between the three countries.

Table A2.1 – **geographical determinants compared**

	UK	USA	Australia
size	245,000 km²	9,826,630 km²	7,617,930 km²
population	61,000,000 (2007)	305,954,000 (2008)	21,619,000 (2009)
climate	temperate (-10 to 35°C) mild and wet	many regions from temperate to subtropical to desert	some desert, some tropical, some temperate
topography	seascape, lowland and some mountains	desert to glaciated mountains to arctic	mostly desert to some mountains, coastal
population in conurbations	15,200,000 (largest five), overall probably 30,000,000 = 50%	79% = 242,000,000	75% = 16,200,000 (coast and cities)
population density	249 per km²	31 per km²	2.84 per km²
main road transport	29,145 miles	46,651 miles (expressway) 2,617,212 miles	176 miles (motorway) 232,899 miles
rail transport	10,375 miles	140,882 miles	22,292 miles

CHAPTER 6 – THE UNITED KINGDOM

Cultural context

Historical determinants

The role of nineteenth century public schools
The **characteristics** of these schools were that they were for the **sons of the gentry**, they were **boarding**, **fee paying**, and **non-local** establishments.

- The non-local feature of these schools was very important in that the developments that occurred in the schools became spread across the nation.
- An informal grouping of the top public boarding schools were paramount in this development. These were the **Clarendon Schools** of Eton, Harrow, Charterhouse, Westminster, Winchester, Rugby, and Shrewsbury - labelled **EHCWWRS**, with additionally St. Paul's and Merchant Taylors as day schools.
- There were also scholars from poorer families and by the 1870s the number of schools had increased to accommodate an emergent middle class.

- There was a delay before similar selective high schools emerged for **upper and middle class girls**.
- By the end of the nineteenth century, there was public or grammar school access for wealthy and bright boys and girls with an active policy for **athleticism**, and the **size** and **provision** to promote it. Other reforms also occurred, such as a broader curriculum, reduced flogging and control of school sport by the Sixth Form.

There were **three** main phases in the development of sports and games in these schools.

Phase one
Initially, the boys brought traditional ethnic sports into the schools, as part of their **free time** experience. **Mob games** (figure 6.1) were played which were dependent on existing facilities.

Phase two
The second phase marked the attempt by head teachers, staff and prefects to condition these activities into a **socially acceptable** form. This resulted in rules and conditions being set and a sports calendar established.

Phase three
Finally, activities in these schools developed into a full expression of **athleticism**, where opportunities were extended and facilities built to encourage sports and games as major educational and cultural vehicles.

figure 6.1 – mob games

Activity development
We can use examples of different activities to **explain** how development occurred. The main popular example is of **mob football** which tended to differ in each school.

- Eton played a field game and a wall game.
- Rugby School played a handling game.
- Harrow and Charterhouse played a so-called dribbling game.
- Local conditions (the availability of large grassy areas or pitches, and whether or not the areas were bounded by fences or walls) at each school largely determined these differences.

Rackets was a game played on the walls of the **Old School at Harrow**. Versions of **fives** (a game played by striking a ball with the hand instead of a racquet) were played at Eton, Rugby and Winchester, with variations in shape and size of court and different rules. Consequently, **unified rules** had to be agreed before inter-school games and individual competitions could be established.

The ethic of **moral integrity** and **physical endeavour** was strongly identified by enlightened head teachers. When the boys left school for Oxford or Cambridge Universities, they had already established an acceptable combination of public schools' rules to produce a **set of rules** which allowed them to play at their university college, and hence unified rules and a stringent organisation for competitions **between** university colleges. Eventually, sets of rules for **inter-varsity** games and contests were produced which became the national and in some cases internationally accepted rules for a sport.

figure 6.2 – William Clarke, gentleman amateur cricketer in 1845

The gentleman amateur
The university college competition structure and the inter-varsity structures remained an elite development and represented the foundation of the **gentleman amateur**. When graduates left university, they entered various careers including industry, the church and the army, and they took their amateur sport with them throughout Britain and the Empire.

For example, a group of university graduates discussed the rules of football and having accepted the divide between the two codes of association and rugby, established the Governing Bodies of the Football Association (FA) in 1863, and the Rugby Football Union (RFU) in 1871.

Different governing bodies gradually reformed their rules to change the class and gender definition of amateurism to a regulation based on **no financial gain**. Meanwhile, several games had acknowledged the place of the professional performer. In cricket and association football, the professional player and club came under the control of middle class administrators, who accepted the code of **physical endeavour and moral integrity** as the basis of all modern games and sports.

Recent moves to change the traditional amateur approach to a more professional approach

The twentieth century brought a further reduction in the elitism of **amateurism**. Though the **barrier** between amateurs and professionals remained strong, several sports like athletics and swimming opened their doors to amateurs from all classes.

Women had their own governing bodies. In athletics for example, the WAAA – **Women's Amateur Athletic Association** – dealt exclusively with female athletics.

All sporting bodies eventually redefined amateurism to encompass the right to **legitimate expenses** which later included **lost time**, and finally to **funding** to achieve excellence.

Meanwhile, **professional** performers were getting higher wages and prize money. The idea of professionals being lower class all but disappeared as middle class competitors were attracted by the rewards and kudos. The media and sponsorship has determined this change, where excellence in a large number of sports means millionaire status for the top performers.

Government policy

Physical Education and School Sport Club Links

The Physical Education and School Sport Club Links (**PESSCL**) strategy (figure 6.3) is a policy jointly delivered by the **DfES** (Department for Education and Schools) and **DCMS** (Department for Culture, Media and Sport). This strategy has eight components:

- Sports Colleges.
- School Sports Partnerships.
- Gifted and Talented.
- Swimming.
- Step into Sport.
- School/Club links.
- QCA PE and School Sport Investigation.
- Professional Development.

figure 6.3 – PESSCL strategy

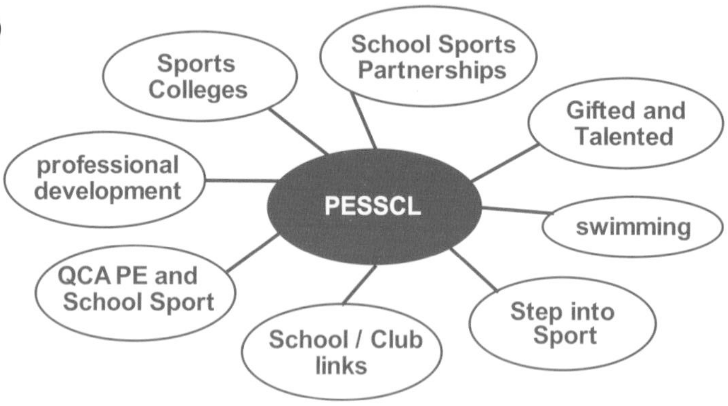

Sports Colleges · School Sports Partnerships · Gifted and Talented · swimming · Step into Sport · School / Club links · QCA PE and School Sport · professional development · PESSCL

The main aim of this strategy is to improve the participation of 5 to 16 year-olds in physical activity. It will be expected that all children will spend at least two hours per week on high quality physical education or sport. A recent survey has found that in 2007 86% of children between KS1 and KS4 achieved the '2 hour offer'. The government is putting into place plans for five hours of quality PE or sport per week for this age group, known as the '**5 hour offer**'. This will include extra-curricular sports or activities.

Commercialisation of sport

Sponsorship and advertising

The so-called '**media golden triangle**' (figure 6.4) links **sport**, **sponsorship** and the **media**.

A sponsor will expect to promote its products by using a performer's image in return for financial support. A contract will be commercial and dependent on the star status of the sportsperson. If the status falls, so might the sponsorship. An example of this is Tiger Woods and his portrayal by the media after his 2009 personal difficulties. These difficulties had nothing to do with his status as World leading golfer, but caused several sponsors to withdraw support.

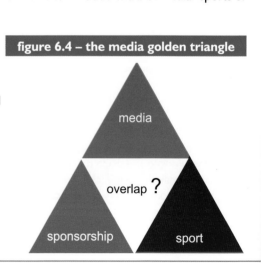

figure 6.4 – the media golden triangle

media · overlap ? · sponsorship · sport

Social determinants

Table 6.1 – discrimination and barriers to progression (SE = socio-economic)

gender	race and ethnicity	disability	social class
women are discriminated against in sport - and in society	black and Asian people discriminated against in society	9% participation in sport (lower than able-bodied)	lack of financial support a big barrier
there are still stereotypical attitudes to female participation	25% soccer premiership players black, hardly any Asians	great success in Paralympics - 2nd in medal table Beijing	parental support important at young age
in Beijing, 45% of participants were female - opportunity	50% UK athletics power event competitors black	elite athletes funded from lottery same as able-bodied	elite amateur athletes funded from lottery - provision
in Athens 40% of British team were women, in IOC only 14% are women, the glass ceiling applies to female participation	no research evidence that black Afro-Caribbean people have higher fast twitch muscle, or less subcutaneous fat	Sports Aid helps performers in 25 disabled sports compared with 50 able-bodied - opportunity	participation from lower SE groups about 55% lower when compared to upper SE groups
women's top soccer is still semi-professional	in UK rugby, very few black players - opportunity	still lack of access to some sports facilities	some activities associated with upper SE status people
before 2007, men's prize money at Wimbledon was more than women's - esteem	in tennis no black and only one Asian competitor in UK top ten - opportunity	age limit for TASS funding raised to 35 compared with 25 for able-bodied	amateur sports have fewer low SE status elite performers
top sportswomen have 14% of income of top men, and find it harder to get sponsorship	hence stereotype of black Afro-Caribbean potential at sport incorrect	low levels of sponsorship - provision	membership of some sport clubs only open to financially independent people
women's boxing, pole vault, triple jump, hammer & weight lifting only allowed since 1987	lack of role models in low black participation sport discourages new participants	lack of media exposure compared to able-bodied sport - lack of esteem	low SE group people have less leisure time than upper SE groups - opportunity
female sport has less social status than male sport	media reflect society's view of black people - self-esteem	media focus on adversity rather than ability	fewer people from low SE groups participate after 16
females get less media space or time than males in the UK	great success from male Asian boxers and cricketers		unless talent identified early, low SE people drop out
women's fitness - hence muscularity - causes media to call into question sexuality	low socio-economic status of many black Afro-Caribbean people prevents participation		
media focus on women's appearance rather than sport			

Values embedded in UK sports ethics

Values of the UK tend to be part of sport, and are summarised in figure 6.5.

Physical education and school sport

Health issues

The focus on physical activity is necessary for the development of a balanced, active and healthy lifestyle. It is a life-time commitment, which involves healthy attitudes in all walks of life.

It would seem that physical inactivity and hence obesity are the result of constant car use, limited physical education on the curriculum or extra-curriculum, the discouragement of vigorous play activities in the playground, and many cases of school fields being sold off or not being fully utilised.

Obesity has also led children to avoid physical activity because of its competitive nature and their discomfort in physical education kit. Programmes are being designed to encourage obese children to join exercise and sports groups and future policies must promote programmes to off-set child obesity, ensuring **opportunity**, **provision** and **self-esteem** for this group.

figure 6.5 – values within UK sport

individuality

overcoming discrimination

democracy

VALUES WITHIN SPORT

fair play

teamwork

participation

competitiveness

Organisation

Sports Colleges

The **Youth Sports Trust** established **Sports Colleges** to bring into action the government policy on school academies for sport in the age group 11 to 16. There are 506 Sports Colleges in England and Wales (in April 2010), each with extra funding for facilities and staff to improve participation and develop excellence in sport among their pupils. Such facilities and expertise are available to feeder junior schools.

These colleges are particularly targeted for the 2 hours per week of PE or sport for every child. They aim to improve the expertise of their staff and make all possible use of new technologies.

School Sport Partnerships (SSPs)

Sports colleges are at the centre of the SSP infrastructure. School Sports Partnerships (SSPs) are groups of schools working together to develop PE and sport opportunities for all young people.

A typical **partnership** consists of:
* A partnership development manager (PDM).
* Up to eight school sport co-ordinators (SSCos).
* Between 30 and 45 primary and special school link teachers (PLTs).
* Competition Managers.
* Further education sports co-ordinators (FESCos).

A **PDM** is a full-time role usually based within a Sports College. They manage the SSP and develop strategic links with key partners in sport and the wider community. For example, part of their role is to link school and local facilities (that tend to operate separately from the schools sector) to large numbers of school pupils who participate in and enjoy physical activity in school, but find it difficult to continue once school finishes. This applies to weekends and school holidays for younger school pupils, as well as what happens when students leave school or college at 16 or 18.

Mass participation

> **STUDENT NOTE**
>
> Mass participation in the context of the sport development pyramid is briefly discussed in AS Revise PE for OCR, ISBN 978 1 901 424 52 2 page 111 onwards.

In terms of **mass participation** in physical activity, the **opportunity** lies within the privately or publicly funded facilities available, or the willingness of the sportsperson to pay for them. In order to **participate**, people must have the **time** and **money**, and be able to **travel** on a regular basis to a facility. Some sports centres give **special rates** to unemployed or elderly people, specifically to improve participation in these groups. Choice of sport may be restricted, depending on where a person lives, and this influences the **provision** for sport.

Sport and the pursuit of excellence

> **STUDENT NOTE**
>
> UK Sport and its part in the structure of sport in the UK is briefly discussed in AS Revise PE for OCR, ISBN 978 1 901 424 52 2 page 109 onwards.

UK Sport and the UK Sports Institute

UK Sport is responsible for managing and distributing public investment and is a statutory distributor of funds raised by the **National Lottery**. This body is accountable to parliament through the Department for Culture, Media and Sport (DCMS) (www.culture.gov.uk). UK Sport's goals are given the title '**World Class Performance**', which are aimed to meet the challenge of London2012.

UK Sport also funds the **UK Sports Institute** (**UKSI**) which co-ordinates elite sport development in the UK. Its **Athlete Medical Scheme** provides the UK's top Olympic and Paralympic athletes with injury treatment. It also organises and sponsors World class **coaching conferences,** which present the UK's top coaches with opportunities to gain new insights and skills to develop future World, Olympic and Paralympic Champions. This provides a pathway into professional sport.

The **UKSI** devolves its regional responsibilities into the **Home Country Institutes**, for example, the **English Institute of Sport** (EIS).

Case studies

Case studies are set out on cricket, rugby league, rugby union, and association football. Students will need to look at current issues in the different sports. Refer to page 28 onwards for some of the details of these sports and their development.

CHAPTER 7 – USA

STUDENT NOTE

An outline of sport in the USA is briefly set out in AS Revise PE for OCR, ISBN 978 1 901 424 52 2 page 103 onwards.

figure 7.1 – the American Way

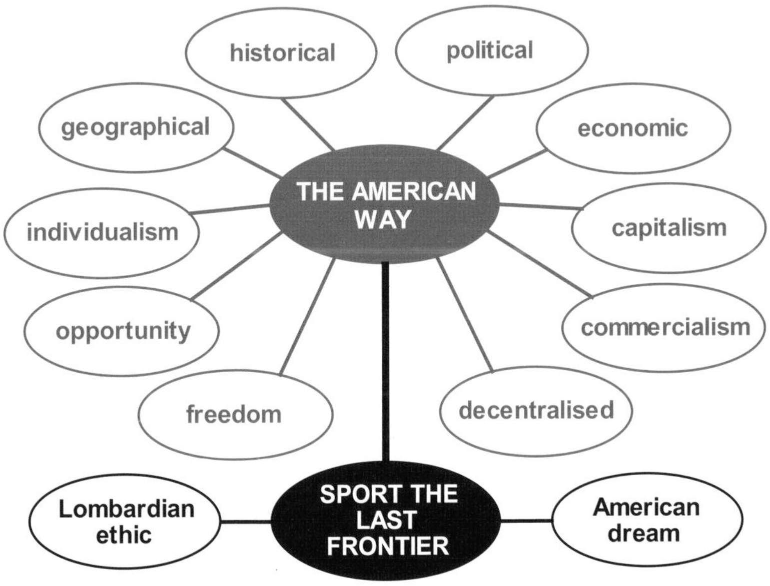

- historical
- political
- geographical
- economic
- **THE AMERICAN WAY**
- individualism
- capitalism
- opportunity
- commercialism
- freedom
- decentralised
- **Lombardian ethic**
- **SPORT THE LAST FRONTIER**
- **American dream**

Historical determinants

After an initial settlement by the Spanish and French on the Atlantic Coast in the 17th century, the 18th century involved substantial British colonisation, cut short by the **War of Independence** in 1776. As a result, the formal control of education and society no longer had a direct association with Britain (and certainly less than in Australia, which stayed within the Empire - later to become the Commonwealth). However, the early development of private education in elite schools had been established, together with sporting developments in the older universities following the Oxbridge model. Many British settlers continued the sporting traditions of their forebears.

- **Independence** did lead to an initial basis of **militarism** and **fitness to fight** in schools (similar to the UK, page 36 above), but was followed by a scientific philosophy which involved a regular daily programme of play and exercise for children along the East Coast. Another phase arose with the diversity of ethnic immigration and the spread of civilisation westward with its outdoor **frontier experiences.**

- As in England, it was **undergraduate enthusiasm** which carried games into American society in a rational form. For example, the first reference to a football club being formed was in 1862 in Boston by young high school graduates. Meanwhile, **baseball** had been played in the 1860s at Amherst College, Massachusetts with written rules being adopted in a similar manner to football.

- Hence the USA is a relatively **young nation.** with independence from Britain being established in 1781. This youthfulness is reflected in the enthusiasm for competitive sport and the promotion of new ideas. Unfortunately, the country went through a period of **isolationism**, which is still evident in the nature of their games. More recently this situation was influenced by **British colonialism** and new ideas from the flow of **immigrants** into the USA.

- The major socio-cultural policy was **pluralism**, a policy which allows ethnic groups to retain their own culture. As a Republic, the US has applied a **decentralised** political system, in which most legislative and administrative function is extended to each state and city.

figure 7.2 – Vince Lombardi, head coach of the Green Bay Packers 1959

- The **capitalist** ethic has resulted in the **independence** of individual organisations, and **free-enterprise** and **individualism** strongly encouraged. This has resulted in the **commercialisation** of sport as an entrenched and valued part of society.

Isolationism and the development of sports unique to the USA

During the late 19th and early 20th century, **isolation** in terms of sport development led to very distinct games being developed as alternatives to those being developed in Britain at that time. Hence **baseball** and **basketball** became major sporting outlets for spectatorism and then commercial exploitation. **Gridiron** football became the major example of how this development happened.

The nature of sport in the USA

The **Lombardian Ethic** (mentioned in figure 7.1 and on pages 46 and 48 below) is based on a statement **'winning isn't the most important thing – it's the only thing'**, made by Vince Lombardi (figure 7.2), a famous American Football coach. This suggests that **outcomes** over-ride the process of **participating**.

The Lombardian ethic is reflected in the way sport is presented, with professional sport **leading** society and only winners being acknowledged. Sport and business are continually linked in that you either win or lose and coming second is to lose!

- This attitude reflects **capitalism** in a superpower with a large population and an organisation to produce enough winners not to have to worry too much about those who have tried, but not reached the top. This is a powerfully promoted concept, but should not be taken as the view held by all Americans. A large minority would **not agree** that 'Nice Guys Finish Last'.

- There is a second ethic known as the **American Dream**. This ethic supports the notion that **anyone** from whatever background, especially the poor and ethnic minorities, can achieve **success** and **wealth** through hard work and talent. This second ethic is often referred to as the **American Way of Life**.

The **American Dream** still promotes a striving society, but in this case recognises sport as an example of that 'dream'.
- Successful sportspeople can have great commercial value as **role models** for young people.
- As role models they enable the promotion of sports clothing and shoes or other lifestyle products, which enables top performers to live a lavish and enviable lifestyle.
- Unfortunately, links with the win ethic are leading the majority of citizens into becoming **spectators** after leaving college, accepting that energetic sport is for the young, and that professional sport is there to be **watched** either at the local stadium or on television.

Geographical determinants

Looking at table A2.1 you will see that the USA has 5 times the **population** of the UK, and about 40 times the land area of the UK. The large population resource, the relatively high standard of living, the diversity of climate and the wide range of natural terrain are such that all sports can be easily accommodated in the USA.

Government policy

Decentralisation of sport in the USA
In a democracy like the USA, the powers to organise and administer sport (alongside other essential state functions such as security, education, health and so on) are delegated to state or city level. Many Americans believe that there is no such thing as an American, but rather **citizens of each State** and large city.

Hence, although general patterns of structure and organisation are similar across the 50 states, each local area or state sees itself as independent and able to organise its own sports events on its own behalf. This applies particularly to the college (university) system, which is the main provider for elite and sub-elite sport across the country, and which are commercial organisations normally paid for by the user.

figure 7.3 – the University of Arkansas Razorbacks stadium

Commercialisation of sport in the USA

The paying for watching of sport by **spectators and viewers** is the foundation of the wealth of professional sport in the USA. This commercialisation gives great power to the **TV companies**, who can dictate start times, break times and lengths, and sometimes the stadium boarding and kit worn by players and others.

Multi-national companies pay the **TV companies** for exposure, and there is a huge take up of sports-brand kit and equipment on the strength of this. But it is the sales potential for every-day items unrelated to sport which inspires the very **large incomes** eventually passed on to professional sport.

Within the **university system**, each college is commercially independent, and has to survive on its own on income provided by students (entirely fee paying) and local communities. Fortunately, sport is able to provide a substantial income because of the giant spectatorship at college football (figure 7.3) and baseball fixtures. This income enables colleges to offer full scholarships to talented sportspeople who in turn will enhance team performance and further income from spectatorship. This is one of the **pathways to professional sport**. **Sponsorship** by shoe companies and college scholarships are the main method of support for elite 'amateur' sportspeople.

Social determinants

Discrimination

Discrimination continues to exist in the USA, despite the law. In a capitalist society, some members of society remain more advantaged than others. This has given rise to a two-tier education system, where wealth influences provision such as in the summer camp system.

Social inequalities do not generally apply to state high school physical education. The process of bussing students into downtown areas has only partly worked to the extent that the provision of facilities, staffing and limited funding results in some athletic departments being better off than others. This wealth differential not only exists at an urban level among ethnic minorities, but in rural areas in some poorer States.

The **American Dream** is linked with the **capitalist** society which implies traditional **inequalities** that have been difficult to eradicate. On the sports scene, this still exists at **opportunity**, **provision** and **esteem** levels.

figure 7.4 – Mia Hamm (L), USA soccer star

Gender issues

Title IX has done a great deal to increase participation opportunities for girls in school, but most of this has been at an intramural level. This legislation states:

> 'No person in the United States, shall, on the basis of sex, be excluded from participation in, be denied the benefits of, or be subject to discrimination under any education program or activity receiving federal financial assistance.'

Though legislation has helped women to participate in sport, particularly in soccer and rugby (figure 7.4), elite sport is still dominated by highly talented, able-bodied **men**. Women compete in the Olympic sports equally as successfully as the men.

Racism and stacking

Disadvantaged groups in the USA still believe in the American Dream, but there is still a **glass ceiling** through which some minority groups have difficulty in breaking. Both wealth and racial inequalities still remain in American society.

The term '**centrality**' has been used to express the problem in which a **WASP** society of **W**hite **A**nglo-**S**axon **P**rotestant immigrants have monopolised the wealth and power of the country.

figure 7.5 – Michael Jordan, best basketballer ever?

This WASP grouping controls sport, and white players have controlled decision-making positions in professional games:

- **WASPs** dominated ownership of clubs because of their wealth.
- **Coaches** and administrators are predominantly white.
- Society is therefore dominated by one section of the community in a country which is striving to be democratic and pluralist through racial and gender equality.
- It takes time and legislation to reduce 'institutional discrimination' and a more even distribution of wealth and opportunity.

The exception to this is basketball, dominated by African American players (figure 7.5) at professional and community level.

Historically, people have looked to the physical advantages of this particular ethnic group, suggesting genetic and physiological advantages.
Today, it is acknowledged that it is **opportunity**, **provision** and the high self-**esteem** arising from black heroes that have stimulated an African American obsession with this sport. Conversely, there has been a '**white flight**' from this game, as a result of real and perceived disadvantage.

The term '**stacking**' is used to describe the lack of opportunity for African American sportsmen to command the best positions and therefore wages in a team. These positions in various games are presumed to have greater skill, decision-making and leadership qualities, and are said to require a master concept of the game as a whole, and a strategic awareness of 'plays' in the game. This element of traditional racism presumes that talented white players will always be better than other races at decision-making and leadership.

Tokenism

Tokenism as practised in American sport was an attempt to eliminate injustice and improve the commercial value of talent. This was a form of positive discrimination, allowing less able candidates from minorities to obtain privileged positions as a compensation for discrimination.

figure 7.6 – Venus and Serena Williams

However, an inferior person promoted to a privileged position (such as quarterback in football) as a token to his racial status, tends to reinforce views of racial inferiority. This process has been dropped in favour of perceived talent and success at sport being the basis of selection for these positions regardless of race.

Athletes like the Williams sisters (figure 7.6) are major icons for both gender and ethnic equality in the USA.

Values

Commercialisation of children's sport has dramatically increased in the USA as it has in Britain, as a result of the transition from amateur to **professional** in so many sports and the impact of career sport. As a **capitalist** economy, there is a dependence on commercial money locally and nationally, stimulated by the massive expansion of the media. This has led to even small rural schools trying to get sport **sponsorships** and families looking for financial support for talented games players to support them through college and into the professional ranks.

Unfortunately there is a rise in drug-taking and other forms of cheating. School PE is at the forefront of the preservation of higher values, but temptations continue to exist for athletic programmes to reduce focus on health and fair play and accept a win-at-all-costs philosophy. Organisations such as **State High School Athletics Associations** (SHSAA) and the **National Collegiate Athletic Association** (NCAA) are all committed to preventing schools and colleges going down this path. The rewards are such that over zealous coaches and parents continue to see winning as the only thing.

American ethics within sport

Although most of the above discussion concerns underpinning values taken for granted by the American public, we should mention three '**ethics**' fighting for attention within American society.

- The **Lombardian Ethic**, which is the dominant sport ethic and supports the notion that **winning is everything**. This rejects the European and Olympic ideal that taking part is most significant and fair play an essential component. The Lombardian ethic almost totally controls the professional sports scene, and remains a central philosophy in most athletic departments in schools.

- The **Radical Ethic** is nearer to the '**sport for all**' European view and is increasingly encouraged in the mass participation of sport. This is particularly so with the more recent encouragement of lifetime or '**lifelong**' sport strategies to encourage popular active involvement in sports. It is evident in school PE departments as educational values to counter the traditional Lombardian focus on achievement. The Radical ethic encourages inter-mural school sport and the educational values of enjoyment, mass involvement in active sporting activity and fair play attitudes.

- The **Counter-Culture Ethic** is the **opposite** to the Lombardian win ethic and is aligned with non-competitive physical recreations. In society it is often linked with the eco-sport movement, with the value of adventurous outdoor activities in the natural environment being emphasised. In the school system it is readily identifiable with the summer camp movement.

As in Britain, there was a period when educationists tried to **take competition out** of school life. Physical educationists in the UK promoted educational gymnastics and dance as non-competitive activities, particularly at primary school level. Today in both Britain and the USA, a **compromise** has been reached, where non-competitive activities sit beside inter-mural sport.

Physical education and school sport

School sport in the USA

A percentage of American children of pre-school age have an opportunity to be taught fundamental sports skills through organised play in a programme called **Smart Sports Development**. This physical education approach is continued by qualified teachers in the elementary schools, where many classes are mixed, movement and dance are taught as well as games skills, and where enjoyment is more important than competition. This is similar to the UK.

The organisation of high school sport

The organisation of high school sport at District and State level is considerable. There is a national advisory body called the **State High School Athletics Association** (SHSAA) with branches in each State and this controls all **interscholastic** athletic (any sport) competition. Each State has its own **Inter-scholastic Association** which is financed by individual school athletic programmes. The sub-division of this is according to the size of the school, where there are five 'conferences' from small schools of some 200 students to the largest schools with around 2000 students.

figure 7.7 – Phoenix Arizona High School football

- In most high schools there are **coaches** appointed for most of the high profile sports (figure 7.7).
- Market forces determine that the coaches' pay is normally higher than that of the teaching staff.
- This reflects the **status of that sport** in the school and community.
- In larger schools, there will be a **team of coaches** in the major sports.
- The coaches are all accountable to the Athletic Director of the school, whose aim is to exclusively **improve sport at the elite level**.

Unlike Britain, where spectators are attracted to professional games only, American **inter-scholastic games** have a **major spectator base**, largely because the size of the country means that the 'local' team is the school team. Consequently, the inter-scholastic **sports facilities are excellent** and include major **spectator seating** and **media** coverage. This gives the school a major source of revenue as well as community significance.

The high prestige of inter-scholastic sport holds a major place in the American psyche and influences:
- The **well-being** of the community.
- The place of **professional** sport in American society.
- The **media** which promotes sport.
- The **morale of the school** which is enhanced by sports success.
- The fact that **spectators and the community** are brought together as well as earning the school considerable revenue.
- The degree of commitment by the cheerleaders.

An example of the commercial impact of inter-scholastic sport is the school district in Colorado which sold the 'naming rights' to its new stadium for $2million.

Mass participation in sport

Over the past 50 years national statistics for the USA show an overall trend of declining total physical activity, despite the growth of jogging and fitness/gym cultures. In 2008 a survey revealed that approximately 16% of 15 year-olds and older take part in some form of daily exercise, whilst the rate of watching television is 5 times higher - a major explanation for the recent increase in obesity in the USA.

The 2003 **HealthierUS** initiative was designed to improve the **health and fitness** of young children. It recommended that young people should be physically active every day, eat a nutritious diet, get preventative screening, and make healthy choices such as avoidance of drugs and tobacco.

Physical fitness testing and measuring form part of the American PE programme and are aimed at increasing the health and fitness of school children.

In the UK, we would look at physical recreation and 'Sport for All' as a necessary experience for the development of a balanced, active, and healthy lifestyle which would involve healthy attitudes in both work and leisure.

In America, the term 'athletic' is a term used to describe high level sport often associated with professionalism and the Lombardian Ethic. On the other hand, the American term **lifelong** or lifetime sport is associated with the British model of '**Sport for All**' and reflects the **Radical Ethic** nurtured in inter-mural sports in schools and colleges.

Lifelong sport as an ambition for the USA?

Additionally, the American love of the outdoors is identified with national pride and **frontier spirit**. This adventurous activity is promoted by the summer **camp school** system, and is also part of adult culture and is identified as **eco-sport**.

Eco-sport consists of healthy exercise and fun in environmentally based (figure 7.8) rather than competitive experiences, and so is adventurously linked with the **Counter-Culture Ethic**.

figure 7.8 – outdoor experiences are valuable

- The distinction between '**athletic**' and '**lifelong**' activity is more clearly defined in the USA than in Britain and Australia. This is because American society has not fully adopted the European amateur sports club approach, with its pyramid of sporting standards in a variety of sports and games.
- As a result the **elite** sports scene is a huge **commercial** enterprise, with the majority of American citizens not participating in lifetime sport.
- Most people therefore **switch off** from **regular participation** in physically challenging sports after leaving college, whilst retaining their love of the outdoors.
- The availability and convenience of **modern transport** and the **media** seems to have distracted the bulk of the American public from the need for regular physical activity which has resulted in a rising problem of **obesity**.

- Recently, the federal government has begun to encourage citizens to participate in active competitive sport. There already are **recreational social groups** like ten-pin bowling, and **country clubs** (for wealthy people only who can afford the fees) for golf and tennis.

But there is little incentive for ordinary people to play the 'big four' American sports because of the violence and the expected degree of ability and commitment (in terms of training for example). Hence it is mainly the **European games** of **soccer**, **field hockey** and **rugby** that are beginning to emerge as mass participant games (in addition to jogging and swimming).

Sport and the pursuit of excellence

Commercialisation of children's sport

The **commercial** development of children's sport dominates the initial development of **sporting values** and **opportunities**. This tends to lie outside the educational system and as such tends to reflect many of the values identified in elite and professional sport in the USA.

- Children's sport is well-organised in the USA, with such titles as **Pop Warner** and **Little League** gridiron football, **Biddy** Basketball and Little League basketball and baseball.
- **Pee Wee** and Little League baseball are both available throughout middle class America.
- With the advent of **Title IX**, there was a marked increase in opportunities for girls.
- There is a strong role taken by **parents**, but a major competitive element can deter less able children.

figure 7.9 – little league baseball

- In the little league sports there are the elements of fun, safe practice and the development of sound attitudes, but there is an under-swell of competitiveness coming from coaches and parents who want their kids to play hard and win trophies.
- This is the '**American Way**', perhaps even the '**American Dream**', where the personal ambition of individual parents to win a mini super-bowl is encouraged by the attention given to **competitive** sport by local **media** and **commercial** companies.

Youth sport

There is also a major policy to supply **sports facilities** and support **organisation** for youth sport, particularly for inner city youth. Though identified as lifelong sport, the **community** motive is to get trouble off the streets. Coaches and players make the games highly competitive, with individuals hoping to get the break into college with a **scholarship** and ultimately into the **professional** ranks.

The latest trend is to include a wide range of games, like soccer and softball, as well as the traditional baseball and basketball. This is controlled by the **National Alliance for Youth Sports**, with an initiative called **Time out for better Sports for Kids** (figure 7.10).

figure 7.10 – children's sport in time out

Pathways to professional sport

University sport and inter-collegiate elite sport

Students graduate from their high school at the age of 17 with a high percentage going on to a two year Junior College programme, with approximately half of these continuing to degree programmes at universities, teachers' colleges and professional schools.

Given the high percentage of children who go on to college education, many young people have access to **outstanding sports facilities**. This is in a system of higher education where **sports scholarships** are available for the most talented and also as an **opportunity** for poorer members of society. The scholarship **regulations** are often **stringent**, demanding considerable commitment to train and play and with conditions of maintaining playing standards. Again, this approach is more **professional** than the normal British university sports club, which has to cater for all who apply for membership and is run on minimal funding.

The problem for these 'sports students' (called 'jocks') is that they have a harsh sport regime to follow and tend to pick 'soft' courses to study alongside their sports programme. This separates them from the student body and although they have huge support from committed spectators (which funds the whole sports programme in most colleges - similar to the high schools - see figure 7.11), people tend to question the **jocks**' academic commitment.

Students accept these conditions because:

* It is an accepted, equitable pathway through college.
* They have been striving for this since the little leagues.
* There is considerable parent enthusiasm and school kudos.
* Successful games players receive adoration from student fans.
* There is the chance of winning a college rose bowl.
* The '**pro-draft**' is a chance to earn a fortune playing professionally.

figure 7.11 – Yale v Harvard at the Yale bowl

Sport scholarships

In statistical terms, the **NCAA** (National Collegiate Athletic Association) suggests that at least 20% of college gridiron and basketball players enter university on sports scholarships. This policy is sometimes called 'special admit', suggesting that some of these candidates are allowed admission on lower grades. There is nothing unusual about this as it occurs regularly in English universities with centre of sports excellence status.

In addition to huge 'multi-universities' and State universities, the **Ivy League Colleges**, akin to Oxford and Cambridge Universities in the UK, offer the **largest scholarships** for the best high school players. Young people and parents are very aware that sporting excellence can get their child into a top university (figure 7.11) with a scholarship to off-set the very high fees.

The quality of performance in specific high level games at college level, depends on producing **winning teams**. This, in itself, attracts large groups of spectators and sponsorship money, which in turn pays for high quality coaches and facilities. With the professional fixtures spread over a huge country, state colleges and universities become the spectator base for most games, leaving professional games to be supported on TV.

The pro-draft

This tradition not only gives collegiate sport a **high profile**, but provides major income as well as **recognition** as the final 'draft' into the **professional** ranks.

- The pro-draft gives the athletic departments considerable wealth and status. Athletic directors, **coaches** and trainers get **larger salaries** than many of the academic staff, because they command a major income from **spectators**, **commercial sponsorship** and **television** rights. If successful, the popularity and status of the institution is enhanced.
- The **pro-draft** is the process of selection of **top college players** in American football and basketball by the **professional major league clubs**.
- Once an athlete has completed a successful 4 years at college (university), he is ranked (by a panel from the colleges) according to ability and potential at his sport.
- This ranking is then accepted by the major professional teams, and the lowest ranked professional team has the **first option** at drafting the **best players**, with the top professional side having to accept lower ranked players (if any).
- The **pro-draft** is the apex of the **American sporting pyramid** set out in figure 7.12.

figure 7.12 – the sporting pyramid in the USA

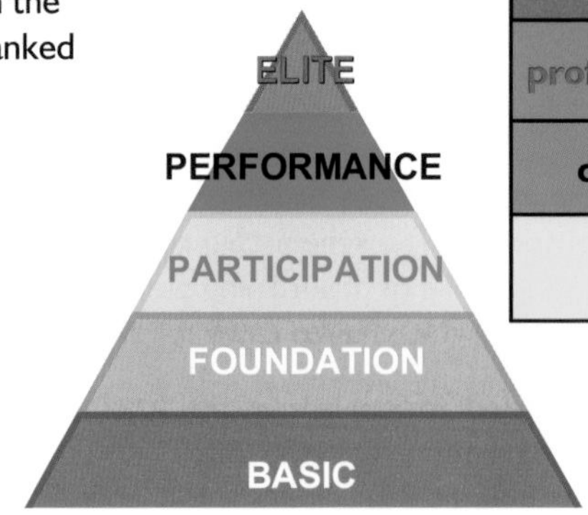

numbers of males participating in the **big four** sports 1994

	numbers	%
professional	3,155	0.164
college	90,629	4.7
high school	1,919,080	100

the big four sports are - football, basketball, baseball, ice hockey.

Most students in this system aspire to being **selected** to play for a professional club or a place in the national Olympic squad. Given the massive following for competitive sport in the USA, it is understandable why so many see the pro-draft as a gateway to higher education as well as a prosperous career. As with soccer in the UK, the drop-out rate is significant, but they do get an education that many English boys sacrifice for a possibly unsuccessful professional sports career.

The totals in figure 7.12 suggest that only 4.7% of high school players get scholarships and only 3.5% of these get onto the pro-draft (which is therefore 0.164% of high school players).

These 'traditional' sporting concepts describing sport in the USA are part of a socio-cultural stage in development rather than a permanent condition. American society and its sport are continually evolving and therefore changing in a global arena.

The historical circumstances behind the USA are gradually being corrected in favour of equal opportunity for all, with major steps in this process being the election of President Obama and the success of Hilary Clinton.

Practice questions

1) Suggest reasons why the USA were so successful in the early Modern Olympic Games.   4 marks

2) How did the American view of amateurism differ from that of the UK in the late 19th century and why was this the case?   4 marks

3) Explain the differences between sport in American schools and colleges, and sport in the UK school and college system.   6 marks

4) Physical Education programmes in the US would appear to be largely 'outcome-orientated' and rely heavily on student scores (e.g. a testing and measurement approach).
   How does this approach compare with PE within the National Curriculum here in the UK? Phrase your answer with reference to the value of the educative process, and the value of 'outcome-led' testing procedures.   4 marks

5) Compare the importance of PE programmes in US high schools with the situation here in the UK. Discuss the advantages and disadvantages in each case.   8 marks

6) Title IX was legislation passed to enable gender equality in educational programmes in the USA.
   Explain the need for this in the context of girls' sport in American high schools.   4 marks

7) Explain the place of testing and measuring in an American PE programme.   5 marks

8) How does the role of summer camps differ in the USA and the UK?   6 marks

9) How does extra-curricular sport differ between the USA and the UK?   4 marks

10) Compare the co-existence of physical education and school sport in Britain and in the USA, giving reasons for the differences you have identified.   20 marks

Mass participation in sport in the UK and the USA

1) a)   The 'frontier spirit' and 'wilderness experience' are two phrases often used in connection with America's 'great outdoors' philosophy. To what extent is this philosophy reflected in the outdoors movement here in the United Kingdom?   2 marks

    b)   How do 'national parks' in the US compare to those in this country?   2 marks

2) Explain the notion of the 'American Dream' in the context of mass participation.   4 marks

3) How does the existence of local games clubs influence participation in the USA and UK?   5 marks

4) Explain the reasons behind the suggestion that little league games fall between two stools?   6 marks

5) Give reasons for the low rate of participation in physical activity in the USA. How does this compare with participation rates in the UK?   6 marks

6) Outline alternative pathways into professional sport that are available to athletes (in its widest interpretation) in the USA and the UK.   6 marks

7) Compare the policy of 'Sport for All' with the American strategy of 'Lifelong Sport' and explain the social problems both face.   20 marks

8) International sporting success is pursued by many countries. Discuss the extent to which cultural factors influence the promotion and achievement of sporting excellence in both the UK and USA.   20 marks

CHAPTER 8 – THE BIG FOUR SPORTS IN THE USA

American football, gridiron

figure 8.1 – primitive American football 1827

History and development
* Early 19th century, mob football brought by English immigrants.
* 1827, Ivy League colleges playing their own style of football (figure 8.1).
* 1840s, Yale vs Princeton, the game banned for roughness.
* 1873, Colombia, Rutgers, Princeton and Yale formed the **Intercollegiate Association for Football**.
* 1874, handling accepted.
* 1876, the **Intercollegiate Football Association**, including Harvard.
* **Middle class** socially privileged student control in the colleges.
* 1882, possession concept included in rules unlike rugby.
* 1900, the **Big Ten** colleges formed a grouping for games.
* 1906, increasing number of injuries and deaths, President Theodore Roosevelt stepped in and demanded that the game be cleaned up.
* Forward pass, blocking, and protective gear included in the rules.
* 1920, first professional league formed.
* Hence completely separate (**isolationist**) development compared with soccer or rugby.
* 1950, NFL (National Football League) formed.
* 1960, AFL (American Football League) formed, hence two conferences.

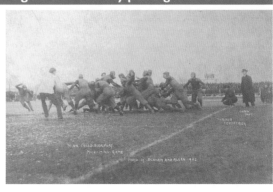
figure 8.2 – socially privileged from 1902

Commercialism
* In the 1960s, a bidding war between clubs and between the two conferences began for the best players from the college draft.
* To counter this, the '**pro-draft**' was introduced (see page 52 above) which was designed to retain a balance in each league and not allow the wealthiest team to buy the best players.
* Totally different from the British soccer leagues, where the richest clubs buy the best players, leading to a Premiership dominated by four or five clubs.
* Massive **commercial influence** of advertising and **media** coverage of all conference teams, so that finance is widely spread to allow each club and their fan base a chance to experience success.
* Franchise system, clubs bought and sold, grounds moved between states to suit owners.
* **Multi-million dollar empire**, attracting over 12 million spectators a season, with TV relays of big games to millions of paying viewers throughout the world.
* **Fans** feel an ownership of a dynamic college or professional team, and therefore provide funds for colleges and corporations via payments at the gate.

figure 8.3 – modern rules

Social determinants
* **Athleticism** is part of the frontier spirit and stimulates both cultural identity and the process of nation building.
* Football reflects the rugged nature of an emerging society which needs aggressive sports to satisfy and absorb its energy.
* The violent nature of the game itself (figure 8.3) appears to be a way in which spectator aggression can be averted (unlike UK soccer).
* The almost complete **lack of spectator violence** and hooliganism may be because **facilities** are excellent, it is popular with **families**, most of the crowd are **middle class,** and there is **continuous entertainment** by cheerleaders and other attractions.
* This compares with the lower class structures of British spectatorism.
* Competitive sport is seen as an instrument for cohesion in a multi-racial society, but in line with the dominant **WASP** sub-culture.

Basketball

History and development

Three games have their origin in North America:

- The Native American game of **baggatoway** (figure 8.4), which colonialists re-introduced as a rule orientated game called **lacrosse**.
- Two games invented by James A **Naismith**, a Canadian YMCA instructor at Springfield, Massachusetts, **basketball** in 1891 (figure 8.5 - the original court) and **volleyball**.

- Basketball was seen as an indoor team game for students to play in the severe New England winters.
- Communications between Naismith and Dartford Ladies College (England) led to the rules of basketball being played in England before 1900, and because the rules of the game were still changing, Dartford interpreted them in such a way as to produce **Netball**, which has retained zonal limits and no dribbling.
- In 1949 the National Basketball Association (NBA) had been established and the following year it began to enrol African American players.
- 1990s, aerial basketball and the 'slam-dunk' was now at its height.
- Great teams like the Chicago Bulls dominated the American scene.
- The 1992 US Olympic 'Dream Team' surpassed all previous teams.

Social determinants

- The popularity of basketball was because of its links with the YMCA.
- It was a game which was also popular with girls and very quickly spread into secondary schools and colleges.
- **Women's** basketball developed alongside the male version and as part of the intercollegiate programme (figure 8.6).
- At this time there was **racial segregation** and so white teams and black teams played separately and belonged to separate clubs and leagues.
- As early as 1907 basketball had become very popular among African Americans in the urban community with such clubs as the Smart Set Club and the Jersey City YMCA.
- Many clubs had **religious** as well as **athletic** associations.
- By 1909 professional black clubs were well established, a parallel to early working class professionals in 19th century English cricket.
- With the game being played in the high schools and colleges by 1912, the best black players were able to join the **Coloured Intercollegiate Athletic Association** (CIAA) and with that the Southern Intercollegiate Athletic Conference.
- Between the World Wars, outstanding **professional African American** teams emerged, raising the standard of play, the best known being the **Harlem Globetrotters** (figure 8.7) formed in 1924.
- The Amateur Basketball Association (ABA) had been formed in 1925, but no black players could join it and so there had been this separate development of a white governing body and teams.
- Northern universities had been including occasional black players before the Second World War, for example Bob Yancy at Boston University in 1937.
- 1950, the segregation laws in the USA began to be broken down, fairly comprehensively in the North, but with many delays in the South.
- The great black players were idolised by a racial group which was discriminated against by advantaged white society.
- **Outdoor courts** were made available for inner city black youth to use for recreation in what had become a cult following.
- This made basketball the flagship for African American sport and eventually led to this racial grouping gaining a place **on merit** in professional gridiron and baseball.

figure 8.4 – the North American Indian game of baggatoway

figure 8.5 – the original basketball court 1891

figure 8.6 – Smith college women's team 1892

figure 8.7 – the modern Harlem Globetrotters

Commercialism

- By the 1920s, talent in basketball was a chance to earn more money regardless of race.
- Throughout this period, intercollegiate basketball was attracting huge crowds, but entirely in the segregated form.
- From 1950 to 1960 the game flourished and its fan base expanded.
- As a result, many great black players made the top rankings with the payment of star players exploding. Such players as Larry Bird and Magic Johnson culminated in probably the greatest player of all time in Michael Jordan.
- By this time the majority of top players were African Americans, with top 'white' coaches earning huge salaries.
- **Most valuable player** awards instituted for the very best.
- **Millionaire salaries** and a huge fan base (1960s onwards).
- Endorsements poured in and the age of 'Nike' and 'Air Jordan' was born.
- Jordan himself established his own marketing company, as well as setting up the Michael Jordan Foundation.
- High schools and colleges had outstanding facilities (both for players and spectators, see figure 8.8).

figure 8.8 – the Chinle Wildcat Den High School basketball facility

Baseball

History and development

The **pre-history** of baseball and rounders occurred in Britain with **mob games** played by Celtic tribes and later Medieval rural communities. These folk games were organised stick and ball games using bases or poles with the English tending to use poles and the Irish and Welsh using bases. These pastimes were taken over to America by early settlers and by the 18th century a baseball-type game was being played with informal rules and improvised equipment.

figure 8.9 – championship baseball 1866 at the Elysian Fields

- 1792, the first recorded evidence of baseball being played in the USA is the mention of a game in Pittsfield, Massachusetts.
- 1823, 'base ball' regularly played on Saturdays near New York in Greenwich Village.
- 1845, first regular team using 'modern' rules, was the **New York Knickerbockers**.
- This was a social club for the upper middle classes of New York. These rules became known as the New York Game as against the Massachusetts Game in the Boston area.
- Compare with English cricket which started as a folk game and was rationalised with rules adopted gradually by the gentry and middle classes.
- 1860s, **rationalisation** of play, with written rules, a **popular** game played by members of the community.
- Professional baseball clubs along the Eastern Seaboard (figure 8.9).
- 1856, the sixteen New York clubs formed the **National Association of Base Ball Players** (NABBP, later NABPL). They held their own championship.
- Beginning in 1869, the NABBP permitted **professional** play, with the Cincinnati Red Socks (1869 to 1871), and the Boston Red Socks (in 1871) the first full professional teams.
- The first National Association for baseball lasted from 1871 until 1875, and the current National League was established in 1876.
- 1885, the first 'black' professional baseball club, the Cuban Giants, was formed.
- **Negro National League** (professional) formed in 1920, but then collapsed with the 1930 Great Depression.

figure 8.10 – a poster from 1902

Development

There were two developmental eras in the game in the 20th century. The period before 1920 has been called the '**dead-ball era**' or the inside game, because it was played over a small area. At this time it was a physically **violent** game, with focus on contact and pitching. From the 1920s with the increase in **spectator accommodation** and enthusiasm, the size of the playing area was increased, violent play controlled and focus moved to 'big hitters' like **Babe Ruth**. Babe could hit the ball into the crowd and he increased the spectacle of hitting '**homers**'.

Commercialism

- By the 1860s, newspapers were heralding baseball as the National Pastime or the National Game.
- Unfortunately, constant breaking of contracts and legal disputes between the two governing bodies caused a bidding war for players, but after 1902, both leagues and the NABPL agreed on a **World Series** between the two major league champions.
- 1920s, there was reward for the most talented players regardless of race at **semi** and **full professional** level.
- From the 1980's onward the major league game has changed dramatically because of their commercial independence, and because of the changes in the marketing and television broadcasting of sporting events. Also the advertising revenue available by brand-naming and player sponsorship deals made a huge difference to the commercial nature of the game.
- Regular television coverage changed a sport predominantly serving a home crowd of local spectators into a sport which was now attracting arm-chair spectators nation-wide. Additionally, the New York Yankees and the Boston Red Socks, for example, also had their own cable network, which beams their games throughout the USA. As a result, this has massively increased the wealth of successful clubs and the wages of top players.
- This wealth also positively stimulated scientific advances in the sport, but on the negative side this has led to players taking performance enhancing drugs.
- There are 71 or more million spectators (figure 8.12) annually (at least equal to the other three professional sports attendance figures put together). Compared to Britain, it has the popularity of soccer, with a format which reflects the socio-cultural differences between the USA and cricket loving Britain.

figure 8.11 – Jackie Robinson 1954

Social determinants

- Baseball is part of community culture, a recreational and sportive **game of the people** not like gridiron football and basketball, which owed much to educational institutions and the YMCA respectively.
- Baseball had become the people's game, as soccer became in Britain.
- Following the Civil War there were over 400 clubs, including clubs as far away as California. These clubs only involved **white players**.
- What initially developed as a **popular urban white immigrant** game, also became an attraction to **African American** and **Hispanic American** members of the **inner city** communities, as a game easily and cheaply set up in any open space.
- A colour bar operated until 1950.
- The major '**World Series**' league for **black** players was revived between 1943 and 1948 and this marked the high point of black baseball. However, **Jackie Robinson** (figure 8.11) signed a contract with the Brooklyn Dodgers in 1947.
- This marked the end of segregated baseball hence talented black baseball players began to play in the white-only major leagues.
- The nature of baseball is such that unlike basketball, smaller ball players could find a place in the professional game. Subsequently, it became a game in which Hispanic Americans could excel.
- **Expansion of the game** took place in high schools and at collegiate level, where baseball has joined the process used by the other three 'big sports'. This process uses educational institutions as a method of grassroots development and as part of the process of identifying and promoting talent.

figure 8.12 – major spectatorship at the Oakland Coliseum 1966

Women's Baseball

- 1943-1954, **All-American Girls Professional Baseball League** (AAGPBL) gave over 600 women athletes the opportunity to play professional baseball.
- 1948, spectators attending women's baseball games reached almost 1 million.
- After the Second World War the major league baseball players came back home and female baseball players were relegated to the job of being a housewife. Hence AAGPBL lost its audience, struggled with finances, and ceased to exist.
- 1997, the professional Ladies League Baseball was born, but then faced financial difficulties through lack of sponsorship.
- Today the **American Women's Baseball Federation** (AWBF) is a non-profit amateur sports organisation formed to promote women's baseball and establish it as a mainstream sport.
- Elite USA female players have access to major global competitions such as the World Cup.
- But are denied the financial rewards and kudos that their male counterparts have.

Ice hockey

The origin of stick and ball games is as old as civilisation. The folk game of **bandy** in Northern Europe and England is the major root of ice hockey, because of its direct association with winter and playing on ice. Part of Celtic culture, the game seems to have been pushed west in Britain as a result of various invasions, and is still played traditionally in Wales and Ireland. Because East Anglia has traditional colder North European winters, the flat landscape lent itself to bandy as a game on ice.

figure 8.13 – mob shinty on ice

History and development
* European immigrants took versions of this mob game to Canada and the eastern seaboard of the USA.
* The earliest records suggest that the game took root in Canada as a winter game, where ice was the natural facility.
* 1810, '**hurly** played on the long pond' by boys at King's College School in Windsor, Nova Scotia.
* The Canadian term 'shinny' derives from the Scottish '**shinty**' and referred to a game played on ice or in the streets, possibly made more **violent** through the influence of early Native American lacrosse.
* 1843, the British Army play in Kingston, Ontario, Canada and later at Halifax, Nova Scotia.
* The use of a piece of ice as against a ball was natural in the earliest folk games, and the term **puck** is very much of Gaelic origin.
* 1870s, **written rules** were made in the schools and universities, the first known at Montreal's McGill University.
* Later than the standardisation of soccer and rugby rules in Britain.
* 1875, first indoor ice hockey appears to have been at Montreal's Victoria Skating Rink.
* 1877, first recognised club, therefore, was McGill University Hockey Club in 1877.
* 1881, first urban club team was Montreal Victorias, using the Victoria Skating Rink.
* 1893, over 100 ice hockey clubs in Montreal alone and leagues throughout Canada, there were some professional players.
* 1925, Sir John Franklin wrote of hockey being played on ice as a community sport (as in figure 8.14).
* Games mostly played on **natural ice**, but in Europe, refrigerated indoor areas were built in most towns as a commercial expansion of free and figure skating, not so far to include ice-hockey.
* The principle of the '**melting pot**' was such that students carried the game with them when they left university and were responsible for the spread of the organised game.

figure 8.14 – ice hockey in 1922

* The game in the **USA** was delayed probably because they weren't inclined to encourage 'colonial' Canadian games.
* 1893, Yale and John Hopkins played their first ice hockey match. This is not to presume that the game was not being played informally during the winter in northern and central states.
* 1896, the Amateur Hockey League founded in New York.
* 1903, first professional team, **Portland Lake Hockey Club**, formed in Houghton, Michigan, and the first **professional league**, the **National Hockey League** (NHL) was established in that year.
* The physicality of the game has retained its basic attraction and social acceptability by having considerable safety equipment (particularly for the goal-minder), and use of the 'sin-bin' to control excessively violent behaviour.

Social determinants
* The game became popular throughout the North and Mid West, with numerous leagues, supervised by the NHL, but it was not until the 1960s that the **professional game** spread to the Southern and Western States.
* This was because of the need for sophisticated facilities in a game which did not lend itself to a warm climate.
* Development of the **women's game** lagged behind the men, but there were pockets of enthusiasm as early as 1921.
* 1998, more than a thousand girls played in National leagues, and in 1999 the **National Women's Hockey League** (NWHL) was formed.
* The rules for the women's game do not allow **body-checking** (penalties are awarded for this offence).

Commercialism

*   The advent of mass media had a huge influence on the expansion of this sport, as the whole country was able to see the speed and thrills of the game. Attendance rates match gridiron football and basketball.
*   The modern game has all the heroes of the other three, particularly the great **Wayne Gretzky** (figure 8.15).
*   The game's speed and physicality includes body checking and the risk from swinging sticks, hard hit pucks in the air, congestion in the goal mouths and the sheer heat-of-the-moment emotionalism. This is attractive to commercial interests.

figure 8.15 – Wayne Gretzky

General summary

Professional Games **Leagues** in the USA are **closed corporation**s with a fixed number of teams. This is called **franchise** and it is possible for these corporations to buy the best teams and **relocate** them to suit the League and associated income. This means that promising professional teams can be moved from one town to another, taken to other states, and brought from Canada to the USA in the case of ice hockey. It is all to do with the wealth and power of the particular corporation and the commercial advantages to the team that moves. This affects a team's national status and the status of the corporation and its commercial earning capacity. Ice hockey has spectacular examples of relocation, with increase in the standard of the game and its popularity in the States. More recently, there has been a relocation of Quebec Nordiques and Winnipeg Jets, both members of the NHL, to the USA.

This phenomenon does not happen in Britain or Australia and seems to reflect the extent to which professional sport is in the hands of private corporations and commercial business interests.

Practice questions

1) Briefly describe the growth of ice hockey in the USA and explain why it was delayed.   4 marks

2) Compare the development of baseball in the USA with cricket in England.   8 marks

3) Analyse the social phenomenon of 'white flight' in the context of American professional basketball.   4 marks

4) Compare the game of American Gridiron Football with British Rugby Union, given that it has the same roots.   20 marks

5) Compare the cultural and commercial development of baseball and soccer in the USA and the UK.   8 marks

6) Compare the cultural and commercial development of ice hockey and rugby league in the USA and the UK.   12 marks

7) To what extent did rugby union and American Football originate as middle class games?   8 marks

8) Compare the role of university sport in the USA and the UK, as a pathway into professional sport.   4 marks

9) It is only recently that elite women athletes have gained enough recognition for their athletic talent and social acceptance as role models to earn a living playing sports.
    Discuss the view that most professional women athletes in the USA and the UK receive very little media coverage or pay when compared with their male counterparts.   8 marks

CHAPTER 9 – AUSTRALIA

Cultural context

STUDENT NOTE

An outline of sport in Australia is briefly set out in 'AS Revise PE for OCR', ISBN: 978 1 901 424 52 2 page 105 onwards.

Historical determinants

Aborigines are the native inhabitants of Australia having arrived during the Ice Age via land bridges linking Asia and Australia. When the water level rose, the Aborigines were isolated on the island of Australia for several thousand years. They lived a spiritual existence in nomadic tribes and created and maintained their own territories. A large number were killed in acts of ethnic cleansing by colonialists, as well as their land being forcibly taken from them.

Sports had a strong religious and ritualistic meaning, based on hunting and games used as preparation for battles (figure 9.1). Activities included:
- Target and distance throwing of sticks, boomerangs, and spears.
- Kangaroo rat or weet weet in which a piece of wood was thrown.
- Wrestling.
- Mungan-mungan, a white stick is placed in an area (representing a girl), young boys had to keep old men from the stick using passing and tackling skills.

figure 9.1 – native Aboriginal games

Colonisation

Australia was similar to the USA in that it is a fairly 'new' country, being 'discovered' in 1606, then colonised in 1788. However, Australia's population is far smaller than that of the USA, and Britain has had a far bigger colonial influence on the development of the Australian nation than the USA.

In 1850, **gold rush fever** indirectly supported the import of the new sports of baseball and basketball by American miners. This was the first non-European influence on Australian sport. There were frequent sporting competitions between settlers and members of the parent stock, and sport provided the opportunity for the colonials to beat their masters (the English Motherland!) at their own game - hence the future development of intense rivalry in sporting matters.

As in the UK at this time, **wagering** was a popular pastime among ex-convicts and working class people. Aboriginal tribes had little political status and were ignored in society as well as in sporting matters.

Australia as a prison
- From 1788, Australia was used as a 'detention centre' for convicted criminals. In 1830, 90% of the population of New South Wales and Tasmania consisted of convicts, former convicts, or relatives of convicts!

- In 1840, the transportation of criminals was abolished, and from then on **free settlements of Anglo-Scottish Protestants** formed alongside ex-convicts aad Irish Catholic workers. 'Colonials' consisted of convict settlers (recent arrivals following deportation from Britain as punishment for quite small criminal offences), the ruling class and first free settlers groups.

- Sport in the pre-Victorian period was developed within the British social structure, which was based on **chivalry**, **gentlemanly conduct** and **moral development**, usually thought to be exclusive to the British aristocratic class.

Development of sport in Australia
By the 1820s Australian cricket had organised clubs, and in 1825 horse racing was established at the Sydney Turf Club. Other English sports introduced were wrestling and football, with the Scots introducing shinty and hurling.

Celtic links may account for the eventual adoption of Aussie rules football (played with an oval ball) with its similarity to Gaelic football (played with a round ball).

In the late 19th century, there was a strong influence from the British tradition of **fair play**, **amateurism** and **muscular christianity** (from British Public Schools). Rowing, cricket, football and rugby cultivated this ethos.

Development of sport

During the 40 years immediately after its federation in 1901, Australia had a **white-Australian policy**, which meant that Asian immigrants were denied entry. During this period, the aboriginal minority were denied access to sporting opportunity - having been fully integrated in the 1860s.

By 1910 there were National Governing Bodies in Australian football, cricket, cycling (figure 9.2), golf, lawn bowls and rifle shooting, with upper class (**WASP**) administrators who exercised control and power in these sporting organisations.

Following the second world war, the Australian economy (previously based on farming communities) emerged as an industrialised and urbanised society which pushed the old amateur ideal to the margins. Immigration led to the diversification of the sporting culture in Australia.

Geographical determinants

Table A2.1 above (page 40) summarises the population and geographical statistics. With a land area roughly the same as the USA and a population less than a tenth, there is a very low population density in the country as a whole. Most of the population is concentrated in major cities on the eastern coastal strip, so facilities for sport (provision) can be available to 75% of the population.

Also summarised in table A2.1, Australia has developed a sophisticated transport system to cope with internal transport needs consisting of highways, airports and railway links.

Government policy

Australia has a **centralised federal administration** (based in Canberra) with devolved State and Territory administrations. Sports administration follows this model, and States express preferences about sports (like Victoria and Aussie Rules Football).

The Australian Sports Commission (ASC)

The Australian Sports Commission is the Australian government body that manages, develops and invests in sport at all levels. The ASC is funded by the Department of the Environment, Sport and Territories (DEST), and received $251.3m in 2007-8, compared with $63.4m in funding in 1993-4.

The range of services provided includes talent ID and promoting and increasing opportunities for participation. In 1989 the **Australian Institute of Sport** (AIS) merged with the ASC and is now aimed at the development of elite athletes.

However, there is a **decentralised** sports administration in which each state has its own sports organisation at elite and mass participation levels. This is not just an extension of the ASC or AIS, for example the Victorian Institute of Sport (VIS).

Commercialism of sport

The nature of sport in Australia

Sport is extremely popular in Australia, and is a massive part of the nation's culture (figure 9.3), with participation (23.5% of Australians over the age of 15 regularly participate in organised sporting activities) and spectator rates rising above most other countries. Hence there is a very broad base to the sport development pyramid which leads to Australians tending to do very well at both the Olympic and Commonwealth Games.

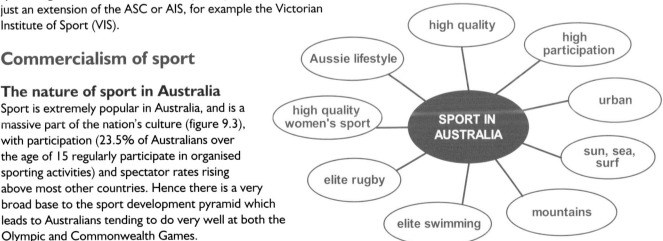

figure 9.3 – sport in Australia

high quality

high participation

Aussie lifestyle

urban

high quality women's sport

SPORT IN AUSTRALIA

sun, sea, surf

elite rugby

mountains

elite swimming

Australia hosted the 1956 Summer Olympics in Melbourne, and the 2000 Summer Olympics in Sydney, and has ranked among the top six medal-takers since 2000. Australia has also hosted the 1938, 1962, 1982, and 2006 Commonwealth Games.

Commercialism of sport

Other major international events held in Australia include the Grand Slam Australian Open tennis tournament, international cricket matches, and the Formula One Australian Grand Prix.

figure 9.4 – Rod Laver, tennis superstar straddled both amateur and professional eras

Sport is **heavily supported** by the government (via the Australian Sports Commission), in the form of excellent funding and organisation. Popular sports include Aussie Rules football, cricket, swimming, athletics, surfing, rugby league and of course rugby union.

Sport provides the Australians with a **key identity** - a way of showing the world the true Australian character, and a major motive for success in Australian sport is the beating of England (as the old Mother country) whenever possible. Hence all test matches (in cricket and rugby union or league) between AUS and ENG (or GBR) are treated with great seriousness! The ashes series at cricket played alternately in England and Australia are fiercely fought by the Aussies - and usually won by them!!!

Australia has strong international teams in cricket, field hockey, netball, rugby league and rugby union, and it performs well in cycling (top of the medals table in World championships 2010), rowing, and swimming.

figure 9.5 – the change in presentation of cricket, Ricky Ponting winning the World cup

Australian success and the media

The highest-rating television programmes in Australia include sports coverage (15% of television time in Australia is allocated to sport), such as the summer Olympic Games, State of Origin games (see page 68 below), and the grand finals of the National Rugby League and Australian Football League.

Some of Australia's best-known people are swimmers (Dawn Fraser and Ian Thorpe), sprinter Cathy Freeman, tennis players Rod Laver (figure 9.4) and Margaret Court, and cricketer Donald Bradman.

The **media golden triangle** (media, sponsorship, sport) applies to Australian sport just as in the UK and the USA (see page 42 above), and the media drive the commercialisation of sport.

In 2002, Orange paid $8.2 million to become the main sponsor for the Australian cricket team until 2007, and Brewers VB also paid a vast amount ($1.7m) to sponsor and name the VB series against England in 2003 which included the 2003 Ashes games.

Influence of media moguls on the style of rugby league and cricket

For example (page 32 above), the TV war between Kerry Packer (Channel 9 and the Australian Rugby League) and Rupert Murdoch (News Corporation and the Superleague) has provided great resources for cricket (figure 9.5) and rugby league in Australia, as well as changed the face and look of these sports as they are played.

Channel 9 currently has sole rights to the national cricket team's games in Australia, which means they are able to decide when and where games are played in exchange for substantial revenue.

Social determinants

Discrimination

In 1971 a policy of **multiculturalism** was an attempt to offer opportunity, provision and esteem for all Australians.
*   **Opportunity** is supposed to be colour blind and gender blind.
*   **Provision** is extensive for most sports within the highly populated coastal strips - but non-existent in the bulk of the central area. Sport is a mostly state run enterprise for the Olympic sports (with some private provision for equestrianism and golf for example), so cost should not be a factor in provision.
*   **Esteem** is very high for those people making the grade - regardless of skin-colour or gender.

Racial inequalities

Aborigines suffered severe discrimination prior to World War II thus affecting their self-esteem. Exclusive Aboriginal National competitions have now been organised (National Aboriginal Australian Rules Carnival, Interstate Aborigine Rugby League Carnivals, Special Aborigine Sports Days).

The **Indigenous Sport Programme** works with 16 national sporting organisations to improve delivery of sports to indigenous populations. The programme offers cultural advice and guidance to sporting organisations via the employment of Indigenous Sport Development Officers. These ISDOs ensure that the delivery of sport within the industry responds to specific needs of the indigenous communities, which is specific provision to establish and raise the esteem of this community.

Gender Issues

Australian women got involved in sport alongside their menfolk at an early stage in Australian development. Unfortunately, the ratio of immigrants in the first (convict) phase of immigration was 5 to 1 (men to women), leading to sexual exploitation on a large scale.

But by December 1934, the Australian women's team played the English women in the first women's cricket test match at the Brisbane Exhibition Ground (figure 9.6).

There have been great **women champions at athletics** including Cathy Freeman - winner of the Olympic gold in the 400m at Sydney 2000 (figure 9.7). Cathy also carried the flame for the Sydney Olympic Games, hence reinforced herself as a role model and icon for indigenous Australians.

Other women's successes are in swimming (with Dawn Fraser and Shane Gould), tennis (Margaret Court), netball, and field hockey (World and Olympic champions).

Australian society has a very masculine dominance, and as a result, the subject of women in sport has a very high profile (compared with the social class traditions in the UK in which the Victorian role of the female was more pronounced).

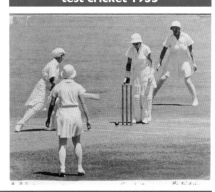

figure 9.6 – Australian women's test cricket 1935

figure 9.7 – Cathy Freeman superstar

Disabled sport

Disabled sport is part of the ASC Sport Performance and Development division, referred to as Disability Sport Unit (DSU). Its mission is 'to ensure that all Australians with disabilities have opportunities to participate in sporting activities at the level of their choice'.

Australia has achieved considerable success in the summer Paralympic Games.

Values

Bush culture

The Bush has always played a central role in Australian society. This is derived from the original aboriginal culture, which is reflected in the present behaviour of some Australians. The term '**bush culture**' describes the community spirit and 'get away from the rat race' notions of Aussie lifestyle. This reflects the slow pace that accompanies life in the bush under (mostly) perfect blue skies, time to relax and reflect, time to look at the wonders of nature, and time for 'fair-dinkum' blokes to have a few tinnies and plenty of laughs. http://www.sandythorne.com.au/wags_2.html

This derives from the fact that the bush was a place of masculine endeavour - men carved out a living from the harsh 19th century environment with little or no separate place for women.

Social melting-pot

This term refers to the fact that the whole of Aussie society is built around **multiculturalism**, reflecting the wide differences in background within the population. The past convict and immigrant status of the population was overlaid by more recent immigration from Britain and Ireland, and was followed by those from Eastern Europe and Asia, all of which have contributed to sports development and attitude to competition and winning.

'Land of the fair go'

This notion followed from a campaign for '**fair dinkum**' fee paying for students. '**Australia, land of the fair go**', is widely perceived as having a student support system that is one of the best and fairest in the world. This notion is that Aussie society is fair and not serving the interest only of the privileged few. There is a very **strong egalitarian strand** within Australia which would extend 'fairness' to everyone. Unfortunately, negative perspectives regarding the Aboriginal minority in society still exist among some people.

The class nature of the society (comparing with the UK) is almost invisible and non-existent.

Physical education and school sport

Fitness, skill and participation levels

As in the UK, Australia had a central concern about physical inactivity and the need to develop a balanced, active and **healthy lifestyle**, because of an increasing problem of **obesity** from over-eating and inactivity. But such is the more dynamic approach to life in Australia and the opportunities for active leisure, that this is far less of a problem than in the UK and the USA.

Sport education and physical education project

- From 1973, in Victoria a wide range of curriculum ideas came from the Ministry of Education and the **Australian Council for Health, Physical Education and Recreation** (ACHPER). The latter is a single unifying organisation which Britain has still not fully achieved.
- Though progressive, Victoria has still not totally achieved its objective of sustaining a daily physical education programme for all primary children. The Federal Government had put its weight behind **Aussie Sport**, a policy promoted by the **Australian Sports Commission** (ASC), and designed to overcome the lack of games skills among **primary** children.
- The Victoria Ministry of Education supported Aussie Sport, and cash has been given to introduce a new programme, **Youth Sport**, for young people between 13 and 18 years-of-age.
- The **joint use of sports facilities** was begun with dual use by schools and clubs. Secondary schools were also encouraged to develop programmes for children who are talented in sport in a similar manner to the Youth Sport Trust in England and Wales. The controlling State of Victoria body is the **Victoria State School Sport Association** (VSSSA).
- Post war, Australia adopted the American system of high schools with the **Higher School Certificate** (HSC) taken in the final two years (similar to A2 for 18 year-olds in England and Wales). The **Victorian Certificate of Education** (VCE) replaced the HSC for successful year 11 and 12 or 17+ students, equivalent to the British AS level (includes PE).
- The federal government operates a Secondary Allowance Scheme which is a means-tested grant available to students for completing their VCE.

A **Physical and Sport Education** (PASE) committee was set up in 1992, and a year later the **Sport Education and Physical Education Project** (SEPEP), which became fully operational in 1995. SEPEP focused on other roles a performer can adopt in sport (rather than the general category of 'player'), such as coach, organiser, administrator, and referee. The objective is to have a daily lesson in either sport or PE, which compares with the 2 hour (present) or 5 hour (future) offers within England and Wales.

The State of Victoria programmes

State of Victoria programmes for the encouragement of participation in physical activity in schools and the community are:
- Sports leader programmes.
- School club links, and Sports linkage scheme.
- Sportsperson in schools project, and Sports search.
- Teacher games.
- State award schemes (**De Coubertin award**).

The De Coubertin award is an initiative of the Victoria Olympic Council and the Department of Education and Early Childhood Development. It is an award in which students must submit an artwork or literary piece that demonstrates what Olympic Values mean to them. In 2008, 166 students from years 10, 11 and 12 and their schools received this prestigious award.

Outdoor adventurous education (OAE)

Size, climate and topography make Australia similar to the USA. But Australia has a small population and vast areas of wilderness which means that an extensive coastline and coastal belt is populated by a number of large cities. The huge interior (or Red Centre) is virtually unpopulated with little prospect of development.

figure 9.8 – Grampians National Park, Victoria

There is no grading system for the various terrains and much of Australia's outback (figure 9.8) is unmapped. Huge tracts of land and coastal waters are owned by the State (as in the USA), and the State Departments of Conservation, Forest and Land manage the parks.

OAE is high on the education agenda due to the vast array of natural environments on offer, their hazards, and the need to educate children on the dangers they may encounter.

OAE

The overall focus is on lifesaving and safety in the outdoors. Victoria schools also make use of the free resources available such as the sea and the outback. Organised trips include:

- Sport climbing, mountaineering and trekking.
- Tandem parachute.
- Orienteering.
- Kayaking or canoeing (figure 9.9).

There are four different types of facility, namely, Outdoor Schools, Environmental Centres, Outdoor Pursuit Centres, and Outdoor Leisure and Environmental Centres.

figure 9.9 – activities at Tharwa Outward Bound school

Mass participation

Australian government policy for participation in sport is called 'Active Australia' which recognised the need for grassroots development, supported by progressive pathways towards excellence. This Australian model is the basis of the UK's Performance Pyramid and the numerous programmes now being operated by UK Sport.

This policy of 'Sport for All' has included the updating to 'More Active Australia' as a strong message that this concept has not yet been achieved, and that a philosophy of active healthy lifestyles is yet to be fully operational in Australia. This programme requires each state government to implement programmes within set guidelines to promote participation.

The main aim of this campaign is to get all Australians involved in some form of activity, either recreation, outdoor recreation, fitness or other initiatives such as Sportstart, Sport It, Sport Everyone's Game, CAPS and Sport for All. Participation figures in Victoria include 480,000 in aerobics or fitness, 1 million in walking, and 320,000 in swimming out of a population of 5.2 million.

Practice questions

1) How is physical education in the Australian State of Victoria influenced by its size, its population density and its desire to promote elite sport? 6 marks

2) In Australia, its many national parks (with the exception of the Great Barrier Reef) are maintained by the State within which they lie. How does this administration, as well as scale and diversity, compare with the 'national parks' in the UK? 4 marks

3) Identify differences in the selection of sporting talent among school children within the United Kingdom and Australia. How are these explained historically? 6 marks

4) Outline two initiatives in the UK and two initiatives in Australia which aim to promote Physical Education and school sport. 4 marks

5) Compare the function of sport in a UK school or college with a typical high school in Melbourne, Australia, explaining why similarities and differences exist between them. 20 marks

6) Identify the governing bodies controlling sport in Australia and Britain and describe their main functions. 4 marks

7) Examine the shared characteristics of the Australian 'More Active Sport' strategy with the British strategies for lifelong sports participation, recognising the main constraints operating in Australia. 5 marks

8) Explain the strategies to improve disabled participation in sport in the UK and Australia, and discuss the cultural problems of opportunity, provision and esteem shared by the two countries. 8 marks

9) Identify major government policies that are currently implemented both in Australia and in the UK that are aimed to promote mass participation and encourage a long active lifestyle. 4 marks

10) Discuss how ethnic minority groups have suffered from discrimination in both Australia and the UK. Give reasons why this has occurred. 6 marks

11) The UK and Australia have to tackle the problem of increasing levels of obesity and inactivity. Compare the efforts being made in these two countries to encourage regular physical exercise and assess the cause of this social problem, suggesting what else might be done. 20 marks

CHAPTER 10 – SPORT and the PURSUIT of EXCELLENCE in AUSTRALIA

The pursuit of excellence at sport in Australia

After winning eight gold, seven silver and two bronze medals at the Munich Olympic Games in 1972, the Montreal Games of 1976 did not produce one Australian winner. This was a stark warning to the Australians, with a great history in competitive sport, that the world had moved on. Unlike many countries, they decided to do something about it. There was a need for better coaching, improved facilities, pre-games international competition and the freedom, both financial and in terms of providing the time for training, to train as hard as the Europeans. The old philosophy 'to do your best' was no longer enough.

The master plan

By 1980, a master plan had been devised, and the concept of the **Australian Institute of Sport (AIS)** was announced, to be based in Canberra (figures 10.1 and 10.2), with comments that it must serve an elite, but not miss out the grass roots. In its first year, of 800 applicants 152 were successful. 72% came from the seaboard cities of Sydney, Melbourne and Brisbane with ages ranged from 13 to 30 in eight sports.

Given the size of Australia, it was deemed necessary to establish a **second administrative tier** at State level. For example the **Victoria Institute of Sport** was established in Melbourne. Once this tier was established, it was agreed that there would also be a **decentralised** activity specialisation established in these State centres, and for example again, Melbourne was nominated as the National Tennis Centre.

A **third tier** was then established in the major towns in each State, where again certain sports were focused, but not to an extent where other sports were ignored. There remained the problem of distance given the size of the country, but this was overcome through **village facilities** being upgraded and **school programmes** being revised with also the provision of **residential facilities**.

figure 10.1 – the AIS at Canberra

figure 10.2 – the pool at the AIS at Canberra

Talent development

With an **administrative pyramid** established and **new facilities** to match, the Australians made sure that what they provided was backed up by **science** and exhaustive **research** of the latest American and European developments. This included the latest **coaching methods**.

The **early recognition of talent** was the final and most important step. **School programmes** were updated with various **competitive sports awards**, and a **testing system** was used to identify young talent. This would lead to early selection for state or national squads and top class coaching.

Pathways to professional sport

- A **Sport Talent Encouragement Programme** (STEP) provides a pathway of financial support, coaching and access to first class facilities for talented 'amateur' sportspeople.
- Progressing to a **Scholarship Sports Programme** (SSP) and then to the **Australian Athlete Scholarship Scheme** (AASS) which provides full financial support and coaching. An AASS player may then progress to a professional club.
- In both Aussie rules football and rugby league, efforts have been made to support minor leagues, but the commercial influence of elite clubs has led to super-leagues. The **draft system** (similar to the USA) used to operate in both sports, but now only in Aussie Rules.
- Many sports have been reluctant to turn pro (similar to UK). But the advantage of being in the southern hemisphere is that performers are able to earn large salaries in Europe during the Australian closed season.

Case studies

Cricket

History

In 1803, the first game was played in Australia. The rules, values, and conventions were brought by English settlers. By 1823, Sydney had its first cricket club (the Australian cricket club), and by 1838 Melbourne Cricket Club was formed. Matches between clubs were occasional because of poor communications and distances to travel.

figure 10.3 – aboriginal touring team 1868

- 1851, the first inter-colonial game took place (Victoria versus Tasmania), and in 1856, Victoria versus New South Wales (**NSW**) at the **MCG** (Melbourne Cricket Ground).
- 1861, the All-England Cricket XI toured Australia, making a substantial impact upon the country.
- 1868, the Australian Aboriginal cricket team (figure 10.3) was the first Australian team to tour England.
- 1877, the various Australian colonies combined to play the first England versus Australia cricket match, which they won!
- 1882, the **Ashes** saga began (see page 32 above and figures 4.11 and 4.12) with England's defeat in England by the Australian side.
- **1892,** the Sheffield shield was established as the premier competition between states.
- 1905, the **Australian Cricket Board** was formed.

figure 10.4 – Don Bradman, greatest cricketer ever?

By the 1920s, Australian cricket was at its best, with **Don Bradman** as probably the best player ever (figure 10.4). His statistics were amazing. Against Queensland at the SCG, Bradman set a world record for first-class cricket by scoring 452 not out in only 415 minutes. He continued until 1948.

- 1932-33 saw the bodyline **Ashes series** in Australia won by England with dubious 'win-at-all-costs' tactics.
- In the 1950s, **Richie Benaud** became test captain and scored centuries and regularly took 5 wickets per innings against England. He became most noted as a commentator (in England) in the 1980s and 1990s.

The modern game and commercialism

- In 1977 the **Channel Nine** (owned by Kerry Packer) cricket rights deal led to a confrontation with the cricket authorities (see pages 32 and 33 above), when top players from several countries rushed to join Packer at the expense of their national sides. Packer's aim was to secure broadcasting rights for Australian cricket, and he was largely successful. Although the global cricket establishment fiercely opposed Packer in the courts, players were paid huge amounts to play in World Series cricket.

- This was a **commercially** led development, and the game was changed by Packer's media-led drive. The whole look of cricket was changed, with coloured kit, a white ball, and limited-over games under floodlights (see page 32 above). This was an attempt to improve spectator appeal, and hence income to Channel Nine via broadcasting advertising.

- Australia have won the last three cricket World cups (1999, 2003, 2007) and are ranked at World number 1 (2009), with great players - Shane Warne, Matthew Hayden, Glen McGrath, and Clive Ponting as captain.

Women's cricket

figure 10.5 – Karen Rolton, the Aussie cricket captain 2009

- 1874, the first recorded Australian women's match was at Bendigo.
- 1886, women's club cricket commenced.
- 1934, the first England versus Australia tests, England won 2-0. Currently, participation in women's cricket is at 12,281 - compared with over 500,000 for the men.
- Australia (figure 10.5) have won the women's World cup 4 times, but England are current champions from 2009.

Rugby League

The size and **isolation** of Australia was a significant factor in the emergence of different games in **different states**. In addition the **racial dominance** of certain immigrant groups may well have caused the game of rugby football to develop in NSW and Queensland, whereas in Victoria, Southern and Western Australia, the Irish influence might have led to the development of Aussie Rules. Post-war patterns of East European immigration led to a much later development of soccer.

- Mid 1800s, the **handling game of football** was being played as 'rugby' in Australia.
- As in England, difficulties began to be experienced by some clubs and players over the need for player payment.
- 1907, the New Zealand 'All Golds' played the English Northern Union (League) clubs in England, and this stimulated the Australians to establish the New South Wales Rugby Football League.
- The 'All Golds' passed through NSW on their return and played against NSW and Queensland - under the new RL rules.
- 1908, nine clubs formed a league - and the **Kangaroos** were formed as the national side.
- 1924, the Australian Rugby League (ARL) was formed to organise and co-ordinate national and international fixtures.

The characteristics of RL in Australia were developed through **working class** associations with the game, through **popular** support by urban spectators, being reinforced by **Polynesian players**, and as a high level **professional** sport.

State of Origin Series
- 1977, Western Australia was scheduled to play Victoria in the **Aussie Rules State of Origin Series**, members of the Rugby League were invited.
- 1980, it was decided to present the inter-state rugby league matches as State of Origin games, where three matches were played annually and players were bound by their state of origin.
- State of Origin was defined as the state of the first senior rugby league club to which they had registered.
- Also players must not have played for any other country.
- The prestige of these games is so high that players will only represent Australia even though they were from another country (this applies particularly to Polynesian players).

From 1980 to 2008, Queensland won 17 to NSW's 12. Over the years the games have had a very bad reputation for violent conduct as well as disagreements between the two state boards. This led to slanging matches between the Queensland 'cane toads' and the NSW 'cockroaches'.

Super League
In 1997 the rugby league premiership was split between the **ARL** and the **Super League**. This was a commercially led development by Rupert Murdoch similar to the Packer development in cricket. In addition to the State of Origin games, a Super League Tri-series was played between NSW, Queensland and New Zealand. These games were selected according to State of Origin rules, but do not count towards the official competition record.

Both NSW and Queensland have internal cup competitions as well as professional leagues supported by urban amateur leagues, where each professional club has an **academy** for the development of young players. This means that unlike Aussie Rules, there is no 'American-style' draft system in operation. Britain has now accepted the principle of academies in most professional games clubs.

figure 10.6 – Darren Lockyer - captain of the Oz team at the 2008 World Cup

However, the biggest influence on the English Rugby League has been the introduction of a professional summer league programme, stimulated by the:
- Establishment of the **Super League** in Great Britain, with regular **TV** coverage.
- Change of season to match up with rugby league in the Southern Continents.
- Resulting in the avoidance of conflict from professional soccer and rugby union.
- Increased global popularity of the game with the World Cup (figure 10.6) and the World Cup Challenge Trophy.

Rugby Union

- 1865, the first football club was the Sydney FC.
- Over the next decade several teams were reported in both NSW and Queensland, but they were organised by 'like-minded young men' rather than as formal clubs.
- 1870, the Wallaroo Club was founded in Sydney, with Richard and Montague Arnold founder members and Old Rugbeians.
- 1874, the Southern Rugby Union was established, administered by Twickenham and handed over to NSW in 1881.
- 1883, the Northern Rugby Union of Queensland (NRUQ) was formed.
- 1892, the Southern Rugby Union represented these two state rugby union organisations.
- 1948, one administrative body was established to represent Australian rather than State Rugby Union.

Since that time membership has spread to all the five states, Tasmania and two territories. Historically, NSW and Queensland have claimed 'ownership' of Australian rugby union, even though Victoria had supplied a number of top players for the Wallabies from the late 1920s. From this time invitations were offered to players from all the States with the appropriate ability.

The national team has become known as the **Wallabies** and the Australian Women's RFU the **Walleroos**.

Amateurism, professionalism and commercialism

- Initially, Australian rugby union football followed the English tradition of being predominantly **middle class.**
- 1895, the **great schism** between rugby union and rugby league occurred in England (see page 30 above).
- 1907, a similar split occurred in Australia based on the same principle of the interpretation of 'amateur' and particularly the notion of gentleman **amateur** and the question of **payment to working class players**.
- After the Second World War the **middle class** values came under fire and **expenses** were given.
- Hence Australian rugby union had problems of **semi-professionalism** throughout its modern development.
- 1996, the transition to the **professional** game was an inevitable pressure from elite clubs, players and international competition.

With increased **commercialism**, the wealth of clubs and the amount that they could pay players eventually influenced levels of success. Rugby League suffered, because they lost their best players to Rugby Union - for example Wendell Sailor.

As with cricket, the **commercial media** became a major source of **revenue**, and brought about **sponsorship** of clubs and international competitions. Full **professionalism** inevitably prevailed at the top level by 2006. This led to the establishment of the '**Super-14**' in 1996, with four Australian state teams, five New Zealand provincial teams, and five South African teams. This will become the Super-15 in 2011, as an extra Australian team is added. Matches are played home and away (round robin), the best four then contest semifinals and so-on.

Competition

- From 1903, there were annual tournaments between Australia and New Zealand.
- In 1931, this became the **Bledisloe cup**.
- From 1996, the **Tri-Nations** became an annual tournament between Australia, South Africa and New Zealand (similar to 6 nations in Europe). Each country plays the others three times.

figure 10.7 – Australia beat England in the 1991 Rugby Union World Cup final

World cup

The World cup began in 1987 with a win for NZ, with Australia winning in 1991 (figure 10.7) and 1999. Australia attaches great significance to success in this tournament, particularly when beating England.

Soccer

Soccer was marginalised in Australia because of the dominance of rugby (both codes) in NSW and Queensland, and Aussie rules in Victoria, South Australia, and Western Australia. Thus, association football did not flourish as it did in the UK.

- 1880, the first recorded game, King's School versus Wanderers.
- 1882, the English Football Association (Australian!) was formed.
- 1911, the EFA became the Commonwealth FA (Australia).
- 1920s, the Australian Soccer Football Association (ASFA) was formed, and the Australian Soccer Federation (ASF) in 1961.

The English professional game developed in high density, industrial towns with large working class crowds, a situation not paralleled in Australia. However, Australian Soccer did have early links with mining towns in Queensland and Western Australia. When the goldfields opened up in the West, British working class families took the game with them to Victoria and South Australia.

Soccer

The post-war development of soccer was promoted by immigrants (to Australia) from Asia and Europe. Italians, Greeks, Serbs and Hungarians flocked to Australia and, settling in ethnic communities, brought their love of soccer with them.

There were issues linked with **racial discrimination** at that time and it coincided with the growth of soccer **hooliganism**. Cultural antagonisms surfaced on the terraces with nationalistic teams, flag-waving and violent acts of racism. Leading clubs like Melbourne Hellas, Adelaide Juventus, Sydney Prague and Perth Azzurri were **ethnically based** and nationalistically defensive.

There was violence on and off the field, which became a legal and political issue and attempts were made to change the names of clubs and their flag-waving to defuse racial tension. Whereas the established games of rugby and Aussie rules had gained a middle class acceptability, already well established in cricket, soccer often became a victim of immigrant group rivalry and a violent lower class youth culture.

World cup

Australia won through preliminary rounds to compete in the 2006 world cup unlike England. This was the high point in Oz soccer - the **Socceroos** did not make it past the first round, losing to Italy 1-0 in their final match.

Australian soccer has never had a high international profile. There is no tradition of international matches as in rugby and Australia has only occasionally qualified for the World Cup. The large number of junior players has not been translated into a large number of professional teams or massive spectator support. This is almost certainly because of the limited population and the traditional standing of rugby and Australian rules football. Soccer is still very much a major part of immigrant culture.

Women's soccer

The Soccer Matildas were formed from the Inaugural National Association in 1978. The 1995 FIFA Women's World Cup saw Australia grouped with USA, China and Denmark. The Matildas' inexperience showed in the opening match to Denmark, losing 5-0, the second match was a 4-2 loss to China, Angela Iannotta scoring Australia's first goal at a World Cup.

Aussie Rules Football

Australian Rules football is a football variant between two teams of 18 players, played outdoors on an oval-shaped grass pitch, often also used in the summer as a cricket ground.

There is evidence of various 'mob games' existing in the gold fields of Victoria in the 1850s, well before any established rules existed in the UK for either football code. The initial format of Aussie Rules arose from the cultures of those playing the game at the time and the environment.

> **STUDENT NOTE**
>
> An outline of Aussie rules football in Australia is briefly set out in 'AS Revise PE for OCR', ISBN: 978 1 901 424 52 2 page 106 onwards.

The rules

- 1856, **Geelong rules** were adjusted to **Melbourne rules** following some experimental matches playing 'foot-ball with a code of laws to keep cricketers fit during winter'.
- There were then several Melbourne and district teams playing in Richmond Paddock, later known as Yarra Park, next to the MCG.
- 1858, a well publicised match between Melbourne Grammar School and Scotch College took place, where records suggest that it was played with a round ball with goals half-a-mile apart and with 40 players-a-side. Similar games were happening in the UK within boys' public schools and between Oxbridge students at about this time.

figure 10.8 – early 'footie' at Richmond Paddock (Yarra Park) 1866 - next to the MCG

- 1861, Melbourne University had a fixture with the Melbourne Club. The Melbourne Football Club Rules (figure 10.8) were written in 1859 and included an award to the Champion of the Colony from the previous season. Herein lies the origin of the **Brownlow Medal**, the present award for the 'best and fairest'.
- There was a strong link with cricket and this may have influenced the aerial nature of the game, although In the early years the cricket field was not used for football.
- The fact that the rules were very similar to Gaelic Football suggests an Irish immigrant link.

The fact of using the same grounds as cricket (pitches are much bigger than the standard soccer or rugby pitch) made the game commercially viable. In 1901 the Federation of Australia was formed, and the Australian Football Council co-ordinated regular interstate (figure 10.9) carnivals.

The modern game and commercialism

The game's appeal lay in speed of play, high scoring and subdued violence.

From the 1960s the wealth of Victoria allowed them to attract the best players from the whole country, giving them a major advantage in inter-state competitions. In 1989, **the Victoria Football League** (VFL) changed its name to the **Australian Football League** (AFL) which caused issues with the governing bodies from the other states.

With the expansion of **professionalism** there was concern by Western Australia that, in the inter-state game with Victoria (figure 10.10) in 1977, it was noted that many of the players selected for Victoria were Western Australian. This gave birth to the **State of Origin** games between the two states, where the state of origin was taken to be the one where players had made their first senior club registration (see page 68 above for the rugby league equivalent).

The Chas. Brownlow Trophy, better known as the **Brownlow Medal** or 'Charlie' is awarded for the 'best and fairest' player in the Australian Football League (AFL) during the regular season. This is determined by votes cast by officiating umpires after each league game. It is not only a prestigious award, but the highest honour in Australian Rules football. The significance of it lies in the fact that not only is the best player recognised, but also the best sportsman. There have been several occasions where poor behaviour has stopped the most skilful player getting the award.

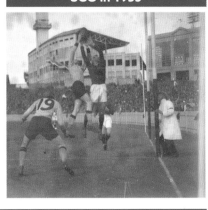

figure 10.9 – Aussie Rules at the SCG in 1933

figure 10.10 – modern Aussie Rules

Practice questions

1) Describe the similarities between rugby league in Australia and the UK and explain why this is the case. 4 marks

2) Explain the development of Test cricket in England and Australia. 5 marks

3) Discuss the development of professionalism in rugby union in the UK and Australia. 6 marks

4) Compare the growth of soccer in the UK and Australia, and discuss the historical and sociocultural influences on this development, with a judgement as to what the future holds for the game in both countries. 20 marks

5) Outline alternative pathways into professional sport that are available to performers in Australia and the UK. 6 marks

6) a) Compare the cultural development of women's cricket in Australia and the UK. 4 marks
   b) How does the women's game differ in commercial development when compared with the men's game? 5 marks

7) In recent years there has been a drastic change of attitude towards people with disabilities. How has this change affected issues of equality and discrimination for elite disabled performers in both Australia and the UK? 8 marks

8) What has been the impact of Kerry Packer on cricket in England and Australia? 6 marks

9) British rugby union and Aussie Rules Football are very popular games within their native countries.
   a) Account for the popularity of these two games. 4 marks
   b) Identify and discuss two social issues which make them different. 4 marks
   c) Account for the lack of development of soccer in Australia. 4 marks

SECTION B: SCIENTIFIC OPTIONS

OPTION B1: SPORTS PSYCHOLOGY

CHAPTER 11 – PERSONALITY and ATTITUDES

Personality

Personality is the term which describes the **unique** characteristics of an individual which makes him or her act as they do. Knowledge about personality is important to ensure **optimum** sporting performance.

Figure 11.1 outlines the main ideas various theorists have used to explain and describe personality and its features.

figure 11.1 – features of personality

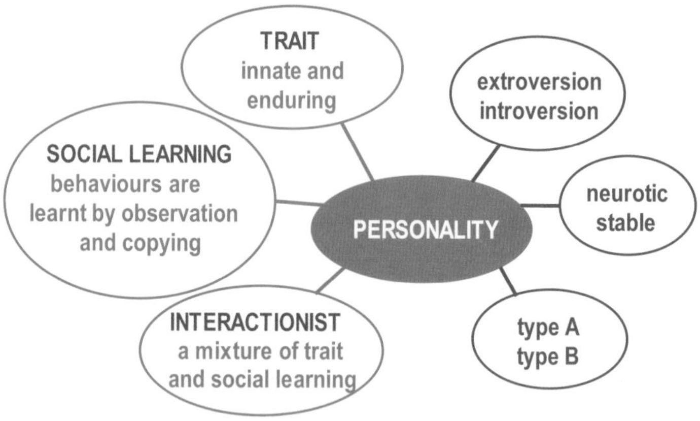

TRAIT
innate and enduring

extroversion
introversion

SOCIAL LEARNING
behaviours are learnt by observation and copying

PERSONALITY

neurotic
stable

INTERACTIONIST
a mixture of trait and social learning

type A
type B

Theories of personality

Trait theories

Trait theories use the idea that a person has always had a feature of his or her personality, and always will have. Such features will be **general** (covering all situations), **underlying** (inside of and part of the person), **enduring** (long lasting), and include **predispositions** (inclinations or motives formed earlier). Such predispositions will tell you how a person will behave when faced with certain situations. For example, the prospect of failure such as losing an important sporting match or competition.

Most trait theories use labels for features of behaviour, and you should remember that such labels (attached to a person) would be intended to last for ever. Some labels for aspects of personality are:

*   **Extroversion** (including liveliness, sociability, impulsiveness, activity, excitability).
*   **Introversion** (including isolation, independence, shyness, quiet).
*   **Stability** (including unchanging behaviour patterns).
*   **Neuroticism** (including the fact that behaviour may change unpredictably).

Eysenck identified a **two dimensional** view of personality as four primary types:

*   A **stable extrovert** would be talkative, outgoing, easy going, carefree, and showing leader qualities.
*   A **neurotic extrovert** would be restless, aggressive, excitable, and changeable.
*   A **neurotic introvert** would be anxious, sober, rigid, or pessimistic.
*   A **stable introvert** would be careful, thoughtful, controlled, reliable, and even-tempered.

At a later date Eysenck added a third scale of **psychoticism** as a measure of how tough-minded a person is, assessed in a test called Eysenck's personality questionnaire.

Which set of characteristics would enable you to predict who would become the next British Olympic champions (figure 11.2)?

Cattell is another trait theorist who identified a much larger number of personality traits which he measured in a questionnaire called Cattell's 16PF.

figure 11.2 – which features of Chris Hoy's personality have led to him becoming a multiple Olympic champion?

Social learning theories

Social learning theory explains behaviour in terms of the reaction to specific situations. The main point of social learning theory is that we learn to deal with situations by **observing others** or by observing the results of our own behaviour on others and by **modelling** our own behaviour on what we have seen. Athletes learn **behaviour** by watching others. This is in addition to the idea of being able to learn skills by watching then copying others (this is the social learning theory of skill development).

Social learning theory

Bandura says that behaviour is determined by the situation. In other words there is social comparison, and a person will behave the same way as the peer group. Social approval or disapproval determines our responses since such behaviour is reinforced or penalised by **the peer group**.

Vicarious conditioning is the learning of emotional responses through observational learning. For example, learning to become angry after a valid referee decision has gone against him or her by watching other players do the same.

Hollander's structure of personality

Figure 11.3 outlines the structure of personality as proposed by Hollander.

In this model:

- The **psychological core** (the inner core of beliefs) describes the beliefs and values that remain more or less permanent. For example, a sportsman's belief that fair play underlies his attitude on the field of play.
- **Typical behaviour** describes the way in which an individual responds in certain situations, for example, to stop fighting at the bell during a boxing bout.
- **Role-related behaviour** describes the fact that in other situations we may behave differently, for example, striking our opponents after the bell when annoyed or frustrated. This is the most changeable aspect of personality.
- **Social environment** describes how the behaviour and expectations of others affect our role. For example, a player argues with the referee because others have done so and he or she has got away with it before.

Interactionist theories

Interactionist theories (figure 11.4) are those which assert that a combination of trait and a person's situation or environment builds up a person's personality, and that traits determine behaviour but can be modified by situations. **Lewin** was the theorist who stated that behaviour is a function of both the person (personality P) and the environment (E), and put this in the mathematical form: $$B = f(P,E)$$

figure 11.3 – Hollander's structure of personality

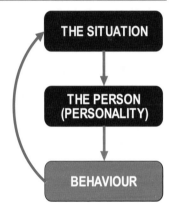

figure 11.4 – the interactionist model of personality

Example of the interactionist theory approach

A young field event athlete shows promise, but worries about competing in important competitions and underperforms in these situations. Her coach works with her on anxiety management strategies and her next competition sees a personal best.

The innate (**trait**) factors of the athlete's personality cannot be changed by a coach, so the coach must therefore get her to view her **anxiety** (which could be a trait which emerges whenever undue stress is placed on her) in terms of the specific situation of the next competition. The anxiety could be channelled into positive images of her technical model, rejecting poor efforts as due to external factors (for example, the weather or the wind), and building on positive images of successful technical elements achieved. The athlete can then build success by focusing on factors other than her own anxiety.

This enables her to adjust her behaviour according to internal factors such as rhythm and fluency, and this strategy should enable the athlete to remove the stress from the situation and hence reduce anxiety - even if she competes poorly.

Types A and B personalities

Table 11.1 – **differences between personality types A and B**

type A characterised by:	type B characterised by:
impatience	relaxed and patient
works at a rapid pace	allows time for tasks to be completed
higher levels of stress	low personal stress
strong desire to succeed	less competitive
easily aroused and shows anxiety in stressful situations	calm and unflappable in most situations
lacking in tolerance	tolerance of others' mistakes
has a need to be in control	delegates easily
makes decisions quickly without much preparation or thought	prepared to wait and assess all options when decisions need to be made

Personality testing or measuring

There are 3 ways of testing or measuring personality:

Interviews
Interviews are before or after the event, are not directly
related to performance, are usually open-ended and flexible, and therefore difficult to quantify accurately.

Questionnaires
Questionnaires are implemented either before or after the event, and are therefore not directly related to performance.

Observations
Observations are made during an actual event, and are therefore directly related to performance.

STUDENT NOTE

Validity and reliability are key issues for discussion when testing or measuring personality.

The profile of mood states (POMS)
This sports-specific questionnaire asks questions which determine the mood of a sports performer and attempts to relate this to the quality of performance. Results are plotted on a chart similar to figure 11.5. Moods are an important aspect of personality which may influence sports performance. The moods assessed by this test are:

- Tension.
- Depression.
- Anger.
- Vigour.
- Fatigue.
- Confusion.

From figure 11.5 you can see that elite sportspeople show low tension, depression and confusion, and they also show high vigour.
Unsuccessful sportspeople show high tension, depression, fatigue and confusion, and lower vigour than the elite athlete.

figure 11.5 – profiles of mood states for good and poor performers

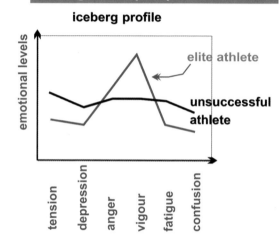

Evaluation of self-report tests
The difficulties with any sort of psychological test are its **validity**, does the test actually measure what it sets out to test, and its **reliability**, does the test measure the same thing every time it is used?

Problems with the tests are:
- Lack of accuracy (**reliability**).
- Participant **honesty**.
- The desire to create a **favourable impression** and therefore give answers which the questioner wants, not what the subject feels.
- Lack of **objectivity** (lack of an accurate means of quantifying data).
- Neurotics tend to **emphasise** certain traits over others.
- **Ambiguous** questions which might confuse the performer or the person making the assessment.
- Interview and observation techniques are usually on a one-to-one basis and hence very **time consuming**.

The answers to questions or observations can be influenced by the personality of the tester, the time of day or month, the previous experience of a test by a subject, and a participant's mood swings. The most important factor, however, is the fact that personality is too complex to be viewed in response to yes or no answers.

Weinberg and Gould (2007) propose 'no specific personality profile has been found that consistently distinguishes athletes from non-athletes'.

In spite of these statements, personality testing is used as part of the UK's sport talent identification programme, since it is accepted that there is a relationship between personality type and sport performance.

Attitudes

Attitudes are combinations of **beliefs** and **feelings** which lead us to think and behave **positively** or **negatively**.

Attitudes are combinations of beliefs and feelings about objects, people and situations (called attitude objects) which predispose us to behave in a certain way towards them. They are learned or organised through experience, and are evaluative (lead us to think and behave positively or negatively) about an attitude object. Sporting attitude objects would include lady bodybuilders as in figure 11.8 below. Attitudes tend to be deep seated and enduring, but can change or be changed.

Components of attitude, the triadic model
This model is outlined in figure 11.6, which lists the **cognitive**, **affective**, and **behavioural** components of attitude.

Influences on formation of attitudes
The major influences on the formation of attitudes are outlined in figure 11.7.

Additionally, **conditioning** (such as the use of rewards such as praise) will tend to strengthen attitudes, and **social learning** will have the same effect, in which people will learn by observing and imitating significant others.

Familiarity with an attitude object can change an attitude towards that object.

Prejudice
Prejudice is a prejudgement of a person, group, or situation, usually based on **inadequate** information, or inaccurate or biased information. This prejudice tends to reinforce **stereotypes**. For example, women are often excluded from male dominated sports clubs or events (historically golf, rugby and snooker clubs have been guilty of this).

Sport stereotypes
In the general population, people form attitudes which are negative stereotypes about certain groups participating in sport.
For example:
* Women in strength, endurance and contact sports, see figure 11.8.
* Participation of the disabled in physical activity.
* Older age groups' interest and ability at sport.
* Participation of particular ethnic groups in specific sports or positions within teams, for example:
    * The black quarterback in American football.
    * The white sprinter.
    * The black skier or swimmer.

Changing attitudes

Sometimes, a coach or sport leader will want to change an attitude of a sports player or performer, particularly if this person displays aggression or negative feelings towards a colleague. There are two generally accepted ways of tackling this.

figure 11.6 – the triadic model of components of attitude

COGNITIVE
knowledge and beliefs
example:
fitness training keeps me fit

ATTITUDE
to regular exercise

AFFECTIVE
feelings and emotions
example:
I enjoy training

BEHAVIOURAL
intended behaviour
example:
I attend training sessions regularly

figure 11.7 – formation of attitudes

media
friends
past experiences
peers
FORMATION OF ATTITUDES
prejudice
family
teachers
coaches

figure 11.8 – participation in some sports has a negative stereotype with some members of the public

Attitude change by persuasive communication

In order for this method to be effective, the subject (the person whose attitude is hopefully to be changed) must pay attention, and must understand, accept and retain the message being given. The coach must be expert and be trustworthy, and the message must be clear, be unambiguous, be balanced between emotion and logic, and be balanced between pros and cons.

Attitude change by cognitive dissonance

Cognitive dissonance occurs when two completely different and contradictory facts affect the behaviour of a sportsperson. The most clear example of this is when a successful sports performer knows that to maintain his or her success, he or she must maximise the use of his or her lungs, and knows therefore that smoking is bad, yet continues to smoke because he or she likes the sensations produced.

In order to change the attitude of such a person (to smoking), he or she must be consistent between cognitive, affective, and behavioural components, and must realise that there is a conflict between the two behaviours (fitness and smoking). At this point, cognitive dissonance will occur and force the performer to change an attitude to smoking (or perhaps to participation in top level sport!).

Evaluation or measurement of attitudes

In order to assess whether or not attitudes need to be changed, it will be important to determine what the attitudes to certain situations or attitude objects actually are (figure 11.9). This can be done in one or more of three ways.

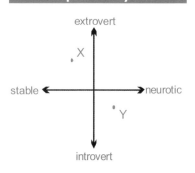

figure 11.9 – good attitudes are important

- By **observation**, which will be related to actual events as they are happening, will be difficult to quantify or measure, and will be open to interpretation by the observer.

- Using **questionnaires**, which are only as good as the questions asked. They are measurable using the Thurstone scale, the Likert scale, or Osgood's Semantic Differential Scale.

- Using **physiological tests**, in which indicators such as blood pressure, skin conductivity, or brain activity (ECG), can be interpreted to indicate whether a sportsperson is telling the truth about an attitude object. These tests are measurable, are independent of an observer, but take a long time to set up, and may require special apparatus.

Practice questions

1) a) What do we mean by the term personality? Why is it important for sports psychologists to know about personality?

    3 marks

    b) Eysenck identified two dimensions of personality as in figure 11.10. Describe the trait approach to personality. What do the traits extroversion and stability mean?   4 marks

    c) From diagram 11.10 describe the characteristics of players **X** and **Y**.

    4 marks

    d) By using an example from sport, outline the social learning approach to personality.   3 marks

    e) What do we mean by the interactionist approach?   2 marks

figure 11.10 – dimensions of personality

extrovert

. X

stable ←——————→ neurotic

. Y

introvert

2) Hollander (1971) viewed personality as a structure with layers of influence. Using examples from sport, explain Hollander's structure of personality.   8 marks

3) What is the iceberg profile and how does it relate to the personalities of elite athletes?   4 marks

4) A rowing coach wants to improve the performance of his squad. In doing so he would want to consider psychological and physiological factors. The coach wants to identify the personality types of the squad members.

    a) What are the limitations of using personality tests? 2 marks

    b) Some rowers behave differently between competition and training. Explain this pattern of behaviour, in terms of interactionist theory of personality. 2 marks

5) a) What do we mean by the term attitude? 1 mark

    b) We often refer to someone as having a positive attitude in sport. Using the triadic model describe the characteristics of a positive attitude. 3 marks

    c) What factors influence our attitudes? 4 marks

6) a) If you wished to change a young person's negative attitude to sport into a positive one, what strategies would you employ? Use psychological theory to back up your answer. 4 marks

    b) What do we mean by the term prejudice and how does it manifest itself in sport? 4 marks

7) Observing behaviour is one method of measuring attitudes. What are the advantages and disadvantages of such a method? 4 marks

CHAPTER 12 – ACHIEVEMENT MOTIVATION, ATTRIBUTION and AGGRESSION

Achievement motivation

STUDENT NOTE

Motivation is discussed on pages 80 and 81 of 'AS Revise PE for OCR', ISBN: 978 1 901424 52 2.

Achievement motivation is the drive to achieve success for its own sake, and is related to competitiveness, persistence, and striving for perfection.

Achievement motivation is influenced by:
- **Personality** factors, which are:
  - The need to achieve (Nach).
  - The need to avoid failure (Naf).
- **Situational** factors, which are:
  - Probability of success.
  - Incentive value of success.

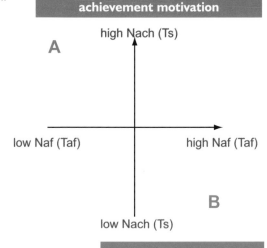

figure 12.1 – personality aspects of achievement motivation

Personality components of achievement motivation

Atkinson and McCelland derived this idea which hinged around:
- The **need to achieve** (**Nach**) or **tendency to approach success (Ts)** personality type likes a challenge, likes feedback, is not afraid of failure and has high task persistence.
- The **need to avoid failure** (**Naf**) or **tendency to avoid failure (Taf)** personality type avoids challenges, does not take risks, often gives up, and does not want feedback.

The chart in figure 12.1 shows **Nach** against **Naf**. Most people participating in sport will occupy a small region of the chart, for example regions **A** or **B** as shown on the chart.

A = someone with a high need to achieve who will probably have a low need to avoid failure. Such a person will choose difficult or demanding tasks which are more risky, for example, the hard route up a rock face (figure 12.2).

B = someone with a high need to avoid failure who will probably have a low need to achieve, and who will choose tasks which are less risky and more easily achieved. For example, this person will take the easy route up the rock face.

figure 12.2 – high Nach?

Situational factors affecting achievement motivation

The chart in figure 12.3 shows probability of success against incentive value of success, and again most people will occupy a small region (examples here are marked **C** and **D**).

C = region of the chart where a task's **probability of success** is **low** (for example, competing against the World champion), and therefore the sportsperson has to strive very hard to win. The **incentive** to **achieve success** is **very high**, and the sportsperson will be highly chuffed if he or she wins.

D = region of the chart where **probability of success** is **high** (for example, competing in local club match), and the sportsperson therefore doesn't need to try as hard to win. Hence the **incentive to achieve** is **low**, because the person expects to win easily, and of course this is not so pleasing to the performer.

What should the coach do?

The prime need for a coach is to improve need and motive to achieve (Nach) in a sportsperson. This is the positive way to deal with motivational issues, and there are strategies he or she could use to **promote Nach**:
- Increase **positive reinforcement** hence increasing pride and satisfaction.
- Ensure that goals are **achievable**.
- Ensure that at least some situations **guarantee success**.
- And subsequently gradually **increase task difficulty** in line with progress.

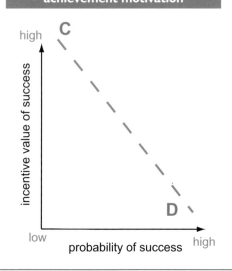

figure 12.3 – situational factors in achievement motivation

What should the coach do?

- Ensure that tasks are **challenging**.
- Ensure that the **probability of success is good**.
- Ensure that the **incentive value of the success is high** (is the race worth winning?).

The coach should also **reduce tendency and motive to avoid failure** (Naf), and this can be done by:

- **Reducing punishment** hence lowering the chance of performer worrying about failure.
- **Focusing negative feedback** on effort rather than ability.
- This avoids the performer tending to believe that causes of failure are internal (due to lack of ability for example).
- And reduces the risk of learned helplessness (see page 80 below).
- **Avoiding** situations where defeat or **failure is inevitable** (such as performing against a much superior opponent).
- If this is not possible **alter the criteria for success** (for example, you will have succeeded if you only lose by 2 goals).

Attribution

Attribution is the process of giving **reasons** for behaviour and ascribing **causes** for events. For example, the player played badly today because the weather was poor.

Weiner's model

Weiner's model has four attributions, **ability**, **effort**, **task difficulty** and **luck** (see figure 12.4).

As in figure 12.4, these attributions are arranged in two dimensions, **locus of causality** and **stability** (with a possible third dimension, **controllability**).

figure 12.4 – Weiner's model of sports attribution

		LOCUS OF CAUSALITY	
		INTERNAL	EXTERNAL
STABILITY	STABLE	ability 'we were more skilful'	task difficulty 'the opposition are world champions'
	UNSTABLE	effort 'we tried hard'	luck 'the court was slippy'

Locus of causality dimension

Locus of causality is the performance outcome caused by:

- **Internal factors** under the control of the performer such as ability and effort.
  - **Ability** is the extent of the performer's capacity to cope with a sporting task.
  - **Effort** refers to the amount of mental and physical effort the performer gives to the task.

- **External factors** beyond the control of the performer such as task difficulty and luck.
  - **Task difficulty** is the term describing the extent of the problems posed by the task including the strength of the opposition.
  - **Luck** describes factors attributable to chance, such as the weather or the state of the pitch.

Stability dimension

Stability refers to the performance outcome caused by stable or unstable factors:

- **Stable** factors are fixed factors which don't change with time such as **ability** or **task difficulty**.
- **Unstable** factors are factors which can vary with time such as **effort** or **luck**.

In attribution theory, **success** is explained by internal attributions, and **failure** is explained by external attributions. **Future expectations** are related to stability. If we attribute success to stable factors, or if we attribute failure to stable factors, then we expect the same next time.

Relationship to sports achievement

- **High achievers** (such as Andy Murray, figure 12.5) tend to attribute **success** to internal factors (such as Andy's incredible state of fitness), and attribute **failure** to external factors (such as the high temperature or strong wind during the match).
- **Low achievers** tend to attribute success to external factors (such as a favourable wind), and attribute failure to internal factors (such as lack of fitness or ability).

- The process of changing attributions is called **attribution retraining**. The point of this is to change a person's tendency to ascribe reasons for success or failure so that it is more like that of a successful performer rather than an unsuccessful performer.
- Attributions affect a sportsperson's **pride**, **satisfaction**, and **expectancy of success**. Some people exhibit **avoidance** tendencies when faced with a sporting situation (they try to avoid participating), and this is called **learned helplessness**.

figure 12.5 – Andy Murray - high achiever

Controllability, the third dimension

The **locus of control** covers attributions under the control of the performer (and sometimes not under the control of the performer). The locus of control dimension relates to the intensity of a performer's feelings of **pride** and **satisfaction**, **shame** and **guilt**.

- **Pride** and **satisfaction** are maximised if success is attributed to internal controllable factors such as ability and effort, and motivation would be enhanced.
- If **success** were attributed to **external** and **uncontrollable** factors such as luck or the fact that the task was very easy, then satisfaction would be less intense and motivation less.
- If **failure** is attributed to internal controllable factors such as **lack of ability** and **lack of effort**, then the overpowering emotion would be dissatisfaction and motivation would be reduced.

The self-serving bias

- This idea crops up because **successful performers** tend to take credit for success. They do this by **attributing success** to their own overwhelmingly outstanding **qualities** (natural ability, **ability** to respond to the competitive situation), thereby enhancing their feelings of pride, self-worth, and self-esteem. They also tend to **blame external factors** for failure.

- Failure is automatically attributed to **avoid internal** controllable and stable factors (even if such factors may be true). This is the **self-serving bias**, people tend to give attributions to **protect their self-esteem** rather than look for true attributions which would reflect the reality of the situation.

- **Unsuccessful performers** do not always attribute failure to external factors and therefore do not protect their self-esteem. This tends to reduce motivation.

Figure 12.6 summarises the attribution process.

Learned helplessness (LH)

Repeated failure (or lack of success) can lead to a state known as **learned helplessness**.

This is explained as a **belief** acquired over time that one has no control over events and that failure is inevitable (for example, if a batsman repeatedly gets a duck, he may feel that he no longer has the skill to succeed at sport). It is characterised by a feeling of **hopelessness** in which a person with the physical potential to achieve highly at sport no longer feels that it is possible for him or her to do so.

This is what is behind the common belief that if you fall off a bike, you must get back on straight away, otherwise you may never do so (figure 12.7 overleaf).

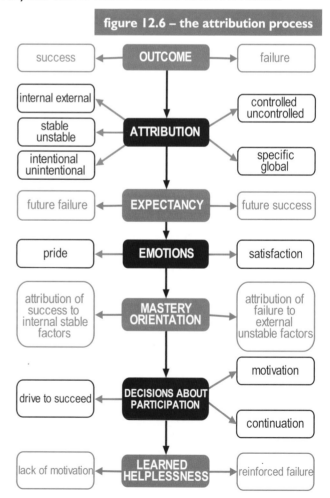

figure 12.6 – the attribution process

General and specific learned helplessness

- **General (global) learned helplessness** occurs when a person attributes failure to internal and stable factors, and this feeling of failure is applied to all sports. For example, the comment 'I am useless at all sports'.

- **Specific learned helplessness** occurs when a person attributes difficulties to internal and stable factors, and this feeling is applied to one specific sport. For example, the comment 'I am good at soccer but useless at racquet games'.

figure 12.7 – get back on the bike straight away

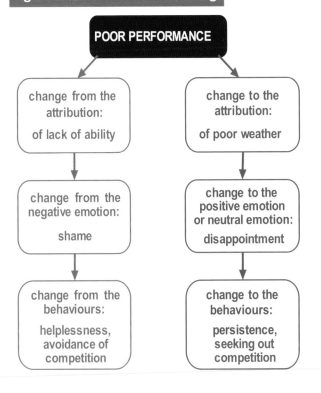

figure 12.8 – attribution retraining

POOR PERFORMANCE

change from the attribution:

of lack of ability

→

change from the negative emotion:

shame

→

change from the behaviours:

helplessness, avoidance of competition

change to the attribution:

of poor weather

→

change to the positive emotion or neutral emotion:

disappointment

→

change to the behaviours:

persistence, seeking out competition

Attribution retraining

Figure 12.8 summarises the process which must be undertaken if learned helplessness is to be avoided or recovered from. Following failure, low achievers need to learn to attribute success and failure to the same reasons as high achievers, namely:

- Success should be attributed to stable internal factors.
- Failure should be attributed to unstable external factors.

This would raise the **self-efficacy** (see page 93 below) of the performer for his or her sport.

Hence attribution training will influence how the performer deals with a situation.

The positive and negative applications of attribution theory on performance and sustaining a balanced, active lifestyle is summarised in table 12.1 below.

The link between motivation and attribution

Table 12.1 – **motivation, attribution and behaviour**

	high achiever	low achiever
motivation	high motive to achieve success low motive to avoid failure focuses on pride and on success	low motive to achieve success high motive to avoid failure focuses on shame and worry about failure
attributions	ascribes success to stable internal controllable factors ascribes failure to unstable external uncontrollable factors	ascribes success to unstable external uncontrollable factors ascribes failure to stable internal controllable factors
goals adopted	adopts task oriented goals	adopts outcome oriented goals
task choice	seeks challenging tasks and competitive situations	avoids challenge, seeks very difficult or very easy tasks or competition
performance	performs well in front of evaluative audiences	performs badly in front of evaluative audiences

Aggression

Aggression (figure 12.9) involves arousal and anger and intention to harm outside the rules of a game or activity.

- **Assertion** has no intent to harm and uses legitimate force within the rules, displays unusual effort, and may carry unusual energy. This is sometimes called **channelled aggression** (figure 12.10).

- **Hostile aggression** has the intent to harm. The goal is to harm with arousal and anger involved.

- **Instrumental aggression** has the intent to harm with the goal to win. This is used as a tactic and is commonly named '**dirty play**'. There is no anger involved and is illegal in all sports except boxing (and other martial arts sports).

figure 12.9 – aggression - the details

intention to harm another participant, player, spectator or umpire

verbal aggression if intended to embarrass or hurt

outside the rules of the sport

AGGRESSION

not including accidentally injuring or harming

not including eyeballing or intentionally damaging equipment

Causes of aggression

- **Physiological arousal** in which anger towards another person causes an increase in arousal. This is because the sportsperson is highly motivated.
- **Underdeveloped moral reasoning** in which players with low levels of moral reasoning are more likely to be aggressive.
- **Bracketed morality** in which there is a double standard of condoning aggressive behaviour in sport, but not in life in general. This way of dealing with aggressive behaviour may retard a player's moral development.

Other **causes of aggression** include:
- High environmental temperature.
- Home or away, reaction to a hostile crowd.
- Losing, frustration at poor performance.
- Physical pain.
- Unfair officiating.
- Playing below capability.
- Large score difference, again frustration at poor performance.
- Low league standing, low self-esteem.
- Later stage of play (near the end of a game), fatigue and niggles.
- Reputation of opposition (get your retaliation in first).
- Retaliation to an incident.
- Copying the behaviour of others.
- Excessive pressure to win.

figure 12.10 – aggression or assertion?

Theories of aggression (figure 12.11)

- **Instinct theory** (due to Lorentz) suggests that aggression is innate and instinctive - caused by a 'survival of the species' response to situations as they arise. In this theory, sport releases built-up aggression, and the aggressive response is cathartic - it gets the aggression out of the system, and purges the person of aggressive intent.

- **Frustration-aggression theory** (due to Dollard) states that aggression is caused by frustration as the sportsperson is being blocked in the achievement of a goal. This causes a drive towards the source of frustration.

- **Social learning theory** (due to Bandura) suggests that aggression is **learned** by observation of others' behaviour. Then imitation of this aggressive behaviour is reinforced by social acceptance of the behaviour.

- **Aggressive cue hypothesis** (due to Berkowitz) states that frustration causes anger and arousal which creates a readiness for aggression. The aggression itself can be initiated by an incident during the performance or game (the cue), so that the aggression is a learned response. For example, a player sees a colleague fouled then decides to join in.

figure 12.11 – theories of aggression

frustration

social learning

THEORIES OF AGGRESSION

instinct

aggressive cue

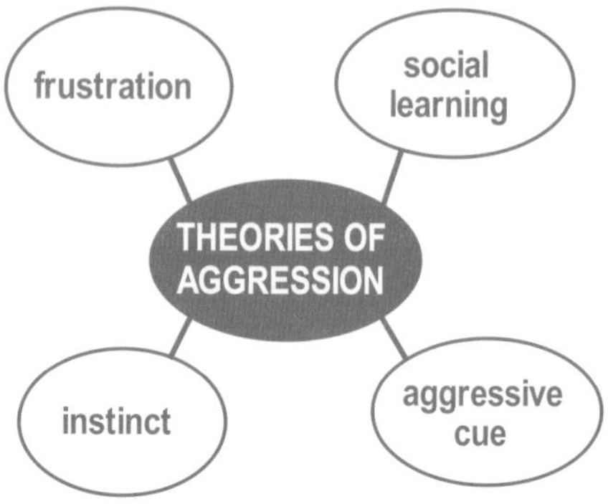

Deindividuation

The theory of deindividuation concerns the fact that people sometimes behave differently when by themselves, as compared with behaviour in a football crowd. There is a contrast between the behaviour of people in the workplace as compared with the terraces.

Responsibility for aggression

Responsibility for aggression lies within the factors listed in figure 12.12. Influential others can exert a moderating influence on the performer, but the performer must accept that aggression is the wrong thing to do, and modify behaviour accordingly. **Reinforcement** of good behaviour will be important to ensure behavioural change.

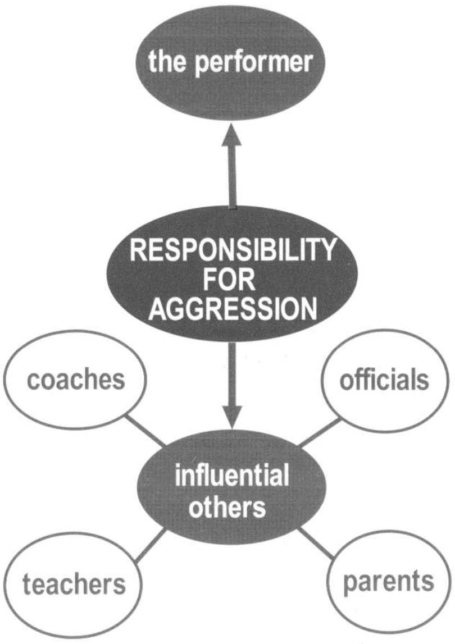

Strategies for control of aggressive behaviour

Governing bodies

Governing bodies are responsible for **player codes of conduct** which should involve coaches, players and officials. They will:

- Use strong officials where appropriate.
- Alter rules of games and implement punishment (remove league points, use sin bins and so on).
- Reward non-aggressive acts (for example, the FIFA fair play award).
- Encourage suitable use of language.
- Attempt to reduce media sensationalism in connection with aggression on or off the field of play.

A coach education programme is essential to reduce and control aggressive behaviour among players.

Coaches and players

- **Coaches and players** (figure 12.13) should promote ethical and sporting behaviour.
- They should control aggressive behaviour using stress management strategies and **relaxation techniques** among players.
- Coaches should initiate **self-control** strategies, and attempt to reduce levels of arousal in players.

- Both coaches and players should maintain a **healthy will-to-win** without winning being everything, and set **performance goals** rather than outcome goals.

- Coaches should **remove players** from the field if it is decided that he or she (but usually he!) is at risk of aggression.
- The tactic would be to **channel aggression** towards a performance goal, and to use **peer pressure** to 'avoid letting the side down'.

figure 12.12 – responsibility for aggression

the performer

RESPONSIBILITY FOR AGGRESSION

coaches

officials

influential others

teachers

parents

figure 12.13 – controlling aggression?

Practice questions

1) a) What do you understand by the term achievement motivation? Explain the different types.   3 marks

   b) How could a coach use the different types of achievement motivation with a group of beginners?   2 marks

2) a) Describe the characteristics of the positive motive: 'the need to achieve'.   4 marks

   b) Describe an example from sport of someone who has a high motive to avoid failure.   3 marks

   c) Identify factors which could affect the use of motives to achieve and to avoid failure in sporting situations.   3 marks

3)   How would you promote the need to achieve motive, rather than the need to avoid failure motive?   8 marks

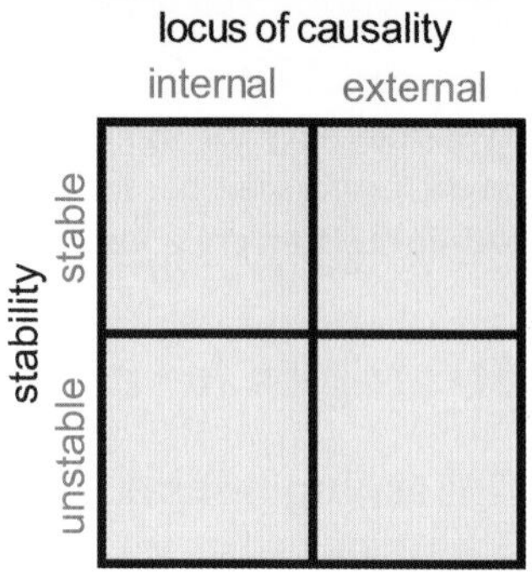

4)   a)   Figure 12.14 partly illustrates Weiner's model of attribution.
           Explain the term attribution using a sporting situation.   2 marks

     b)   Explain the terms locus of causality and stability when applied to
           attribution theory.   4 marks

     c)   Redraw the model and place on it relevant attributions for each of
           the four boxes.   4 marks

     d)   What attributions would you encourage if your team were playing
           well but often losing?   5 marks

figure 12.14 – Weiner's model of attribution

5)   a)   Many young people claim to be hopeless at gymnastics. Suggest three reasons why these youngsters might have a
           negative attitude to gymnastics.   3 marks

     b)   What is meant by learned helplessness (LH) and how is it caused?   3 marks

     c)   How would you attempt to attract beginners to a gymnastics class, and then change any negative attitudes?
                                                                                                                 4 marks

6)   Those who achieve little in sport often attribute their failure to factors outside their control and learned helplessness
     can result. Using examples from sport, explain what is meant by learned helplessness and identify how self-motivational
     techniques may help to limit the effects of learned helplessness.   6 marks

7)   a)   What do we mean by the term aggression in sports psychology? Give an example from a sport or game which would
           illustrate your answer.   2 marks

     b)   Using examples from sport, briefly describe the differences between aggression and assertion.   2 marks

     c)   Some team players display unwanted aggression. What are the possible causes of such aggression?   4 marks

8)   Explain in detail what is meant by social learning when applied to aggression.
     How can aggressive tendencies be eliminated in a sports situation?   10 marks

9)   a)   The aggressive cue hypothesis (Berkowitz 1969), is a theory which explains why aggression may be experienced by
           sports performers. Using an example from sport, describe the aggressive cue hypothesis.   4 marks

     b)   Using examples from sport, explain the frustration-aggression hypothesis.   4 marks

10) Discuss how theories of aggression can be applied to sport.   6 marks

CHAPTER 13 – GROUPS, LEADERSHIP and SOCIAL FACILITATION

Groups and teams

A **group** (figure 13.1) consists of two or more people **interacting** with one another so that each person influences and is influenced by the others. A group will have a **collective identity** and a sense of **shared purpose**, and is a **social aggregate** involving **mutual awareness** and **potential interaction** with structured patterns of **communication**. For example, a crowd at a soccer match, a soccer team or parents watching their children swim.

Successful groups:
*   Have a strong collective identity in which members have an opportunity to **socialise** and who **share goals**, **ambitions** and **ownership** of ideas.
*   Will have members who are able to **communicate effectively** (on the same wavelength).
*   Will have strong **cohesion** (see below).
*   Have members who **value relationships** within the group.
*   Have a **successful coach** or leader who ensures that **members' contributions** to the group are **valued**.

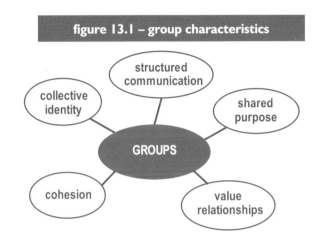

figure 13.1 – group characteristics

Group cohesion

Cohesion points at the way in which group members **gel** together, or feel **collective affection** for one another, or feel a strong **sense of sharing** whatever it is that the group does. It is the extent to which members of a group exhibit a desire to **achieve common goals** and **group identity**. The two themes of co-operation and co-ordination are strong elements of this idea.
*   Sometimes this can mean selection of less skilled but more co-operative players for a team.
*   Unfortunately, friendship groups can have negative effects.

figure 13.2 – cohesion is important for some teams

Cohesion has both **task** and **social** elements:
*   **Task cohesion** is about people who are willing to work together (see figure 13.2) whether or not they get on personally, hence the group would have the potential to be successful.
*   **Social cohesion** covers the notion that teams with high social cohesion but low task cohesion are less successful.

Carron's model

This model (figure 13.3) outlines **four** factors that affect the development of cohesion:
*   **Environmental factors** which bind members to a team, for example, contracts, location, age, eligibility. To make cohesion stronger, you should avoid a star system and provide opportunities for socialising.
*   **Personal factors** which feature things that members believe are important, and include motives for taking part. To optimise on cohesion, a coach should give opportunities for motives to be realised, and develop ownership feelings and social groupings within the team.
*   **Leadership factors** which are about the behaviour of leaders and coaches. Coaches should use all leadership behaviours to influence different individuals.
*   **Team factors** relating to the group, including team identity, targets, member ability and role, creation of team short- and long-term goals, and the rewarding of individual and team efforts.

figure 13.3 – Carron's model of cohesion

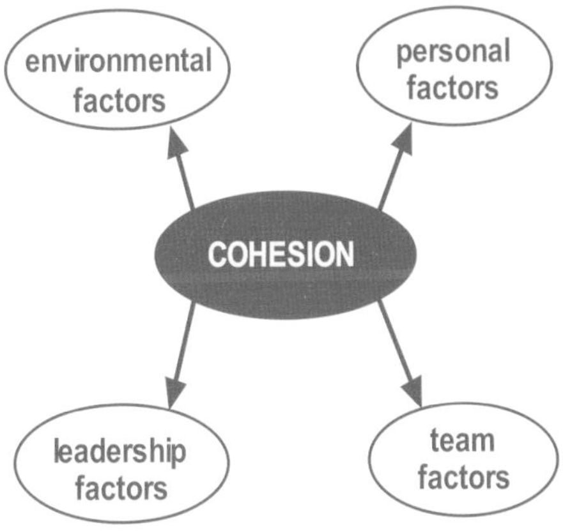

Steiner's model of a group or team

This model states that:

team success = (potential for success) - (co-ordination and motivation problems)

- **Potential for success** revolves around the issues that usually skilful individuals make the best team, and usually individual success (of team members) correlates with overall team success.

- **Co-ordination problems** (for players) occur if there should be a high level of interaction between players, but one (or more) player is being selfish or aggressive, or if a defence is not working together, and hence overall team performance suffers.

- **Motivation problems** occur because people seem to work less hard in a group than they do on their own. For example, in rowing, times of winning double sculls are often only slightly faster than single sculls. This is **social loafing**, 'the **Ringlemann Effect**'.

- **Motivational losses** occur because individuals may not share the same motives. This leads to loss of group cohesion, for example, some players may play a game for social reasons, others in order to win.

Social loafing, the Ringlemann Effect

- **Social loafing** is the term which describes the fact that individuals appear to **reduce their effort** when in a group (figure 13.4), and can **hide their lack of effort** amongst the effort of other group members.

- It can be eliminated if the contribution of an individual **can be identified** as with **player statistics** (American football, rugby league, cricket, basketball).

- The **need** for interaction between players varies between sports.

- **Co-operation** between players can be significant in eliminating social loafing.

figure 13.4 – social loafing

Leadership

A leader can influence the behaviour of others towards required goals and will influence effective team cohesion. He or she will also help fulfil the expectations of a team, and will develop an environment in which a group is motivated, rewarded and helped towards its common goals.

- **Emergent leaders** come from within a group because of their skill and abilities or through nomination or election.
- **Prescribed leaders** are appointed by a governing body or agency outside the group.

Theories of leadership

These theories centre around the **nature** or **nurture** debate.

The 'great man' or trait theory
This is the '**nature**' theory, that leaders are born (figure 13.5) not made, and have relevant innate personality qualities.

Social learning theory
This is the '**nurture**' theory, in which leaders learn their skills through watching and imitating other people (models). This theory says that leaders are formed throughout life by social or environmental influences.

According to this idea, learning to be a leader starts by observation of a model, then continues by imitation or copying of the behaviour of the model. The effectiveness of this process would depend on the model having high status.

figure 13.5 – who is the leader of this group?

The Chelladurai continuum

The Chelladurai continuum theory covers the notion that there are three types of leader, and that an actual leader may adopt all three of the types in different situations depending on the circumstances. These three types of leader are:

- The **autocratic authoritarian** leader who makes all the decisions.
- The **democratic** leader who shares the decisions (with members of a group or team), and seeks advice from the group itself. He or she will be prepared to change his or her mind based on this advice.
- The **laissez-faire** leader who lets others make decisions and is prepared to go along with whatever they decide.

Martin Johnson (figure 13.6) leads by both example and by his own trait qualities. The following discussion outlines how someone like Martin can lead by his authority, based on his past history as a player.

figure 13.6 – what style of leadership is shown here?

Factors affecting leader effectiveness

The following **leadership qualities** will determine a leader's effectiveness:

- Ability to communicate.
- Respect for group members.
- Enthusiasm.
- High ability.
- Deep knowledge of the sport and techniques or tactics.
- Charisma.

Figure 13.7 summarises the three broad groups of factors affecting the effectiveness of a leader with any given group or team.

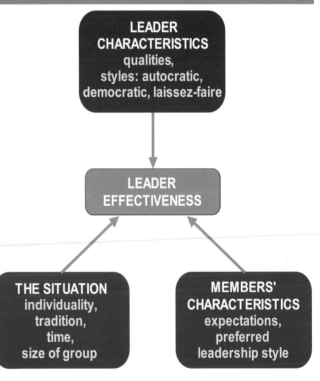
figure 13.7 – factors affecting leader effectiveness

LEADER CHARACTERISTICS
qualities, styles: autocratic, democratic, laissez-faire

LEADER EFFECTIVENESS

THE SITUATION
individuality, tradition, time, size of group

MEMBERS' CHARACTERISTICS
expectations, preferred leadership style

Fiedler's contingency theory

Fiedler's theory states that there is a continuum between:

- **Task-centred leadership**, which would be best for the most favourable or least favourable situations.
- **Person** (or relationship) **centred leadership** which would be best for moderately favourable situations.

Whether or not the task-centred or person-centred approach should be used depends on whether relationships are warm, if the task has a clear structure, or if the leader is powerful and people will do exactly what he or she says. There would also be the pressure of time which might affect the choice of leadership style.

Situational factors within leadership

- If things are going **well** for the team, or things are going **badly** (for example there are poor facilities or no support), then a leader needs to be **task-oriented**.
- On the other hand, if things are going **moderately well**, then a leader needs to be **person-centred**.

- In **team sports**, a leader should be **directive** (task-oriented) and would organise and structure group tasks according to a plan (tactics or game strategy, for example).
- In **individual sports**, however, we would look for a person-oriented leader, who would empathise with athlete problems and be sympathetic to individual difficulties.
- The **size of group** will affect leadership style, since the more members in a group, the less likely individual needs will be taken into account.

Situational factors within leadership

- If a **decision needs to be made quickly** (for example in a dangerous rock climbing situation), then an **autocratic** style of leader would be essential to ensure that the correct action is taken immediately (people will need to be told what to do to avoid danger).

- **Tradition** can sometimes play a part in which style of leadership should be used, since within some groups, group members might tend to resent change. Sometimes change is essential, and it would be necessary to be **autocratic** and **task-centred** to implement change (the leader would not try and explain why change is needed, just that it needs to be done for the good of the team).

Members' characteristics within leadership

A good leader will adapt to the expectations, knowledge and experience of group members.

- If members of a group are **hostile**, then a leader would adopt an **autocratic** style.
- If members of a group are **friendly**, then the leader would adopt a more **democratic** and **person-centred** style.

Problems arise if the strategies for preparation used by a leader do not match group expectations (for example, if members of a team do not feel that the proposed strategy will achieve a win in the next match against a particular opposing team).

Chelladurai's multidimensional model

Chelladurai set out the model in figure 13.8, which sets out the links between **leader**, **situation** and **member** characteristics, and **required**, **actual** and **preferred** leader behaviour. All these factors will affect the eventual performance of a team or group, and the satisfaction gained or perceived by both group members and the leader him or herself.

The point made by the model is that all the factors discussed above are linked in a real situation.

Chelladurai's five types of leader behaviour

- **Training and instruction**, in which behaviour is aimed at improving performance. This type of leader behaviour is strong on technical and tactical aspects.

- A **democratic** approach, in which the leader allows decisions to be made collectively.

- An **autocratic** approach, in which a leader uses his or her personal authority. This type would be least preferred if the leader or coach does not show that he or she is aware of sportspeople's needs and preferences.

- The **social support** approach, in which concern is shown for the well-being of others. This might be preferred by youngsters.

- The **rewards** approach in which a leader uses positive reinforcement to gain the authority of leadership.

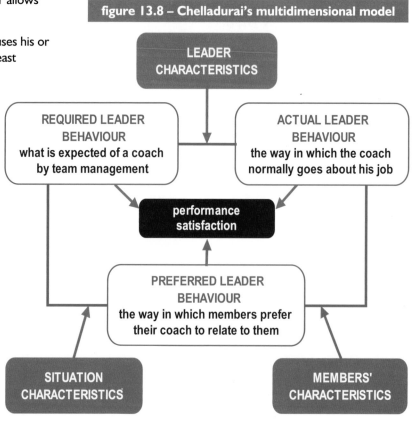

figure 13.8 – Chelladurai's multidimensional model

Social facilitation and inhibition

figure 13.9 – effects of audience?

Social facilitation

Social facilitation concerns how people other than the performer can influence his or her attitudes and behaviour.

The effect that the presence of spectators has on the way sportspeople play or perform can be positive (called **facilitation**), or negative (called **inhibition**). For example, a crowd (figure 13.9) encourages a team playing well (positive or facilitation), or the crowd jeers at a team not playing well (negative or inhibition).

Facilitation
Facilitation of a performance by an audience tends to lead to the fact that high arousal leads to improved performance by a highly skilled or extrovert performer. Gross or simple skills tend to be improved by audience effects. See the link between arousal and performance in drive theory (see page 97 below).

Inhibition
Where the presence of an audience **inhibits performance**, high arousal tends to lead to reduced performance by novices whose skills are not well-learned. This also applies to introvert performers. Fine and complex skills requiring great concentration will also tend to have performance levels reduced by negative audience effects.

Different types of audience

figure 13.10 – ball-boys as co-actors

Passive others (social facilitation) are audience and co-actors, and **interactive others** are competitors.

Co-actors
Co-actors are a passive form of audience involved in the same activity and at the same time as the performer, but not competing directly. For example:
* Officials, umpires or referees.
* Members of a player's own team.
* Ball-boys (figure 13.10) or helpers during a performance.

Factors affecting performance
* **Size of audience** - larger crowds create more arousal.

* **Proximity of audience** - the closer the audience the greater the arousal.

* **Intentions of the audience** - can be positive or negative. If spectators are negative about a player (shouting or jeering) this may suppress arousal or increase arousal depending on the personality of the performer.

figure 13.11 – fine skills or gross skills

Factors affecting performance
* **Skill level** or **difficulty** of the task - performance improves for a well-learned skill and decreases if the skill is not well-learned.
* **Personality** of the performer - extroverts perform better when aroused, but introverts can be over-aroused.
* **Type of task** (figure 13.11) - fine skills need lower levels of arousal whereas gross skills could be improved by increased arousal.

Zajonc's model

Zajonc's theory says that the mere **presence of others** creates **arousal**, which then affects performance negatively if a skill is poorly-learnt (early in the learning curve - figure 13.12).

In this case, arousal causes an incorrect response because the incorrect response is dominant.

On the other hand, if a skill is **well-learnt** (later in the learning curve), then **arousal** causes a **correct response** because the correct response is dominant.

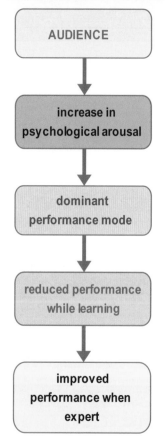

figure 13.13 – the process of evaluation apprehension

Evaluation apprehension

This theory (due to Cottrell - figure 13.13) explains that an **audience is perceived as evaluating** (assessing the value or worth of) performance. This **causes anxiety** - which in turn causes arousal.

> **figure 13.12 – a learning curve**
>
> high
>
> performance
>
> correct response dominant
>
> incorrect response dominant
>
> low
>
> time

> **STUDENT NOTE**
>
> Look at inverted U theory for the connection between arousal and performance on page 82 of AS Revise PE for OCR, ISBN: 978 1 901424 52 2.

The distraction effect

Baron's distraction-conflict theory says that **distraction** is an aspect of concentration (or **lack of concentration**). Attentional focus is very important for the effective sportsperson and if this is disrupted then he or she is distracted from his or her task. Audience and evaluation apprehension can act as a distraction. The sportsperson needs therefore to practise in distracting circumstances, and practise switching attentional focus when faced with potentially distracting circumstances.

Homefield advantage

Home or away effect on performance concerns the fact that more teams win at home than away.

A crowd may be judged as supportive or hostile (facilitation or inhibition), and high levels of anxiety caused by hostility may reduce performance.

The environment of their own stadium or playing situation is familiar to home teams, therefore home players are more comfortable. This limits anxiety and enables a worry-free and hopefully successful performance (figure 13.14).

figure 13.14 – World Cup 1966 - Wembley, 97,000 spectators, homefield advantage?

Strategies for coping with evaluation apprehension

Strategies include:

* Stress management (see page 100 below).
* Mental rehearsal (see page 100 below).
* Selective attention (away from evaluators). See page 72 of AS Revise PE for OCR, ISBN: 978 1 901424 52 2.
* Lowering the importance of the situation.
* Training with an audience present.

Practice questions

1) a)   What is meant by cohesion in the context of teams?   4 marks

   b)   What factors stop a team ever performing to its true potential?   6 marks

2) a)   Explain what is meant by social loafing by using examples from sport.   3 marks

   b)   What advice would you give a coach of a team to ensure maximum productivity?   5 marks

3) a)   What is meant by a leader and what sort of qualities would you expect to see in a leader within the context of sport?
                                                                                                                     4 marks

   b)   Using psychological theories describe how an individual becomes a leader.   4 marks

4) a)   Name three leadership styles.   3 marks

   b)   What factors should be taken into consideration when deciding upon which leadership style to adopt?   6 marks

5) Look at figure 13.8 (on page 88 above) of Chelladurai's multidimensional model of leadership.

   a)   Explain each part of the model using examples from sport.   3 marks

   b)   Behaviour of the group associated with leadership can be viewed from three perspectives. Briefly name and explain
        each of these perspectives.   3 marks

   c)   Discuss the statement 'Good leaders are born not made', and explain whether you agree or disagree in the light of
        psychological theory.   5 marks

6) Fiedler's Contingency Model suggests that the effectiveness of a leader can change depending on the situation.
   Use sporting examples to explain this theory.   4 marks

7) a)   What is meant by social facilitation and what is its main effect?   3 marks

   b)   What effects can be experienced by an individual if there is an audience present?   6 marks

8) a)   What is meant by evaluation apprehension?   2 marks

   b)   As a coach of an individual who is affected adversely by the presence of an audience, how would you help him or her
        to overcome the negative influences?   4 marks

9) Two groups of male sportspeople (of the same age) undertook an arms-length weight hold endurance test. Success at this
   exercise was measured by the length of time the weight was held. Table 13.1 below shows the average times for group 1
   (who did the exercise alone) and group 2 (who did the exercise in the presence of an audience).

Table 13.1 – **time for a weight hold endurance test**

	group 1 no audience	group 2 with audience
average time held in seconds	46.5	50.5

   a)   What effect (if any) did the audience have on the performance of the exercise?   1 mark

   b)   How would you account for this effect (or lack of effect)?   4 marks

   c)   The audience in this exercise (for group 2) was not known to the participants. Explain any effect you think there would
        be if the audience was known to the group.   6 marks

10) Using examples from sport, explain what is meant by evaluation apprehension and outline the causes of it.   3 marks

CHAPTER 14 – GOAL SETTING and SELF-CONFIDENCE

Goal setting

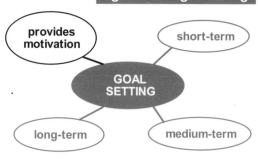

figure 14.1 – goal setting

The main function of goal setting (figure 14.1) is to increase **motivation**. The feeling of satisfaction gained from achieving a goal brings about this motivation. Goal setting can also be used as a means of **managing anxiety** or stress.

Goals can be **short**-term, **medium**-term or **long**-term. Short-term goals can be used as targets for single training sessions, or what can be expected after a period of training. Long-term goals may or may not be achieved, but are placed in the background of a performer's mind and can underpin everything he or she does. Kelly Holmes had the ambition (goal) of getting an Olympic gold, and she **eventually** did this – twice! This goal motivated Kelly to keep going through injury and disappointment, to keep her training through bad weather and good times.

Goals (figure 14.2) should be:
- **Easily** attained initially and therefore **realistic**.
- **Incremental**, a little bit at a time.
- **Challenging** but **achievable**.
- **Progressively** more difficult.
- **Training goals** should be planned around **overall goals**.

figure 14.2 – goals should be?

Goals are either:
- **Outcome oriented**:
- Towards the end result of the sporting activity. For example to win a race.
- **Performance oriented**:
- Judged against other performances. For example to beat his or her best time.
- **Process oriented**:
- To obtain an improvement in techniques.

Effective goal setting

Goals (figure 14.3) should be:
- Stated **positively**.
- **Specific** to the situation and the performer.
- **Time phased**, to be achieved in one week or two months for example.
- **Challenging**.
- **Achievable**.
- **Measurable**, so that you can actually say exactly whether or not a goal has been achieved.
- **Negotiated** between sportsperson and coach.
- **Progressive**, from short-term to long-term.
- **Performance oriented** rather than outcome oriented.
- **Written** down.
- **Reviewed** regularly (with downward adjustment if necessary - in the case of injury).
- **Achievement oriented** rather than failure oriented.

figure 14.3 – effective goals

Failure to achieve goals should be followed by the resetting of goals to maintain the performer's **self-esteem**.

S.M.A.R.T.E.R. goals

SPECIFIC
> directly related to a sporting situation.

MEASURABLE
> progress can be assessed.

ACCEPTED
> by both performer and coach.

REALISTIC
> challenging but within the capability of the performer.

TIME PHASED
> a date is set for completion.

EXCITING
> inspiring and rewarding to the performer.

RECORDED
> written down.

For example, the **smarter** goal of running a 400m in 48 seconds. This would be achieved after 5 racing attempts, agreed by both performer and coach, assessed at an 80% success rate, providing an exciting challenge, with a record of training and racing times.

figure 14.4 – mental preparation for sports performance

COMMITMENT

↓

SELF-CONFIDENCE

↓

CONCENTRATION

↓

EMOTIONAL CONTROL

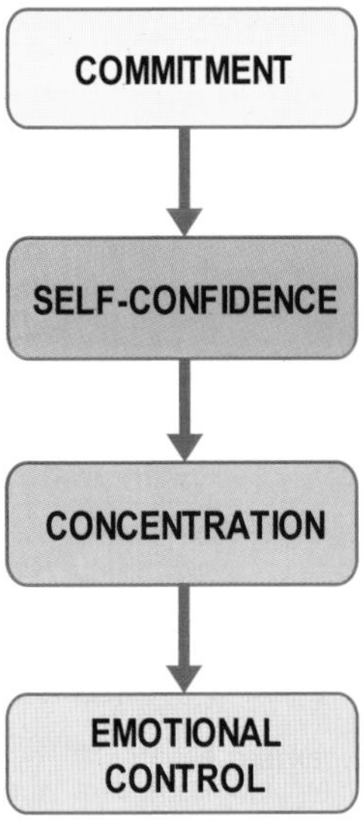

Self-confidence

Confidence

Confidence is an element of mental preparation for sports performance, as outlined in figure 14.4.
The explanation of how confidence affects us includes:
- It arouses **positive** emotions.
- It facilitates **concentration**.
- It enables **focus** on the important aspects of a task.

figure 14.5 – self-confidence and self-efficacy

Self-confidence is a feature of a sportsperson's attitude to his or her sporting activity which boosts personal self-worth and self-belief as outlined in figure 14.5. This belief centres around the notion that he or she can win or perform well.

Self-efficacy is a situational form of self-confidence. It is specific to the sport or activity which a person is undertaking.

Confidence (figure 14.6) arouses positive emotions which allow the athlete to:
- Remain **calm** under pressure.
- Be **assertive** when required.
- **Concentrate** easily.
- **Focus** on the important aspects of a task.
- Set challenging but realistic **goals**.
- Increase **effort**.
- Devise effective game **strategies**.
- Keep psychological **momentum**.

A confident player plays to win even if it means **taking risks**, will take each point or play at a time, and **never gives up** even when defeat is imminent.

figure 14.6 – self-confidence

Sport confidence

Vealey's **sport confidence** is the level of belief a person has in his or her ability to be successful at sport.

- Success in sport could be related to winning (**outcome orientation**), or performing well (**performance orientation**).

- Different performers have different ways of enhancing sport confidence. Their **competitive orientations** can be varied according to the situation whether a performer is motivated towards a performance goal or an outcome goal.

Vealey's model

Table 14.1 – **sport confidence**

factors influencing sport confidence	definition
trait sport confidence	the level of sport confidence a person usually has
competitive orientation	the perceived opportunity to achieve a performance or outcome goal
state sport confidence	the level of sport confidence a performer has in a specific sport situation

Trait sport confidence example, a discus thrower is generally confident about making a throw.
Competitive orientation example, the discus thrower is motivated by a national championships to throw well.
State sport confidence example, the discus thrower feels confident because the wind is in the right direction.

Relationship of confidence to attribution

A performer's attribution of success or failure will relate to sport confidence. Attributing success to factors like ability and effort will increase a performer's sport confidence, by increasing his or her future expectancy of success.

Results of research

- **Males** (in the general population) have a higher sport confidence than **females**.
- **Elite performers** have high sport confidence.
- Elite sporting females have the **same level** of sport confidence as elite sporting males.
- Therefore elite sporting females are **less affected** by **traditional female stereotyping** and roles.
- Elite performers are more **performance oriented**, which means that their feelings of confidence are based more on how well they perform than whether they win or lose.

Self-efficacy

Bandura's **self-efficacy** model (figure 14.7) outlines **four** factors relevant to the self-efficacy of a sports performer.

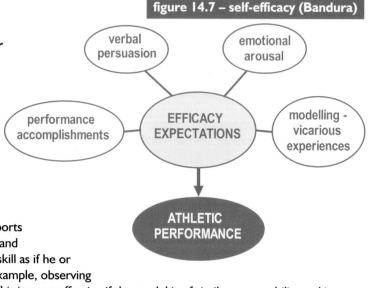

figure 14.7 – self-efficacy (Bandura)

- **Performance accomplishments**
  Performance accomplishments consist of **past experiences**, for example, a previously performed skill at dribbling a soccer ball. If this is successful, then this leads to greater self-efficacy at this particular task in the future.

- **Vicarious experiences**
  Vicarious experiences consist of what has **been observed in others** performing a similar skill (the sports performer experiences the same feelings of mastery and competence by watching another person perform a skill as if he or she has performed the skill himself or herself). For example, observing another player in your team dribbling a soccer ball. This is most effective if the model is of similar age or ability and is successful. This may lead to greater self-efficacy.

- **Verbal persuasion**
  Verbal encouragement can lead to greater self-efficacy if the person giving encouragement is of **high status** compared with the performer.

- **Emotional arousal**
  If **arousal** is too high, then **state anxiety** (anxiety produced by the specific situation of an activity - otherwise known as **A-state**) can be too high. This could lead to low self-efficacy. Mental rehearsal or physical relaxation techniques could lead to greater confidence and a calmer approach - this also contributes to self-efficacy.

Lack of confidence

Lack of confidence can cause **stress** under pressure. What tends to happen is that attention and concentration tend to focus on outside stressors such as mistakes (falling during an ice-skating or gymnastics programme), or spectators (shouted comments or applause on a neighbouring court).

figure 14.8 – over-confidence can lead to injury

- What also tends to happen is the setting of **goals** which are either **too easy** or **too hard**.

- Lack of confidence also causes the athlete to try to **avoid mistakes** (fear of failure or tendency to avoid failure, see page 78 above about achievement motivation).

- Non-confident athletes find it difficult to reverse negative psychological momentum, so that once things start to go wrong it is difficult to think positively.

Over-confidence or false confidence

Over-confidence is dangerous because it can lead to inadequate preparation (the athlete thinks he or she is better prepared than is actually the case).
Low motivation and low arousal can occur, which are difficult to correct when competition (figure 14.8) is under way.

Role of the coach in boosting self-confidence

The coach should develop self-confidence and self-efficacy through successful achievement.

He or she should ensure early and continued success by careful selection of goals, tasks and levels of competition, focusing on successful personal performance, not on winning.

Practice questions

1) a) Show what is meant by short-term goals and long-term goals by using examples from sport. — 4 marks

   b) What are the main positive effects of setting goals in sport? — 2 marks

   c) As a coach how would you ensure that your goal setting was as effective as possible? — 6 marks

   d) How does performance profiling assist in goal setting? — 3 marks

2) Explain the meaning of the acronym S.M.A.R.T.E.R. in relation to goal setting. — 7 marks

3) a) What is meant by the term self-efficacy when applied to sports psychology? — 1 mark

   b) Bandura suggested that self-efficacy is influenced by four factors. Identify and apply these factors to a sport of your choice. — 8 marks

   c) As a coach of a sports team, how would you raise an individual's level of self-efficacy? — 4 marks

4) Drawing on your knowledge and understanding of sports psychology, examine the theories and methods that you might use to raise the levels of confidence of a sports performer. Illustrate your answer with practical examples. — 20 marks

CHAPTER 15 – ATTENTIONAL and EMOTIONAL CONTROL

Attentional control

STUDENT NOTE

Look at page 72 of AS Revise PE for OCR, ISBN: 978 1 901424 52 2 for an introduction to the ideas behind perception and attention.

Attention

Attention relates to:
- **Amount of information** we can cope with, since the amount of information we can attend to **is limited**, and therefore we have limited **attentional capacity**.
- **Relevance of the information**. The performer must therefore attend to only **relevant information**, and **disregard irrelevant** information. This is called **selective attention**.

Selective attention

This is the process of sorting out **relevant** bits of information from the many which are received. Attention passes the information to the **short-term memory** which gives time for **conscious analysis**. A good performer can **focus totally** on an important aspect of his or her skill which **can exclude other elements** which may also be desirable. Sometimes a performer may desire to concentrate on several different things at once.

When some parts of a performance become **automatic**, the information relevant to those parts does not require attention, and this gives the performer **spare attentional capacity**. This allows the performer to attend to new elements of a skill such as tactics or anticipating the moves of an opponent. The coach will therefore need to help the performer to make best use of spare attentional capacity, and will also need to **direct the attention** of the performer to enable him or her to **concentrate** and reduce the chance of **attentional switching** to irrelevant information or distractions.

Concentration

Concentration is a state of mind in which attention is directed towards a specific aim or activity. Concentration and **attentional focus** (**control of attention** towards a task) are essential components of a sportsperson's armoury of mental techniques to assist performance.

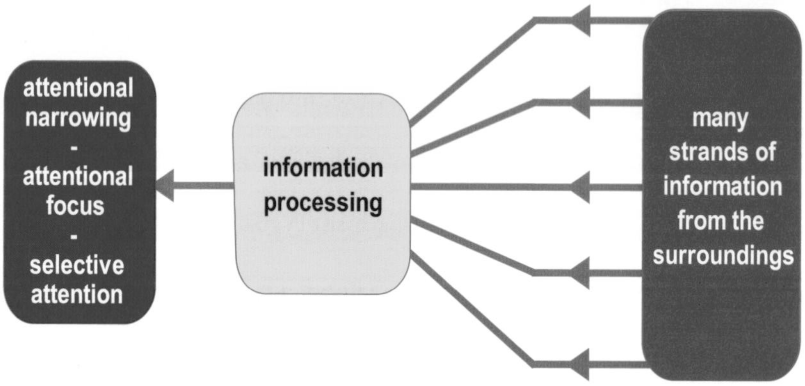

Attentional narrowing (concentration, figure 15.1) occurs when some parts of a performance become automatic. The information relevant to those parts then does not require attention, which gives the performer spare attentional capacity. This **spare capacity** will allow the performer to attend to **new elements** of a skill such as tactics or anticipating the moves of an opponent.

figure 15.1 – attentional narrowing

The **coach** will need to help the performer to make best use of spare attentional capacity, and direct the attention of the performer to enable him or her to concentrate. This would reduce the chance of **attentional switching** to irrelevant information or distractions.

Use of cognitive techniques to assist concentration

Cognitive techniques such as imagery and mental rehearsal or relaxation can be used to direct the sportsperson's mind towards a specific task (see page 100 below). These techniques can be used to manage the stress of the situation, or to manage anxiety in a productive way.

Cue utilisation

Cue utilisation (Easterbrook) describes a situation in which cues can be used by the sportsperson to direct attention, and to trigger appropriate arousal responses. This would enable attentional focus at a relevant moment. Sometimes, **narrowing of attentional focus** by an aroused player will cause lack of awareness of broader play issues.

Attentional control training (ACT)

Attentional control training is a personalised programme which targets a performer's specific concentration problems. It assesses the demands of the sport, the situation, and the personality of the performer.

Nideffer's attentional styles

On the graph in figure 15.2, the axes represent attentional styles that are narrow to broad and internal to external, and a particular event or sports activity will have a mixture of all four styles.

The following attentional styles are highlighted:

- **Narrow** (A), in which a player concentrates on one aspect of the game, for example the goalkeeper who has predominantly closed skills.
- **Broad** (B), in which a player concentrates on the whole game, with all players' positions and movements. This applies to open skills of this type.
- **Internal** (C), in which a player decides to concentrate on his own technique.
- **External** (D), in which a player focuses on the position of his opposite number.

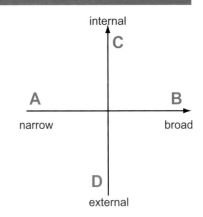

figure 15.2 – attentional styles

Emotional control

Arousal

STUDENT NOTE

Look at page 81 of 'AS Revise PE for OCR', ISBN: 978 1 901424 52 2 for an introduction to arousal as it affects sports performance.

Arousal is a state of **mental** and **physical preparedness** for action. This is the level of inner drives which forces the sportsperson to strive to achieve. It needs to be under control and at the right level depending on the task and is closely related to **anxiety**. The symptoms of arousal are:

- A faster **heart rate**.
- Faster **breathing rate**.
- **Sweating**.
- Ability to focus (**concentrate**).
- Response to danger (**fight or flight** adrenaline response).

The **reticular activating system** (RAS) is a system within the brain which causes arousal. Extroverts have lower levels of intrinsic arousal than introverts, hence extroverts seek situations of high arousal whereas introverts seek low arousal situations.

Theories linking arousal and performance

Drive theory (summarised by figure 15.3) describes the simple situation where the **higher** the **arousal** level, the **higher** the achievement or **performance** level.

Inverted U theory (summarised by figure 15.4) is attributed to Yerkes and Dodson, and states that there is an **optimum arousal** level. As arousal increases, performance increases up to a certain point. If aroused more than this, the performance will **go down**.

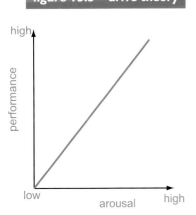

figure 15.3 – drive theory

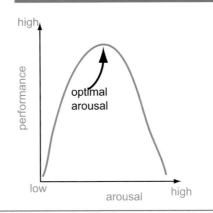

figure 15.4 – inverted U theory

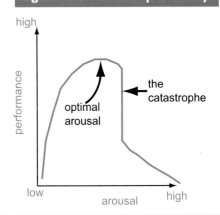

figure 15.5 – catastrophe theory

Arousal and performance

Catastrophe theory (summarised by figure 15.5) is a variation of inverted U theory in which performance **increases** as arousal **increases**, but if **arousal** gets **too high** a **complete loss of performance** occurs (the catastrophe).

Peak flow theory

Csikzentmihalyi derived a theory which asserts that flow is an **optimal experience** which is intrinsically rewarding. Figure 15.6 shows the relationship between the task demands and the skill level of the performer, and you will see that there is a **zone** in which these two factors combine to produce an effective performance.

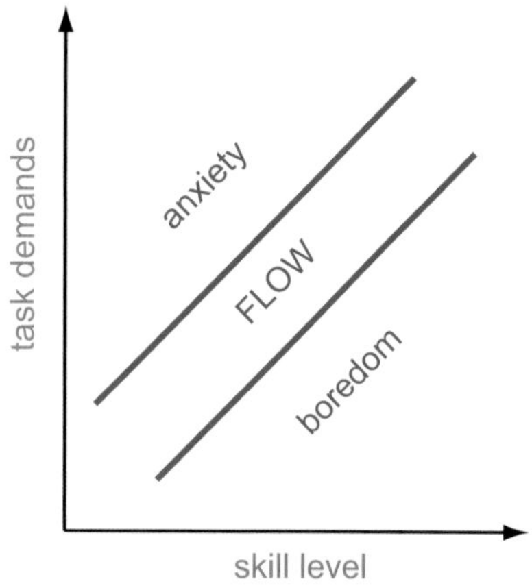

Flow is a period of peak performance, when the performer feels totally involved without effort, and without having to concentrate. If skill level exceeds task demands (task is too easy), the performer is bored, and if task demands exceed skill level (task is too hard), the performer becomes anxious.

Peak flow occurs when:
- The demands of the task match the skill level of the performer.
- Actions of a performer become automatic.
- Concentration is total without effort.
- The performer feels in control without effort.
- The performer loses self-consciousness.
- Time appears to speed up.
- Or time appears to slow down.
- The performer feels exhilarated by the activity.

Peak flow is achieved when:
- The performer has a positive mental attitude.
- The performer controls his or her anxiety.
- The performer maintains concentration and confidence (maintains focus).
- Peak fitness is maintained.

Perhaps Usain Bolt (figure 15.7) was both **in the Zone** and had **peak flow** when setting his multiple World records at the Beijing Olympics 2008, and the Berlin World championships 2009.

Zone of optimum functioning

Hanin worked out that the optimum level of arousal is not always at mid-point of the inverted U, and that best performance will vary between sportspeople. For example, some athletes will peak at low arousal, and other athletes will peak at medium or high arousal.

Also, an athlete's best performance will be in a **zone** (not just a point of optimum performance - figure 15.8), and different athletes will have **different zones of arousal** for optimum performances depending on **personality**, **skill** or **task** and degree of **habit**.

Habit is defined as the strength and **permanence** of a correctly learned skill.

Effects of arousal on technique
- The **point of optimum arousal** is of crucial importance to the learning and stability of a sportsperson's technique.
- Technique is the sequence of actions which enables a performer to successfully perform the skill of his or her event.
- Trying too hard (overarousal) can cause a performer to change his or her technique in an uncontrolled way - with a resultant loss of performance.
- This can be made worse by the anxiety which would accompany a major event - such as a major at tennis or an open at golf.

figure 15.6 – peak flow

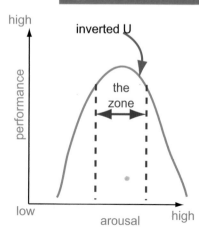

figure 15.7 – Usain Bolt with peak flow?

figure 15.8 – the zone

Choking and overarousal

High arousal can cause a performer to have negative thoughts. **Negative thoughts of failure** or lack of success can creep in if a performer is **over-aroused**. These thoughts can affect the performer's confidence and create an almost complete inability to perform skills properly. This is **choking** and is an aspect of inverted U theory.

Examples are:
- The snooker player who misses an easy shot when in the final frame of an important match.
- The golfer who misses the fairway from the tee when in the lead in a competition.
- This particularly applies to sports which use a fine skill.
- Choking can be controlled by **cognitive management techniques** (see page 100 below).

Anxiety affects arousal, and these theories can also apply to how anxiety affects performance.

Anxiety

Anxiety can be explained as an emotional state similar to fear, associated with:
- **Somatic (physiological)** arousal - connected with raised heart rate, raised breathing rate, sweating and so on.
- **Cognitive (psychological)** arousal - worry and negative feelings about the situation, feelings of nervousness, feelings of **apprehension**.

Anxiety is closely linked to arousal, since an anxious person is more likely to become aroused than a calm person. Hence the various theories linking arousal with performance (drive, inverted U, catastrophe) can also apply to link anxiety with performance.

It can have **behavioural** consequences - in which a person will experience:
- Tension.
- Agitation.
- Restlessness.

Trait anxiety - A-trait (Speilberger)
Trait anxiety is an inbuilt (**trait**) **part of the personality** which gives a person:
- A tendency to be **fearful** of unfamiliar situations.
- A tendency to perceive competitive situations as **threatening**.
- A tendency to respond to competitive situations with **apprehension** and **tension**.

State anxiety - A-state
State anxiety is an emotional response to a **particular situation**, characterised by feelings of nervousness and apprehension which is often **temporary** - as you might expect if the anxiety is related to a certain situation which of course will change as daily activities change.

Stress

Stress and **anxiety** are closely linked, with stress being a major cause of health issues in our society. Figure 15.9 outlines the main factors associated with stress and stressors.

Stress is a response of the body to any demands made on it. The symptoms of stress are **physiological**, **psychological** or **behavioural** (see table 15.1 below for details).

figure 15.9 – stress and stressors

Stressors
Stressors are the cause of stress and are:

- **Social** including the disapproval of parents or peers, the rejection by peers or parents, or isolation from normal social interactions.

- **Chemical** or **biochemical** in which harm is inflicted by ingestion of nasty substances.

- **Bacterial**, which would be an illness caused by micro-organisms.

Stressors

- **Physical** in which a person would suffer injury, pain or exhaustion.
- **Climatic** in which extremes of weather are experienced, such as hot weather for endurance activities, or rain and cold on bare skin.
- **Psychological**, in which there is a mismatch between the perception of the demands of a task and the ability of a person to cope with these demands.

Symptoms of stress

Table 15.1 – **symptoms of stress**

physiological symptoms	psychological symptoms	behavioural symptoms
increased heart rate	worry	rapid talking
increased blood pressure	feeling overwhelmed	nail biting
increased sweating	inability to make decisions	pacing
increased breathing rate	inability to concentrate	scowling
decreased flow of blood to the skin	inability to direct attention appropriately	yawning
increased oxygen uptake	narrowing of attention	trembling
dry mouth	feeling out of control	raised voice pitch
		frequent urination

Control of stress and anxiety

Stress and anxiety management techniques become important for sports performers when performances fall, or failure is experienced.

Cognitive relaxation techniques

These techniques use the power of **thought** to redirect attention away from failure or perceived failure. A performer will take **control** of emotions and thought processes, will **eliminate negative feelings**, and will develop **self-confidence** (self-efficacy, see page 93 above).

- **Imagery relaxation**, in which a performer will think of a place with associations of warmth and relaxation, then imagine the activity or technique. This process involves practice in non-stressful situations, and will be used prior to competition.

figure 15.10 – mental practice or rehearsal

mental picture of a skill

imagine success or avoid failure

mental warm-up, readiness for action

simulate a whole movement sequence

must be as realistic as possible

USES OF MENTAL PRACTICE

used during rest periods

control arousal before performance

prevents wear and tear

building self-confidence

focus attention on important aspects of skill

small muscle contractions same as actual practice

- **Thought stopping**, in which when negative thoughts or worry (about failure) begin, a performer should immediately think '**stop**', and substitute a **positive thought**.

- **Mental rehearsal** or practice (visualisation), in which the mental or cognitive rehearsal of a skill without actual physical movement is undertaken by a performer. The performer will consciously imagine a performance or rerun a past experience, and will continue with a preview of hoped-for success. This process helps concentration, and helps the performer to focus on strengths and weaknesses. This technique is used by most top level sportsmen, and is often prompted by video or talk from a coach. The point of this in stress or anxiety control is that it brings an activity away from the actual performance, and therefore away from any anxieties associated with the performance itself. Figure 15.10 outlines the main features of this process.

- **Concentration** (see page 96 above).

Cognitive relaxation techniques

- **Attentional control training** (ACT) (see page 96 above).
- **Cue utilisation** (see page 96 above).

- **Self-talk** is a procedure where a person will talk through the process of a competitive situation, talking positively and building self-confidence.

Somatic relaxation techniques

Somatic relaxation techniques control the physiological symptoms of stress and anxiety.

figure 15.11 – John McEnroe used centring

- **Progressive muscle relaxation**, sometimes called **self-directed muscle relaxation training**, enables a performer to focus on each of the major muscle groups in turn, then to allow breathing to become slow and easy. The athlete will visualise the tension flowing out of a muscle group until it is completely relaxed. Eventually a sportsperson will be able to combine muscle groups, and achieve total relaxation quickly.

- **Centring** involves the control of physiological symptoms of stress by focusing on control of the diaphragm and deep breathing. The famous John McEnroe (famous for throwing tantrums on court 'you can't be serious', then going on to win Wimbledon titles, figure 15.11), used centring to bring himself down from a major row with a court official to playing the perfect serve or shot - within 10 seconds!

- **Biofeedback** is the process of monitoring skin temperature (cold if stressed, warm if unstressed), and the galvanic skin response in which the electrical conductivity of skin increases when moist (tense muscle causes sweating). A further measurement is made by electromyography, in which electrodes are taped to specific muscles which can detect electrical activity and hence tension in muscle. The point is that these measures are perceived by the sportsperson during a performance, and he or she can then alter his or her behaviour to reduce the symptoms of stress or anxiety.

Practice questions

1) Explain the link between selective attention, concentration on a sports task, and the idea of attentional narrowing.
8 marks

2) Describe how a coach might use cognitive techniques to assist concentration.
6 marks

3) Explain how Nideffer's attentional styles describe how a sportsperson can direct attention to a relevant aspect of a game or sport.
8 marks

4) The catastrophe theory is used to explain a golfer's disastrous failure to win a match having been 3 strokes in the lead coming up to the last green. Explain this situation and why this theory might be useful in preventing a repetition.
4 marks

5) A number of PE students are attending trials at their chosen sport. Describe the Inverted U theory and explain how it might affect a student's performance at the trials.
5 marks

6) a) What is meant by the term stress? 2 marks
   b) Explain two psychological symptoms of stress. 2 marks
   c) Identify three main stressors in the context of sport. 3 marks
   d) What is the difference between state and trait anxiety? 2 marks
   e) What coping strategies should the anxious performer draw upon? 5 marks

7) a) Discuss the possible relationships between anxiety and performance in sporting activities. 7 marks
   b) High levels of arousal have often been linked with stress. Sketch a graph showing the relationship between the performance of a complex skill and level of arousal. 2 marks
   c) Add a second curve to your graph showing how the performance of a simple skill might be affected by arousal.
   2 marks

8) Many elite athletes identify an emotional response called the peak flow experience that is associated with success. Describe what is meant by peak flow experience and give reasons why it might occur.
5 marks

9) With reference to sporting performance, explain how cognitive and somatic anxiety differ.
5 marks

SECTION B: SCIENTIFIC OPTIONS

OPTION B2: BIOMECHANICS

CHAPTER 16 – LINEAR MOTION

Newton's laws of motion

figure 16.1 – a sprinter at constant speed

Newton's first law
Newton's first law of motion describes what happens when **zero net force** acts, which means that all forces acting must cancel out. In figure 16.1 the forces (green arrows) **cancel out**. The vertical forces are the same size (arrows are the same length) but in opposite directions. The horizontal forces are also of the same size and in opposite directions, hence all forces cancel out.

When there is zero net force acting on an object:
* The object is **stationary**.
* **Or** the object moves at **constant velocity**.
Hence when any object moves at constant velocity, all forces must cancel out, the net force must be zero.

Inertia
The first law is also known as the law of **inertia**. The concept of inertia is that a massive object will remain at rest and will require a force to shift it, and once moving, will require a force to change its motion (accelerate or decelerate it). Sometimes, the word **inertia** is used to represent the **mass** of a body or object.

figure 16.2 – a sprinter decelerating

Newton's second law
Newton's second law of motion describes what happens when a **net force acts** on a body. **A net force** produces **acceleration** or **deceleration** of the body or changes the direction of the body (swerving). In the motion of a sprinter the acceleration is produced by the net force applied, which must be forwards if the sprinter is accelerating forwards. When the sprinter **decelerates**, there is a net **force backwards**. In figure 16.2, the vertical arrows (representing vertical forces) are the same length but in opposite directions, and hence cancel out. The horizontal forces are both acting backwards, therefore there is a net force acting backwards on her. This means that she is **decelerating** (horizontally!).

* Newton's second law also says that the bigger the **net** force, the greater the **acceleration** of the person.
* Hence a **stronger** sprinter should be able to **accelerate** out of the blocks quicker.
* However, the more mass an object has, the less the acceleration for a given force.
* Hence a heavier (more massive) sprinter will accelerate less than a lighter sprinter.

This is expressed mathematically as: $\mathbf{F = m \times a}$ (force = mass x acceleration)

As discussed above, slowing down (**deceleration**) is also caused by force. Hence a bike hitting a barrier encounters a large force, since a large deceleration slows the bike very quickly, possibly wrecking it and hurting the rider. However, if the cyclist had applied the brakes moderately, he or she would have encountered less deceleration, taking longer to stop, but would do so safely.

Newton's third law
Newton's third law of motion describes what happens when **two bodies** (or objects) exert forces on one another. Action and reaction are equal and opposite and always occur in pairs.

figure 16.3 – a swimmer pushes away the water

Weight and mass

These two ideas are often confused. **Mass** is a scalar and represents the total quantity of matter in an object. **Weight** is the force due to gravity on a mass (with a direction towards the centre of the Earth) and can be calculated from the fact that the gravitational field strength at the Earth's surface is approximately 10 newtons for each kilogramme of mass. Hence if the mass of the sprinter in figure 17.3 is 50 kg, then her weight would be 50 x 10 = 500 newtons towards the centre of the Earth.

> **STUDENT NOTE**
>
> If this sprinter were to obtain astronaut status and visit the moon (where the gravitational field strength is 1.67 newtons per kilogramme), then her mass would still be 50 kg, but her weight would be 50 x 1.67 = 83.5 newtons towards the centre of the moon.

Types of force

Reaction forces

Reaction forces are forces acting via Newton's third law as explained on page 102 above. When one object pushes on another, the first object experiences a force equal but opposite in direction to the second (figure 17.4):

- **a**, the jumper pushes down on the ground (black arrow), the ground pushes up on the jumper (red arrow).
- **b**, the weight lifter pulls up on the weight (black arrow), weight pulls down on lifter (red arrow).
- **c**, the swimmer pushes backwards on the water (black arrow), the water pushes forward on the swimmer (red arrow).
- **d**, canoeist pushes backwards on the water (black arrow), reaction force thrusts the canoe forward (red arrow).
- **e**, sprinter pushes back and down on the ground (black arrow), the ground pushes upwards and forwards on the sprinter (red arrow).
- **f**, in cycling, the tyre on the rear wheel pushes backward on the ground (black arrow), the ground pushes forward on the rear wheel (red arrow).

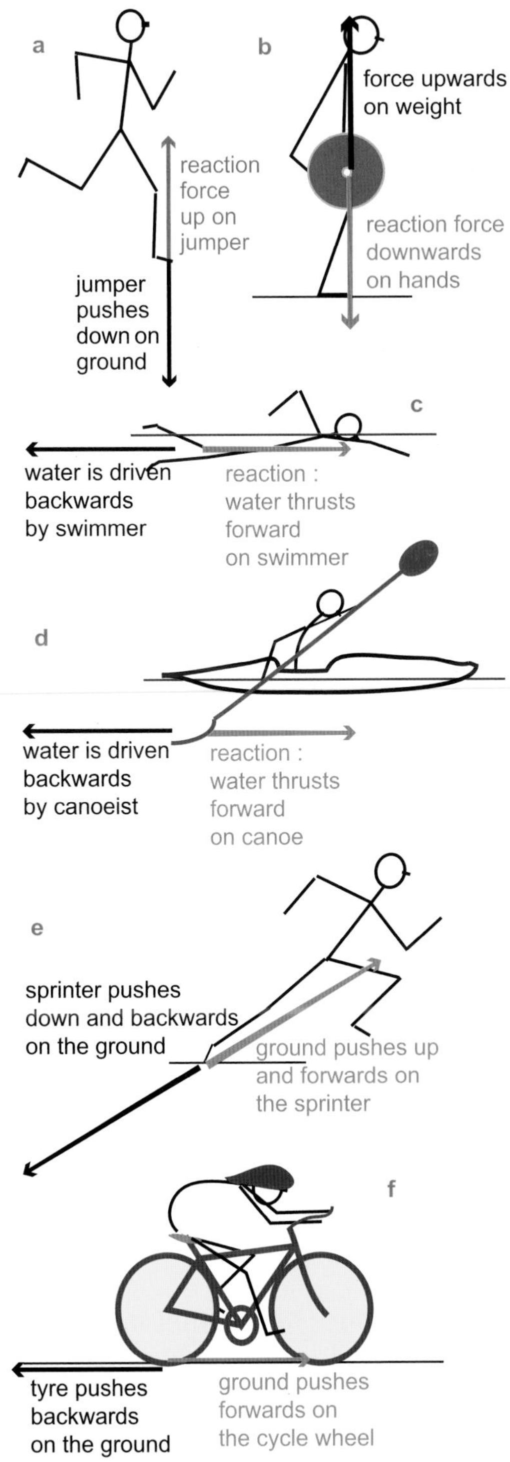

Friction

Friction is a force which acts sideways between two surfaces which tend to slide past one another. This force enables sportspeople to accelerate, slow down, swerve, walk, and run.

The magnitude of friction depends on the **grip of footwear** on floor surface, and the **nature of the surface** itself (rough, smooth, slippy, greasy and so on), for example:

- **Studs and spikes** increase friction to enable better swerving and accelerating and decelerating in games or track situations. This applies to soft or wet surfaces.

- For **dry hard surfaces**, solid smooth rubber soles can give better friction as in discus or hammer shoes, rock climbing shoes, or tennis shoes for concrete surfaces.

- In **snow and ice**, long slender footwear (skates or skis) have low forward friction, but high sideways friction.

Note that friction acts forwards on the feet of the accelerating runner (see figure 17.5).

figure 17.4 – examples of reaction forces

a

reaction force up on jumper

jumper pushes down on ground

b

force upwards on weight

reaction force downwards on hands

c

water is driven backwards by swimmer

reaction : water thrusts forward on swimmer

d

water is driven backwards by canoeist

reaction : water thrusts forward on canoe

e

sprinter pushes down and backwards on the ground

ground pushes up and forwards on the sprinter

f

tyre pushes backwards on the ground

ground pushes forwards on the cycle wheel

figure 17.5 – friction

friction acts forward on the foot of the accelerating sprinter

Friction

Friction depends on the force pressing the surfaces together, but not on the area of contact. For example:

*   The inverted wings on racing cars increase the down force on wheels. This increases cornering friction between the wheels and the ground.
*   When riding a mountain bike up a steep hill, you should sit back over the rear wheel to increase downward force on the rear wheel, so that there is more friction between the rear wheel and the ground.
*   Friction also enables swerving by games players in rugby, soccer, hockey, and tennis. The friction force then acts sideways to the direction of motion, and changes the direction of motion.
*   The direction taken after a bounce by a spinning bal depends on the direction of spin and the friction between the ball and the ground (see page 117 below).

Rolling or sliding friction

*   **Rolling friction** is the term which describes the force between surfaces which do not move relative to one another, like a wheel rolling over a surface, or a foot driving and pushing without slipping. The friction can be anything from zero up to a maximum just before slipping occurs. As soon as slipping occurs, the friction force falls, and would not be enough to keep a sportsperson upright (so he or she slips over!).

*   **Sliding friction** occurs when the two surfaces are moving relative to one another, and is always less then the maximum rolling friction. This is why ABS (advanced braking systems) will reduce braking force on wheels if sensors detect the beginning of sliding.

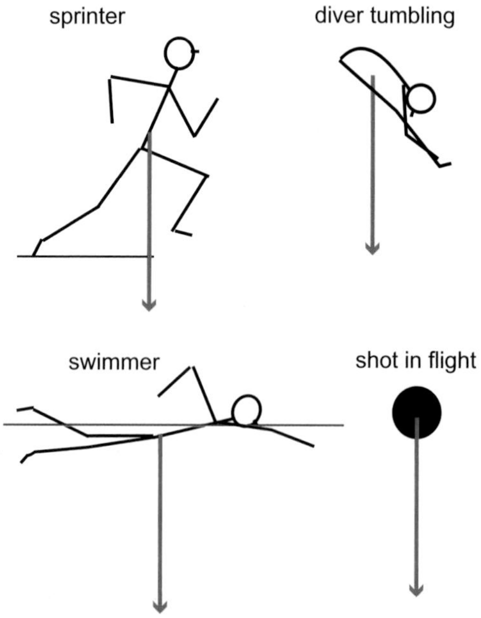

Weight

As discussed on page 107 above, **weight** is the force pulled downwards towards the centre of the Earth on any object by gravity. Weight will vary slightly over the surface of the Earth depending on the gravitational field strength.

The gravitational field strength changes slightly depending on the thickness of the Earth's crust, the longitude, the proximity of large mountains, and the height above sea level. Weight is approximately 10 newtons for each kilogramme of mass, and will act on the centre of mass of a body (the point which represents the averaged position of all the mass of a body), with examples shown in figure 17.6.

Weight is also the predominant force acting on an object projected into flight (see page 113).

figure 17.6 – weight of various bodies

sprinter   diver tumbling

swimmer   shot in flight

Fluid friction

Fluid friction (or **drag**) is a term applying to objects moving through fluids (gases or liquids). The force acts in the opposite direction to the direction of motion (discussed in detail on page 112 below).

Free body diagrams

figure 17.7 – pin-man or free-body diagram

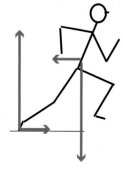

Pin men (free body) diagrams are used to represent the human body with forces acting on it when answering exam questions. Free body diagrams are a way of doing this without any anatomical details.

In figure 17.7, a runner is represented by a pin man, with forces depicted by red arrows. The figure shows four forces acting, 2 forces acting up on the foot and down on the body, and 2 forces acting backwards on the body and forwards on the foot. Longer arrows mean greater force.

The **point of action** of a force is also important, remembering that drag forces will act over the whole body but are usually represented by a single arrow acting somewhere in the middle of the body. A friction force will act on the foot of the runner, and the weight will act on his or her centre of mass. Reaction forces act at the point of contact between two objects (on the foot of the runner in figure 17.7).

Impulse

Impulse is another concept derived from Newton's second law.

$$\text{force} = \text{rate of change of momentum}$$
$$= \frac{\text{change of momentum}}{\text{time taken to change}}$$

Hence force x time $=$ total change of momentum

Impulse is defined as **force x time**, therefore

$$\text{impulse} = \textbf{total change of momentum}$$
$$\text{unit } \textbf{newton second (Ns)}$$

This is useful when large forces are applied for short times. Examples of the use of impulse:

- A **cricket fielder** catching a hard cricket ball. The incoming cricket ball will change its momentum from some high value when travelling, to zero when caught. This fixes the impulse (force x time), so if you catch the ball in a short time, a large force will be exerted, and the ball will smack the hands and hurt! If, on the other hand, you let the hands go with the ball, you would increase the time over which the momentum of the ball would change, and therefore reduce the force of impact. The hands would no longer hurt!

- A **bat, racquet, stick, golf club striking a ball**. If you use follow-through during a strike you would increase the time of contact with the ball, therefore increase the impulse, and increase the change of momentum of the ball. The ball would therefore leave the bat with greater velocity.

- A **footballer kicking a ball**. Again, follow-through will increase the time of contact and therefore increase the outgoing velocity of the ball.

- The **turn in the discus throw**. The turn increases the time over which force is applied, and therefore increases the impulse, and increases the final momentum of the discus. This therefore increases the speed of release and the distance thrown.

Impulse and force-time graphs

The formula: **impulse** = total change of momentum = force x time

can be used to calculate change of momentum if force and time the force is acting can be measured.

Using total change of momentum $=$ force x time

Or total change of momentum $=$ impulse
$=$ **area under graph** of force against time

Once you have calculated the change of momentum, you can calculate the change of velocity (by dividing by the mass of the object experiencing the force).

Force-time graphs

The area under this graph is the **impulse**, and in the graph in figure 17.8 of the force between foot and ground during a foot strike when sprinting, the bigger the area under the graph, the bigger the impulse, and the greater the change of momentum of the runner (and hence the greater the acceleration and therefore the change of velocity).

The sprinter

Figure 17.9 overleaf continues the theme started above of the 100 metre sprinter.

The graphs in figure 17.9 show the force-time graphs for the horizontal force acting on a single foot of a sprinter at four stages of a 100 metre sprint.

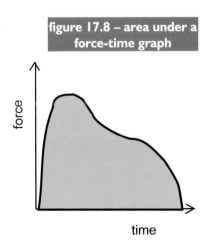

figure 17.8 – area under a force-time graph

The sprinter

- **a** when the runner is in contact with starting blocks or immediately at the start.
- **b** when he or she is accelerating during the first two to three seconds of a run.
- **c** when the runner is running at approximately constant speed during the middle of a run.
- **d** during the slowing down at the end of a run.

- In figure 17.9a, the area under the **force time curve** is above the horizontal axis (and hence **positive**), which means the force is acting **forwards** on the runner. The force lasts for a relatively long time, therefore the impulse is high and positive and would cause large forward acceleration and change of forward velocity of the runner.

- In figure 17.9b, some of the area of the graph is below the horizontal axis and therefore **negative** but the **overall impulse** is **positive**, meaning that the runner is still accelerating forwards but not now as much as in case (a).

- In figure 17.9c, the **positive** area above the horizontal axis is exactly **cancelled** by the **negative** area under the axis. This means that the **horizontal impulse is zero** so the sprinter would not be accelerating or decelerating and would be running at **constant speed**.

- In figure 17.9d, the **negative** area below the axis of the graph is **bigger** than the **positive** part and hence the **overall impulse is negative**. This means that the runner will be experiencing an overall **force** (averaged over the stride) **backwards** and hence would be **decelerating** or losing speed.

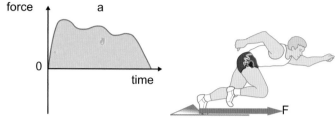

figure 17.9 – horizontal foot impulse during a sprint

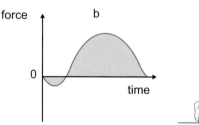
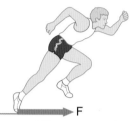

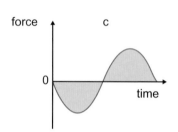
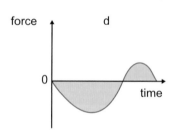

In Figures 17.9 b, c and d, the parts of the graphs which show a negative impulse (area below the horizontal axis of the graph) correspond to the situation where the foot placement is in front of the runner's centre of mass and so exerts a backwards force for a short time. This is immediately followed by the centre of mass moving forward over the contact foot which then applies a forward force on the runner and hence a positive impulse for the latter part of the foot contact.

Practice questions

figure 17.10 – forces acting on a runner

1) a) What characterises a vector quantity? 2 marks

   b) Figure 17.10 shows the forces acting on a runner at the start of a race. Use a vector diagram to show how you could work out the resultant force acting. 3 marks

   c) Sketch a pin man drawing of a person standing still showing all the forces acting on him. 2 marks

   d) Sketch a second diagram showing the vertical forces acting on a basketballer just before take-off while performing a jump shot. Represent the relative sizes of any forces you show by the length of the force arrows on your diagram. 2 marks

e) Use this second diagram and your understanding of Newton's laws of motion to explain why the basketballer is able to take off. If the vertical upward ground reaction force on him is 2000N, and his weight is 800N, estimate the net upward force acting on him.

4 marks

2) The four man bobsleigh develops a large momentum during the first few seconds of its run.

a) Explain the meaning of the term momentum, and explain why the four man bobsleigh travelling at a speed of 28 ms⁻¹ has a different momentum to a skier moving at the same speed.

2 marks

b) Explain using Newton's laws of motion how the bobsleigh acquires its large momentum during the first part of a run.

4 marks

3) The follow-through is an important aspect of a forehand ground stroke in tennis.

a) Sketch a graph of the force applied by the racquet (y axis) against time (x axis). Show the effect of a follow-through on your graph.

2 marks

b) Explain how the use of a follow-through would affect the motion of the ball.

4 marks

4) a) In a tennis match, the ball travels towards a player at 35 ms⁻¹. The ball has a mass of 80 g and the racket head has a mass of 0.6 kg. The racket head moves towards the ball at 10 ms⁻¹.
Calculate the momentum of the racket and the ball before contact.

3 marks

b) If the player stops the racket moving on contact with the ball, calculate the velocity of the ball after contact.

3 marks

c) The graphs in figure 17.11 show the forces acting on a runner's foot during a 100m sprint. For each graph, describe the resultant impulse force and the motion that occurs.

6 marks

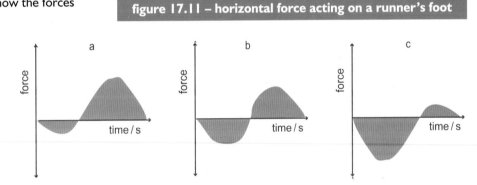

figure 17.11 – horizontal force acting on a runner's foot

5) Tennis players have to change direction quickly during a match to recover to the centre of the court. Figure 17.12 shows a tennis player just after hitting a forehand and then starting to recover to the centre of the court in the direction shown.

a) Draw a pin diagram of the tennis player as he pushes off the court surface to recover to the centre of the court, showing all forces acting on the tennis player at this point. All forces must be clearly identified.

3 marks

figure 17.12 – a tennis player moves between strokes

b) Explain the factors that affect the horizontal force at this point. Apply Newton's second law of motion to explain the effect of this force on the player. 4 marks

moving

6) A sprinter uses her calf muscles to push on the blocks at the start of a run. Sketch a pin man diagram of the forces acting and use this to explain how this produces a forward force on her.

3 marks

7) Explain the nature of the reaction force which provides forwards impulsion for a cyclist.

4 marks

CHAPTER 18 – FLUID MECHANICS

This chapter looks at all the forces which act via fluids (gases or liquids) through which a body or sports object moves (discus, javelin, car, bike, boat and so-on).

Air resistance (drag, fluid friction)

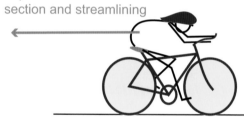

figure 18.1 – factors affecting fluid friction

As mentioned above (page 108), **fluid friction** (or **drag**) is a term applying to objects moving through fluids (gases or liquids). The force acts in the opposite direction to the direction of motion.

Fluid friction force depends on the shape and size of the moving object, the speed of the moving object, and the streamlining effect (summarised in figure 18.1).

Drag

In order to minimise drag, the following developments affect sport:
*   The body position and shape for a swimmer.
*   The shape of helmets for cyclists.
*   The use of lycra clothing.
*   The shape of sports vehicles (cars or bikes).

Low values of fluid friction

This discussion concerns **low values of drag** compared with other forces. Examples are:
*   Any sprinter or game player for whom air resistance is usually much less than friction effects and weight. Therefore streamlining is seen as less important.
*   A shot or hammer in flight, in which air resistance would be much less than the weight, and therefore the angle of release should be around 45°.

High values of fluid friction

High values of drag will occur for any sportsperson or vehicle moving through water, and hence fluid friction is the critical factor governing swimming speed.
*   Body shape or cross section, and clothing (surface material to assist laminar flow, see below), are adjusted to minimise fluid friction.

A cyclist (figure 18.2) travels much faster than a runner and therefore has high fluid friction:
*   He or she crouches low to reduce forward cross section.
*   The helmet is designed to minimise turbulent flow.
*   Clothing and wheel profiles are designed to assist streamlining.

Cross sectional area is the area of the moving object as viewed from the front. The smaller the better to reduce drag, hence cyclists crouch down, and keep elbows in!

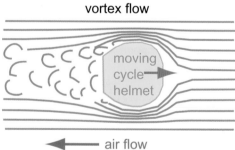

figure 18.2 – a cyclist needs good streamlining

fluid friction (drag) depends on forward cross section and streamlining

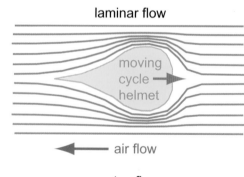

figure 18.3 – laminar flow and vortex flow

laminar flow

moving cycle helmet

air flow

vortex flow

moving cycle helmet

air flow

Laminar flow and drag

Fluid friction (or drag) depends on **laminar** flow, the smooth flowing of air or water past an object. Laminar means flowing in layers, and streamlining assists laminar flow. Figure 18.3 shows images of a streamlined helmet, and a non-streamlined helmet. The point of the streamlined shape is that the air moves past it in layers whereas in the case of the non-streamlined helmet, vortices are formed where the fluid does not flow smoothly. When this happens bits of fluid are flung randomly sideways which causes drag. The drag is caused by bits of fluid being dragged along with the moving object (the cycle helmet).

Projectiles

This section looks at the motion of objects in flight, such as human bodies (during the flight phase of a jump), throwing implements (shot, discus, javelin or hammer), and soccer, rugby, cricket, tennis or golf balls.

The flight is governed by the forces acting, the weight, air resistance, Magnus effect, aerodynamic lift, and the direction of motion. If weight were the only force acting, the flight path would be parabolic in shape, and some flight paths are similar to this (shot or hammer, the human body in jumps or tumbles or dives, where weight is the predominant force acting).

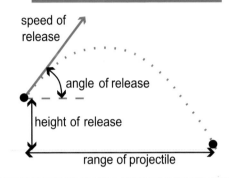

figure 18.4 – factors affecting distance travelled

Distance travelled by a projectile

Figure 18.4 summarises the factors which influence the distance travelled, the angle of release, the speed of release, and the height of release.

Components of velocity during flight

Figure 18.5 outlines the vertical and horizontal components of the velocity during the flight of a projectile.

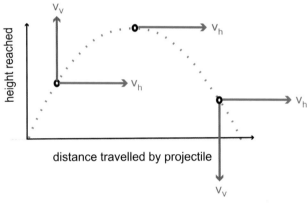

figure 18.5 – components of velocity during flight

Near the start of the flight:
- There is a large upward vertical component v_v.
- But a fixed horizontal component v_h.

At the middle of the flight:
- There is zero upward vertical component, since the object moves entirely horizontally at this point.
- There is still a fixed horizontal component v_h, which is the same as at the start.

Near the end of the flight:
- There is a large downward vertical component v_v, which is almost the same as the horizontal component since the object is travelling at approx 45° to the horizontal downwards.
- There is still a fixed horizontal component v_h, which is the same as at the start.

The relative size of forces during flight

The forces acting during flight are: the weight of the object, the air resistance (the faster the projectile travels the greater will be the air resistance), **aerodynamic lift** (see page 114 below), and the **Magnus effect** or Bernoulli effect (see page 114 below).

If the shapes of the flight path differ from a parabola then some combination of these forces must be relatively large compared with the weight (remembering that a flight of an object with only weight force acting would be a parabola).

For example:
For a badminton shuttle **struck hard** (figure 18.6a), the air resistance is very large compared with the weight, because the shuttle is moving quickly. The resultant force will therefore be very close to the air resistance. This would make the shuttle slow down rapidly over the **first part of the flight**.

Later in the flight of the badminton shuttle (figure 18.6b), when the shuttle is moving much more slowly, the air resistance is much less and comparable with the weight. This pattern of the resultant force changing markedly during the flight predicts a pronounced asymmetric path.

figure 18.6 – forces on a badminton shuttle

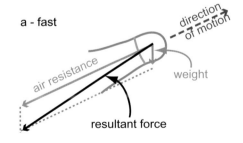

a - fast

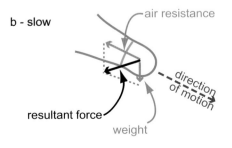

b - slow

Lift force

Lift forces are caused by bulk displacement of fluid and are similar to air resistance. They are caused by a wing-shaped object moving through the air (like a discus, ski jumper, javelin, rugby ball, American football, and a frisbee). As it moves forward and falls through the air, it pushes aside the air, creating a higher pressure underneath the object and a lower pressure over the top of the object.

This creates a lift force which is similar to the force which enables a stone to skip over the surface of water.

The Bernoulli effect

The force which gives lift to aircraft wings, and down-pressure on racing car bodies (figure 18.7, enabling greater friction between wheels and the road, and hence faster cornering speeds) is called the **Bernoulli effect**.

This effect depends on the fact that fluids which move quickly across the surface of an object cause a reduced pressure when compared with slower moving air across another surface.

Hence, in figure 18.7, the laminar flow of air across the **lower** surface of the wing (or car body shaped like an inverted wing) is **quicker**, because the air has to travel **further** in the same time as the air moving a shorter distance across the upper surface of the wing. Hence the shape of the wing is crucial to create the Bernoulli lift or down force.

Spin

Imparting spin on a ball

This is done by exerting a force (or striking, hitting or kicking) on the ball whose direction does not pass through the centre of mass of the ball (as in figure 18.8). This is called an **eccentric force**, and skilful performers can kick or hit a ball in such a way to cause a swerving, soaring or dipping path of the ball.

The Magnus effect

As a **spinning ball** moves through the air (from left to right on figure 18.9), the air layers which flow round the ball are forced into the path shown in the diagram. Here you can see that the air flow is **further** round the top of the ball, and hence the air flow is **faster** over the top of the ball than the bottom. This means that the **air pressure** will be **less** over the top of the ball than the lower half of the ball (following from the Bernoulli effect), hence the ball will experience a force upwards in the view of figure 18.9.

Hence **top-spin** as shown in figure 18.10, would cause a dipping effect on the ball in flight.

Similarly, **side-spin** will cause a swerve in the flight whose direction is in the same sense as the spin of the ball.

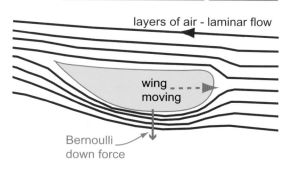

figure 18.7 – Bernoulli effect on an inverted wing

layers of air - laminar flow

wing moving

Bernoulli down force

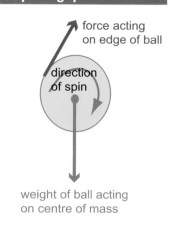

figure 18.8 – imparting spin on a ball

force acting on edge of ball

direction of spin

weight of ball acting on centre of mass

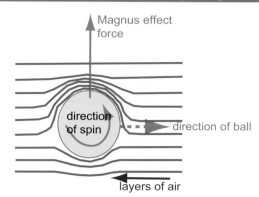

figure 18.9 – Magnus effect on a spinning ball

Magnus effect force

direction of spin

direction of ball

layers of air

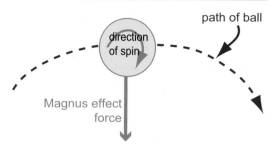

figure 18.10 – flight of a spinning ball

path of ball

direction of spin

Magnus effect force

The spinning bouncing ball

The spin on a ball will cause a change in the amount of friction between the surface of the ball and the ground surface in which it is bouncing. This friction will cause the ball to spin further and change its direction (compared to the direction it would have moved had there been no friction, see figure 18.11).

The change in direction of the bounce can be predicted by noting that an extra backward force will tend to make the ball bounce behind its normal path, and a forwards friction force will cause the ball to bounce in front of and below its normal path.

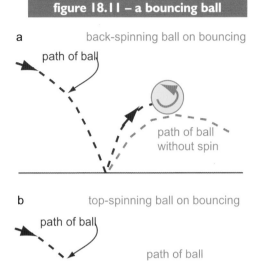

figure 18.11 – a bouncing ball

a   back-spinning ball on bouncing
path of ball
path of ball without spin

b   top-spinning ball on bouncing
path of ball
path of ball without spin

Practice questions

1) a) Using examples, explain how the shape of an object can alter its flight path.   4 marks

    b) Explain the effect of air resistance on the flight of two badminton shuttles, one of which has been struck hard and the other gently.   10 marks

    c) Briefly explain why the flight path of a shot in athletics is so different from the flight of a badminton shuttle.   4 marks

2) a) Identify three physical factors (not skill factors) which govern a swimmer's speed and explain how one of these occurs.   3 marks

    b) Describe the factors which determine the amount of fluid friction acting on a swimmer.   4 marks

    c) Explain how you would minimise turbulent flow (high drag) of the water past the swimmer's body.   2 marks

    d) Give three examples, each from a different sporting context, to show how fluid friction affects the sportsperson.   3 marks

    e) How would you attempt to reduce fluid friction?   3 marks

    f) Look at figure 18.12 showing the vertical forces acting on a swimmer during a stroke. Explain why it is difficult for a swimmer to keep a horizontal floating position.   4 marks

3) a) Fluid friction is a force which acts on a bobsleigh once it is moving. Identify the nature of the fluid friction in this case and explain how this might limit the maximum speed of the bob.   3 marks

    b) Explain the term 'turbulent flow', and how the bobsleigh is used to minimise this factor.   3 marks

figure 18.12 – forces acting on a swimmer

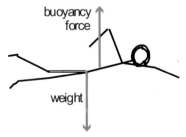

buoyancy force

weight

4) a) Sketch a diagram to show the flight path of the shot from the moment it leaves the putter's hand to the moment it lands.   2 marks

    b) State and briefly explain three factors (excluding air effects) which should be used by the putter to optimise the distance thrown.   6 marks

    c) Explain why the turn in a discus throw produces greater horizontal range than the standing throw.   3 marks

5) a) The Bernoulli effect states that a faster flowing liquid or gas exerts less pressure than a slower moving liquid or gas. Using figure 18.13, show how the Bernoulli effect explains the swerve of a spinning ball. 4 marks

b) Use diagrams to show how your explanation relates to the flight of a table tennis ball with side, back and top spin. 3 marks

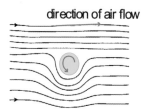

figure 18.13 – Bernoulli effect on a spinning ball

direction of air flow

c) Sketch a vector diagram of all forces acting on a table tennis ball in flight with back spin, and explain how the resultant force on the ball predicts the actual acceleration of the ball. 4 marks

d) Identify one sport other than a ball game, in which the Bernoulli effect plays a part. 1 mark

CHAPTER 19 – STABILITY and LEVER SYSTEMS

Stability

Centre of mass

Centre of mass (CofM) is the single point (on a body) which represents **all the spread out mass** of the body. So, since gravity acts on mass to produce weight, the weight acts at the centre of mass of a body. In figure 19.1, the weight is marked as a green arrow, and it acts downward on the CofM. The CofM can be defined as **'the point of balance of the body'**. As limbs are moved, or the torso changes shape (as when bent over for example), so the position of the centre of mass of the body will move as in figure 19.1. Note that the CofM does not always lie within the body shape, when the torso is bent, it can lie well outside the body mass.

Note that the right hand image in figure 19.1 is that of the layout position for the Fosbury flop high jump technique. The CofM lies underneath the body, and can be below the bar even though the athlete clears the bar.

| figure 19.1 – centre of mass position changes with body shape |

centre of mass

weight acts at the centre of mass

Balance

The CofM must be **over the base of support** if a person is to be balanced. In figure 19.2, with the leg stuck out sideways, the centre of mass moves to a position to the left of a vertical line through the foot. So, the weight (force) acts downwards through the centre of mass, and will topple the person to the left. Therefore to maintain balance, the person must lean to the right (as we look at her), and thereby bring the CofM back vertically over the supporting foot.

Toppling

Toppling is caused by the weight acting vertically at the CofM and therefore to **one side** of the near edge of the base of support. This fact can be used by divers or gymnasts to initiate a controlled spinning (twisting) fall. And hence lead into somersaults, cartwheels or twists.

| figure 19.2 – a gymnast topples to the left |

weight causes toppling to the left

Lever systems

The term **internal forces** describes the forces acting (figure 16.4 on page 103 above) when a muscle pulls on its **origin O** and **insertion I**. The force on the origin (in red) is equal in size but opposite in direction to the force on the insertion (in black). This changes the **shape** of the person.

Levers

A lever is a **means of applying force at a distance** from the source of the force and has a **fulcrum (pivot)**, **effort** and **load**. In the human body, usually a **joint** and the **attached limbs** or bones act as a lever. **Force** is applied as **effort** by a **muscle** or group of muscles. The **load** is the **force applied** to the **surroundings** by the lever.

Classification of levers

Class 1 lever

This is a see-saw lever with the fulcrum in between the effort and the load. It is found rarely in the body, for example the triceps/elbow/forearm lever (see figure 19.3), or the atlas/neck muscles used in the nodding movement.

Class 2 lever

This is a wheelbarrow lever where the load is bigger than the effort, and the fulcrum is at one end of the lever with the load in between the effort and the fulcrum. This is found rarely in the body, the main example being the Achilles tendon/calf muscles (gastrocnemius and soleus) and ankle joint lever (see figure 19.4). This is used in most running or walking movements with the fulcrum underneath the ball of the foot as it drives the body forward.

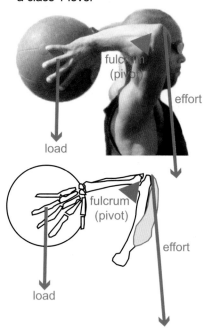

figure 19.3 – elbow/triceps lever

a class 1 lever

figure 19.4 – ankle/calf lever

a class 2 lever

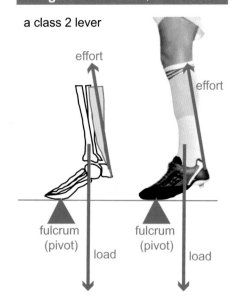

Class 3 lever

This class of lever again has the fulcrum at one end of the lever arm, with the effort in between the load and the fulcrum. It has a mechanical disadvantage, the effort is bigger than the load and is the most common system found in body. For example the elbow/biceps/forearm lever (see figure 19.5), or the knee/quadriceps/tibia/fibula systems (see figure 19.6).

figure 19.6 – knee/tibia/quadriceps lever

a class 3 lever

figure 19.5 – the elbow and forearm lever

a class 3 lever

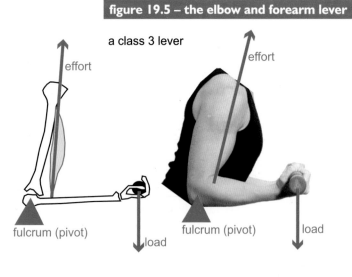

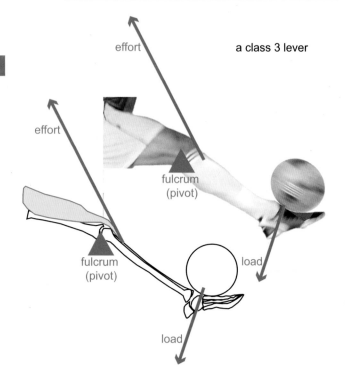

Effects of the length of lever

The **length of the lever** or **resistance arm** of the lever (**d** in figure 19.7) affects the **load** able to be exerted by the lever, and the **speed** at which the hand can move. The longer the lever **d**, the smaller the value of the load for a given biceps strength and value of the **effort arm** (distance between effort and pivot). The longer the lever arm **d**, the faster the load can be applied (as the limb moves through its range - a longer limb - the hand would move further in the same time).

This means that the hand of a thrower with long arms will be moving faster than the hand of a thrower with short arms if each is turning (rotating) at the same speed.

The **shorter** the **effort arm** the less load can be exerted. The shorter the load (resistance) arm of a person the bigger the load can be. This is why successful weightlifters tend to have short arms.

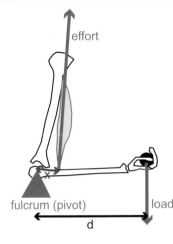

figure 19.7 – the length of a lever arm

effort

fulcrum (pivot)

load

d

Torque or moment of force

Torque (also called **moment of force**) is the turning effect of a force on a system. In the case of the forearm system of figure 19.7, the load force exerts a turning effect (in this case turning clockwise) on the forearm about the elbow joint as its axis of rotation.

The turning effect can be measured by the torque calculated by:

> **torque = force × distance**

Where the distance from the turning axis is measured at right angles to the direction of the turning force, as marked in figure 19.8 where:

> **torque = F × d**

figure 19.8 – moment of force

So in the case of the load in figure 19.7:

> **torque = load × d**   (clockwise moment)

And in the case of the effort in figure 19.7:

> **torque = effort × x**   (anticlockwise moment)

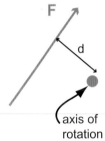

F

d

axis of rotation

Principle of moments

For a balanced system of forces acting around an axis of rotation (fulcrum in the case of a lever):

> **anticlockwise moment = clockwise moment**

This means that there is zero net torque acting on the system (it is balanced).

For the elbow forearm biceps system in figure 19.7:

> **effort × x = load × d**

Hence if you measure **load**, **d** and **x** you can estimate the effort in the biceps muscle (see questions 9 and 10 on page 122 below for worked examples of how to do this).

Rotation

Effect of line of action of a force on subsequent motion

The line of action of a force on a jumper before take-off determines whether or not he **rotates** in the air after take off. If a force acts directly **through the centre of mass** of an object, then **linear** acceleration will occur (Newton's second law), no turning or rotating. For example, for a **basketballer** (figure 19.9), the **take off force acts through the CofM** therefore the jumper does not rotate in the air, and is able to land on his or her feet easily. Of course, the bigger the force, the greater the acceleration during take-off and the higher the jump.

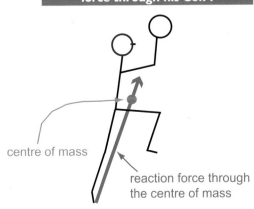

figure 19.9 – a basketballer has a force through his CofM

centre of mass

reaction force through the centre of mass

Eccentric force

A force which acts **eccentrically** to the centre of mass of a body (**to one side**) will cause the body to begin to rotate. For example, for a **high jumper** (figure 19.10) the **take off force acts to one side of the CofM** therefore the jumper tumbles and twists in the air, and will land on his or her back. In figure 19.10, the force acting to the right of the CofM tends to topple her body to the left, turning her body anticlockwise.

Of course, the bigger the force, the greater the acceleration during take-off and the higher the jump.

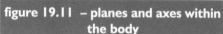

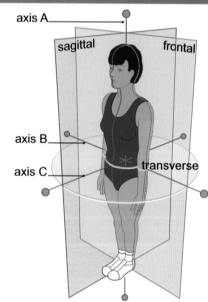

figure 19.10 – a high jumper – force not through CofM

centre of mass

reaction force to side of the centre of mass

Axes and planes of rotation

To simplify the description of how sportspeople rotate during their sporting movements, it is usual to define **three planes of motion** within which a movement will occur, and to define **three axes of rotation** about which these movements occur.

Three imaginary planes
Refer to figure 19.11.

Frontal (coronal) plane
- A vertical plane that divides body into **front and back** sections.
- Movements in this plane are abduction and adduction, as for example in a cartwheel.
- And spinal lateral flexion, as for example in side flexion trunk bends.

Sagittal (median) plane
- A vertical plane that divides the body into **left and right** sides.
- Movements in this plane include flexion and extension, as for example in somersaults, biceps curl, pole vault take-off, sprinting, dorsiflexion, and plantarflexion.

Transverse (horizontal) plane
- A horizontal plane that divides the body into upper and lower sections.
- Movements are rotational movement patterns such as supination, pronation, and spinal rotation.
- Example movements would be twisting/turning, the spinning skater/discus/ hammer/ski turns.

figure 19.11 – planes and axes within the body

axis A

sagittal

frontal

axis B

axis C

transverse

Axes of rotation

An axis of rotation is defined as '**an imaginary line about which the body rotates or spins, at right angles to the plane**'. Look at figure 19.11, axes labelled A, B and C.

Three imaginary axes
Longitudinal axis
- **Axis A** on figure 19.11.
- This axis runs vertically from the top of the head to a point between the feet.
- Movements in the transverse plane about the longitudinal axis are rotational movements.
- Examples of sporting movements would be the spinning skater and the hammer throw.

Transverse axis
- **Axis B** on figure 19.11. This axis runs horizontally from side to side across the body between opposite hips at right angles to the sagittal plane.
- Movements within the sagittal plane about the transverse axis are flexion, extension, hyperextension, dorsiflexion and plantarflexion.
- Sports movements about this axis include sit ups, and the high jump Fosbury Flop flight phase.

Frontal axis
- **Axis C** on figure 19.11.
- This axis runs horizontally from front to back between belly button and lumbar spine.
- Movements in the frontal plane about the frontal axis include abduction, adduction and spinal lateral flexion.
- Examples of sports movements about this axis are a cartwheel, and the bowling action in cricket.

Practice questions

figure 19.12 – a long
jumper in flight

1) Explain with diagrams what is meant by the centre of mass of a body.
Explain with the aid of pin-man diagrams how the centre of mass of a long jumper changes
from the take-off position to the flight phase shown in figure 19.12.   5 marks

figure 19.13 – swimmer
starting a race

2) Figure 19.13 shows a swimmer holding a balance
just before the start of a race. Explain how the
position of the centre of mass can affect the
swimmer's balance. Describe how the swimmer
in figure 19.13 can use his knowledge of balance
to achieve his most effective block start.
5 marks

figure 19.14 – long
jumper taking off

3) Sketch the lever system which would represent
the action of the biceps muscle in flexing the
arm. Show on your diagram the resistance arm
of the lever.   3 marks

4) In figure 19.14 of a jumper taking off, name,
sketch and label the lever system operating at
knee **B** during this action.   3 marks

5) In softball, what order (class) of lever is shown in the hitting action in figure 19.15?
State **one** disadvantage and **one** advantage of reducing the bat length for a beginner.
3 marks

figure 19.15 – softball bat

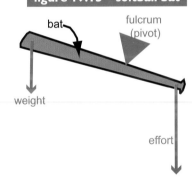

6) Name, sketch and label the lever system which is operating at the ankle of leg **C**
when doing the sprint set action illustrated in figure 19.16.   3 marks

figure 19.16 – ankle
lever system

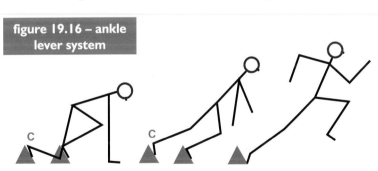

7) a) Figure 19.17 shows an elbow joint A of a person performing an exercise.
Draw a simplified sketch to show the lever system, indicating the various forces operating.   4 marks

b) On your diagram draw and label the effort and resistance arm.   3 marks

figure 19.17 – a press-up

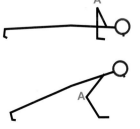

8) During physical activity the performer uses a combination of levers to produce movement. Explain why the length of the lever will affect performance.

3 marks

9) a) Figure 19.18 shows an elbow joint of a person performing an exercise.

Work out the clockwise moment provided by the force of 200 newtons about the elbow as a fulcrum, then, assuming the arm is stationary, use the principle of moments to calculate the effort force exerted by the biceps muscle. Show your working.

6 marks

figure 19.18 – elbow joint and biceps lever

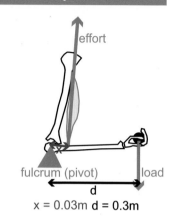

x = 0.03m d = 0.3m

b) Diagram 19.19 shows the elbow joint and the position of the triceps muscle in relation to it when supporting a load (a shot) behind the head. Draw a simplified sketch to show the lever system, indicating the various forces operating.

4 marks

c) Using the values shown in the diagram and the fact that the mass of the shot is 8 kg, calculate the load. Neglecting the mass of the ulna, estimate the effort needed to balance the system. (Take the gravitational force on 1 kg to be 10N).

4 marks

figure 19.19 – elbow joint and triceps lever

d = 0.3m   x = 0.03m

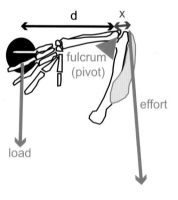

10) Figure 19.20 shows a diagram of a sportsperson's foot pivoting at a point under the ball of the foot. Use your knowledge of the principle of moments applied to this lever to calculate the effort force in the calf muscle. Show all your working. 4 marks

figure 19.20 – ankle joint and calf lever

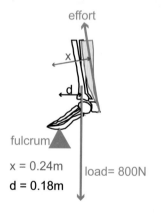

x = 0.24m
d = 0.18m
load= 800N

CHAPTER 20 – ANGULAR MOTION

Describing angular motion

Angle (angular displacement)
To be scientifically correct angle should not be measured in degrees, but in radians, see figure 20.1.

$$\text{Angle} = \frac{\text{arc length}}{\text{radius of arc}} = \frac{l}{r}$$

360 degrees	$= 2 \times \pi$ radians	$= 6.28$ radians
180°	$= \pi$ radians	$= 3.14$ radians
90°	$= 1/2\ \pi$ radians	$= 1.57$ radians
30°	$= 1/6\ \pi$ radians	$= 0.52$ radians

and so on (see maths text book for more).

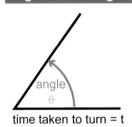

figure 20.1 – angle

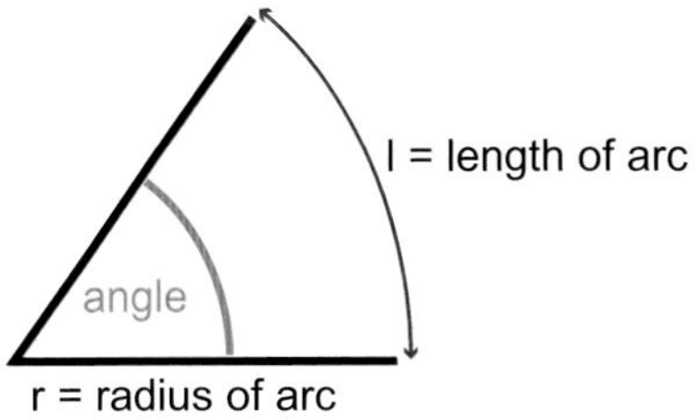

l = length of arc

angle

r = radius of arc

Angular velocity
Angular velocity = angle turned through per second (figure 20.2).

$$\omega = \frac{\text{angle turned through}}{\text{time taken}} = \frac{\theta}{t} \quad (\theta = \text{symbol for angle})$$

ω = Greek letter omega.   (ω = symbol for angular velocity)

This is **rate of spin**, most easily understood as revolutions per second (revs per sec).

Revs per sec would have to be converted to the unit radians per second (radians s^{-1}) for calculations.
1 rev per second $= 2 \times \pi = 6.28$ radians s^{-1}.

figure 20.2 – angular velocity

angle
θ

time taken to turn = t

Rates of spin apply to:
*   Tumbling gymnasts.
*   Trampolinists (piked straight and tucked somersaults).
*   Discus and hammer throwers.
*   Spinning skaters.
*   Skiers turning and twisting between slalom gates.

Moment of inertia

figure 20.3 – moments of inertia of different shapes

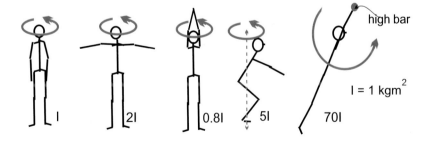

Moment of inertia is the equivalent of mass for rotating systems, it is rotational inertia. The mathematical formula is
$$\text{MI} = \Sigma\ mr^2$$

Objects rotating with large MI require large moments of force (torque) to change their angular velocity, and objects with small MI require small moments of force (torque) to change their angular velocity or ω.

high bar

I = 1 kgm^2

The formula above means that moment of inertia depends on the spread of mass away from the axis of spin, so as the body shape changes, the moment of inertia of the shape changes. The more spread out the mass, the bigger the MI.

The unit of MI is kilogramme metre squared kgm^2.

*   Bodies with **arms held out wide** have large MI, the further the mass is away from the axis of rotation increases the MI dramatically.
*   Sportspeople use this to control all spinning or turning movements.
*   Pikes and tucks are good examples of use of MI, both reduce MI.

Values of moment of inertia

In figure 20.3, I is the MI for the left most pin man and has a value of about 1.0 kgm^2 for an average male person. From this diagram you can see how control of the arms will make a big difference to the value of MI, and that a tuck or pike can also change MI dramatically.

figure 20.4 – the sprinter's leg

The sprinter's leg

This is an example of how a sportsperson uses moment of inertia to control his or her movement.

- From figure 20.4 you can see that when the leg is straight, the leg has high MI about the hip as axis. This therefore requires a large force or torque in the hip flexor muscles to swing the leg.
- On the other hand when fully bent, the leg has low MI, which therefore requires a low force or torque in the hip flexor muscles to swing the leg.
- Hence a sprinter tends to bring the leg through as bent as possible (with the heel as close to the backside as possible), and he or she will find that it is easier and faster the more bent the leg.

hip

large torque required

hip

small torque required

Angular momentum

Angular momentum is a quantity used to describe what happens when bodies spin and turn, it is defined as:

> angular momentum = **moment of inertia** x **angular velocity**
> = **rotational inertia** x **rate of spin**
> **H** = **I** x ω

figure 20.5 – a spinning skater

Conservation of angular momentum

The **law of conservation of angular momentum** is a law of the universe which says that angular momentum of a spinning body remains the same (provided no external forces act).

- This means that a body which is spinning, twisting or tumbling will keep its value of **H** once the movement has started.

- Therefore if moment of inertia (**I**) changes by changing body shape, then angular velocity (ω) must also change to keep angular momentum (**H**) the same.

- So, if MI (**I**) **increases** (body spread out more) then ω must **decrease** (rate of spin gets less).
- And conversely, if MI (**I**) **decreases** (body tucked in more) then ω must **increase** (rate of spin gets bigger).

- Strictly, this is only exactly true if the body has no contact with its surroundings, as for example a high diver doing piked or tucked somersaults in the air, but it is almost true for the spinning skater!

figure 20.6 – a slalom skier

Sporting examples of conservation of angular momentum

- **The spinning skater**. If the arms are wide, the MI is large and the skater spins slowly. If the arms are brought in, MI is small and the skater will spin more quickly (figure 20.5).

- **The tumbling gymnast**. With the body position open, the MI is large and the gymnast (or diver or trampolinist) will spin slowly. When he or she creates a tucked body position, the MI is small and he or she will spin more quickly.

- **The dancer doing a spin jump**. The movement is initiated with arms held wide which would therefore have the highest possible MI. Immediately he or she has taken off, the angular momentum is conserved, and so by tucking the arms across the chest, this will create the lowest possible MI. This then means that he or she will acquire the highest possible rate of spin, so that more spins can be completed before landing.

- **The slalom skier**. The slalom skier crouches on approach to the gate and therefore will have a large turning MI. As he or she passes the gate, he or she stands straight up (reducing MI). This enables the person to turn rapidly past the gate, then he or she crouches again (figure 20.6) - increasing MI which will resume a slow turn between the gates.

Practice questions

1) Define the term angular velocity.   2 marks

2) a) A diver can make a number of different shapes in the air. Table 20.1 shows three of these. Explain the meaning of moment of inertia (MI) in this context.   4 marks

Table 20.1 – **data for shapes of diver during flight**

phase of dive	shape of diver	time during flight	MI of shape kgm²
1	Z	0.0 - 0.5s	18
2	Y	0.5 - 0.7s	9
3	X	0.7 - 1.0s	3
4	Z	1.0 - 1.1s	18
entry	axis of rotation = ●	1.1s	

b) During a dive a diver goes through the shapes shown in table 20.1.
Explain how the rate of spinning (angular velocity) would change through the dive.   5 marks

c) Sketch a graph of this rate of spinning against time. Your sketch need only be approximate.   4 marks

d) State the relationship between angular momentum, moment of inertia and angular velocity.   2 marks

e) Name the law of conservation which accounts for these variations in rate of spin.   1 mark

f) Explain and sketch the arc described by the diver as he or she falls.   3 marks

3) a) Describe in detail the body shape and movement within a chosen sporting situation where rates of spin are affected by body shape.   6 marks

b) How would you stop the spinning in this situation?   2 marks

c) Figure 20.7 shows a sportsperson's leg in two different positions. The values quoted are the moment of inertia of the leg as it rotates about the hip joint (shown as a red dot on each diagram). Explain the implications of these data for the efficiency of running style in a sprinter and long distance runner.   7 marks

figure 20.7 – shape of leg

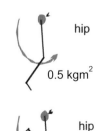

hip

0.5 kgm²

hip

0.25 kgm²

4) a) Figure 20.8 shows a gymnast undertaking a forward somersault following a run up. Sketch three traces on a single graph to represent any changes in angular momentum, moment of inertia and angular velocity for the period of activity between positions 2 and 9.

3 marks

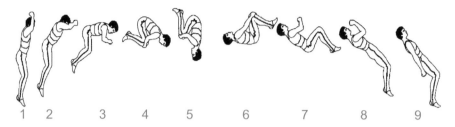

figure 20.8 – shapes of a gymnast

1   2   3   4   5   6   7   8   9

b) Explain the shapes of the traces on the sketch graph that you have drawn.

6 marks

c) Table 20.2 sets out measurements of angular velocities (rates of spin) of the gymnast at successive frames from the start of the somersault.

Estimate from this table the ratio of angular velocities at times X and Y.

1 mark

d) If the moment of inertia of the gymnast is 8 kgm² at time X, estimate the moment of inertia at time Y, using data from table 20.2.

2 marks

Table 20.2 – **data for angular velocity of gymnast**

	frame	angular velocity (degrees s⁻¹)
	1	650
X	2	750
	3	850
	4	1100
	5	1400
Y	6	1500
	7	1000
	8	850
	9	650

figure 20.9 – shapes of a gymnast

5) a) Figure 20.9 shows a spinning skater in various positions. Under each diagram is an approximate value for the moment of inertia of the skater spinning about his or her central vertical axis.

The angular velocity of the skater in position **W** is 2.0 revolutions per second. What is the formula for calculating the skater's angular velocity?

Calculate the angular velocity for the skater in position **Z**.

2 marks

W   X   Y   Z

MI=1.0 kgm²   MI=2.0 kgm²   MI=4.5 kgm²   MI=6.0 kgm²

b) Sketch a figure showing a possible position which could cause the skater to attain an angular velocity of 3.0 revolutions per second and calculate what the moment of inertia of this shape must be.

2 marks

c) Principles of angular momentum can be used to improve performance in a variety of sports. With the use of diagrams explain how a slalom skier turns through the gates at maximum speed.

4 marks

d) Explain with the use of diagrams how a dancer manages to complete a triple spin in the air before touching the ground.

4 marks

SECTION B: SCIENTIFIC OPTIONS

OPTION B3: EXERCISE AND SPORT PHYSIOLOGY

CHAPTER 21 – ENERGY SYSTEMS and the RECOVERY PROCESS

Energy definitions
Energy is the capacity to do work, and work has a mechanical definition, namely **work = force x distance** moved in the direction of the force. Energy and work are measured in joules (J).

Chemical energy is energy that is produced by a complex series of chemical reactions, which can then be made available as **kinetic energy** (energy due to movement which results from muscular contractions), or **potential energy** which is stored energy due to gravity.

Power is the **rate** at which energy is used, or the energy used per second which is measured in watts (W). Power can be calculated using the formula: **power = energy (in joules)**   **answer in watts**
                                                                                     time (in seconds)

Energy sources
We derive our energy from food, namely carbohydrates (CHO), fats, and to a lesser extent proteins.

The energy derived from carbohydrates, fats and proteins is stored in bodily tissues in the form of a high energy compound called **adenosine triphosphate** (ATP).

Adenosine triphosphate (ATP) and its resynthesis

ATP is the compound which stores energy and is therefore the energy currency linked to **intensity** and **duration** of physical activity. ATP exists in every living tissue and its breakdown gives energy for all life functions - this includes the action of the liver and the brain for example, as well as the contraction of muscle tissue. All muscular activity requires the availability and breakdown of ATP (figure 21.1).

The energy released during tissue respiration is stored in the chemical bonds in ATP, and this energy is released during the reaction: **ATP → ADP + P_i + energy**

where ADP is adenosine diphosphate, and P_i is a free phosphate radical. **ATPase** is an enzyme which facilitates this reaction, which is **exothermic** - it releases energy.

figure 21.1 – all muscle action uses ATP

The energy stored within ATP is only available as long as ATP is retained within the cells using it. In muscle cells during intense (flat-out) exercise, the stored ATP only lasts about 2 seconds. Therefore the ATP must be replaced as soon as possible so that exercise can continue. There are **three** processes by which this can happen:

- The **ATP-PC** system (also called the alactic anaerobic system).
- The **lactic acid** system (which is also anaerobic).
- The **aerobic** system.

Resynthesis of ATP from ADP uses the reaction: **energy + ADP + P_i → ATP**

This is an **endothermic** reaction since energy is **given** to the molecule to enable the reaction to happen. This energy will be derived from **food fuels**.

Anaerobic energy systems

The ATP-PC system

This system of replenishing of ATP from ADP is the predominant one for activity which lasts between 3 and 10 seconds, which means for high intensity maximum work, for example, flat out sprinting - the 100m sprint.

No oxygen is needed - the process is anaerobic. The chemical reactions within this system are a **coupled reaction** in which ATP is resynthesised via **phosphocreatine** (PC) stored in muscle cell sarcoplasm.

The following reactions take place: **PC → P$_i$ + C + energy**

energy + ADP + P$_i$ → ATP

The two reactions together are called a **coupled reaction** and are facilitated by the enzyme **creatine kinase** (CK).

The net effect of these two coupled reactions is:

PC + ADP → ATP + C

PC is re-created in muscle cells during the recovery process, which requires energy and is an **endothermic** reaction.

STUDENT NOTE

This process does not directly require glucose as an energy source - but the re-creation of PC during recovery will do so.

During intense exercise, peak anaerobic power is attained within the first 5 seconds, and depletion of PC occurs between 7 and 9 seconds.

Look at the graph in figure 21.2 showing changes in muscle ATP and PC. After an initial small fall, the ATP level is maintained, then falls as the PC is used up because the energy from PC is being used to resynthesise ATP.

This causes PC levels to fall rapidly to zero after about 10 seconds. The capacity to maintain ATP production at this point depends on the lactic acid system.

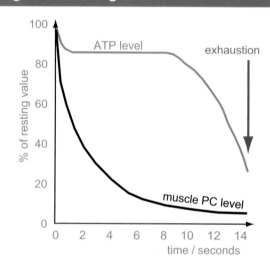

figure 21.2 – changes in muscle ATP and PC

The lactic acid system

This system depends on a chemical process called **glycolysis** which is the incomplete breakdown of sugar. Figure 21.3 shows the schematic layout of glycolysis.

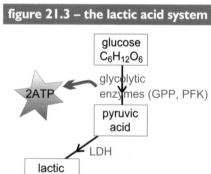

figure 21.3 – the lactic acid system

- **Carbohydrate** from food you have eaten is stored as **glycogen** (in the muscles and liver).

- This glycogen is converted into **glucose** by the hormone **glucagon** released when blood glucose levels fall (when glucose is used during tissue respiration).

- The breakdown of glucose provides the energy to rebuild ATP from ADP.

- This is facilitated by enzymes such as **glycogen phosphorylase** (GPP) and **phosphofructokinase** (PFK).

- The whole process produces **pyruvic acid**.

- **Glycolysis is anaerobic**.

- It takes place in the **sarcoplasm** of the muscle cell.

- No oxygen is needed, and the end product of this reaction (in the absence of oxygen) is **lactic acid**.

- The enzyme facilitating the conversion from pyruvic acid to lactic acid is **lactate dehydrogenase** (LDH).

As work intensity increases, lactic acid starts to accumulate above resting values, which produces **muscle fatigue** and pain. The resultant low pH inhibits enzyme action and cross-bridge formation, hence muscle action is inhibited and physical performance deteriorates.

The lactic acid system is the predominant one used to resynthesise ATP in sport or activities in which the flat-out effort lasts up to 30-60 seconds. For example, a 400m run or a 100m swim.

After exercise stops, extra oxygen is taken up to remove lactic acid by changing it back into pyruvic acid - this is the **EPOC** (**Excess Post-exercise Oxygen Consumption**, sometimes called the oxygen debt), see page 134 below for the details of EPOC.

The aerobic system

The aerobic energy system releases stored energy from muscle glycogen, fats and proteins.

Figure 21.4 is a graphic of some of the details of the aerobic system showing how between 32 and 34 ATP molecules are resynthesised from one molecule of glucose - which is the food fuel created from the food we eat. This process will continue indefinitely until energy stores run out - or the exercise stops.

figure 21.4 – the aerobic system

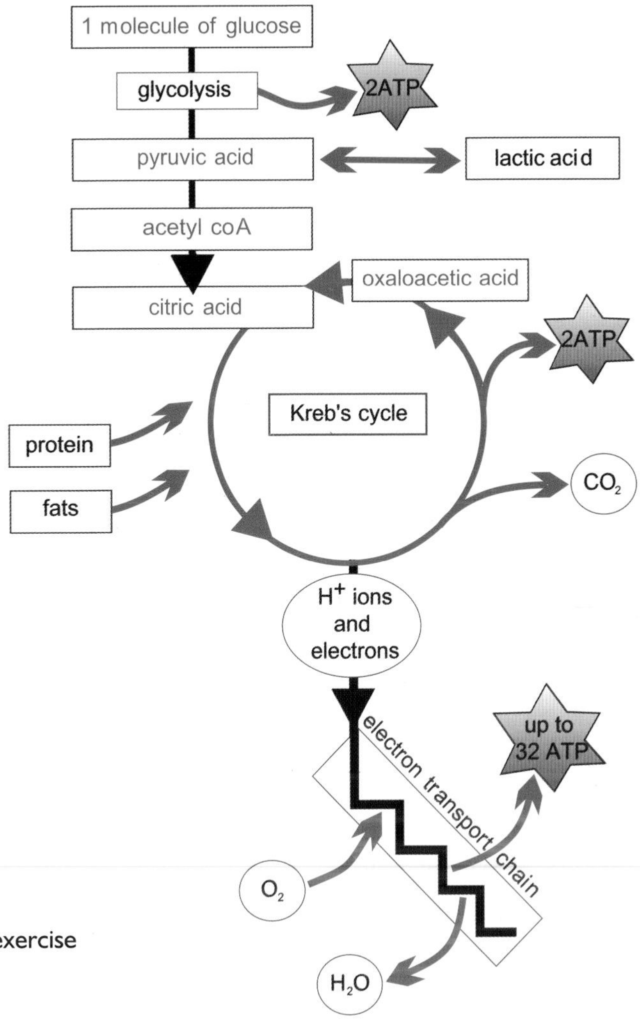

Stage one - glycolysis
This process takes place in the **muscle cell sarcoplasm** and is identical to the lactic acid system (anaerobic). **ATP regenerated = 2 ATP per molecule of glucose**.

Stage two - Kreb's cycle (citric acid cycle)
This stage occurs in the **presence of oxygen**, and takes place in the **muscle cell mitochondria** within the inner **fluid filled** matrix. Here, 2 molecules of **pyruvic acid** combine with **oxaloacetic acid** (4 carbons) and **acetyl coA** (2 carbons) to form citric acid (6 carbons). The cycle produces H^+ and electron pairs, and CO_2 and 2 ATP. Also, free fatty acids (from body fat) facilitated by the enzyme **lipoprotein lipase**, or protein (keto acids - from muscle), act as the fuel for this stage.

The enzymatic catabolism (breakdown) of fat within the muscle cell mitochondria is termed β-**oxidation**. Energy derived from the breakdown of FFAs are the preferred food fuel as the duration of exercise increases.

Stage three - the electron transport chain
The **electron transport chain** occurs in the presence of oxygen within the **cristae** (inner part) of the **muscle cell mitochondria**. **Hydrogen ions** and **electrons** have potential energy which is used to produce the ATP which is then released in a controlled step-by-step manner. Oxygen combines with the final H^+ ions to produce water and 32 ATP.

Aerobic respiration
In summary, the total effect of aerobic respiration is that it is an **endothermic** reaction:

$$\text{glucose} + \textbf{36ADP} + \textbf{36P}_i + \textbf{6O}_2 \rightarrow \textbf{6CO}_2 + \textbf{36ATP} + \textbf{6H}_2\textbf{O}$$

Fat fuels produce 2 ATP less than glucose.

Short-term response to aerobic activity

The aerobic system requires carbohydrate in the form of **glucose** which is **derived from glycogen** stored in muscle cells (mostly slow twitch - SO type I) and in the liver.

The graph in figure 21.5 shows how the rate of usage of muscle glycogen is high during the first 30 minutes of steady exercise - which has to be replaced if a sportsperson is to continue at the same rate. Hence consumption of energy drinks and bananas during a long tennis match.

Short-term response to aerobic activity

Endurance athletes can utilise FFAs during prolonged exercise sooner than untrained people. This training adaptation enables the trained athlete to not use glycogen up immediately, but save it for later on in an exercise effort, or when the intensity of exercise increases. This is called **glycogen sparing** and is illustrated in figure 21.6.

Energy continuum

This describes the process by which ATP is regenerated via the different energy systems depending on the **intensity** and **duration** of exercise. Although **all** the systems contribute to ATP regeneration during any activity, one or other of the energy systems usually provides the major contribution for a given activity. Table 21.1 shows approximate proportions of ATP resynthesised via aerobic and anaerobic pathways for some sporting activities.

Table 21.1 – **percentage contribution of the aerobic and anaerobic energy systems to different sports**

sport or event	aerobic %	anaerobic (all) %
100m sprint	0	100
200m sprint	10	90
100m swim	20	80
boxing	30	70
800m run	40	60
hockey	50	50
2000m rowing	60	40
4000m cycle pursuit	70	30
3000m run	80	20
cross country run	90	10
marathon	100	0

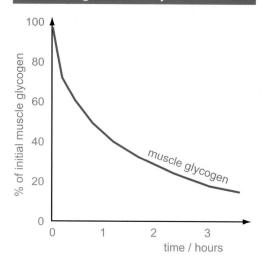

figure 21.5 – change in muscle glycogen during low intensity exercise

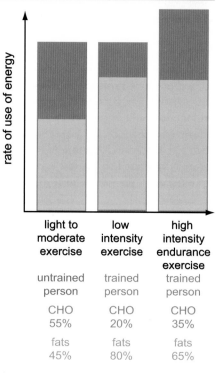

figure 21.6 – contribution of CHO and fats for trained and untrained people

	light to moderate exercise	low intensity exercise	high intensity endurance exercise
	untrained person	trained person	trained person
CHO	55%	20%	35%
fats	45%	80%	65%

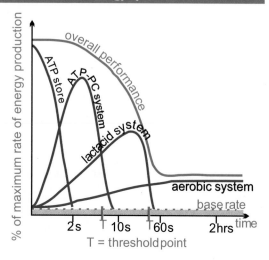

figure 21.7 – variation in contribution of energy systems

The graph in figure 21.7 shows how the different energy systems contribute resynthesis of ATP during flat-out exercise. Obviously, at reduced intensity of exercise, the contributions will be slightly different. But note that **all systems** are contributing from the start of exercise, only it takes some time for the lactic acid and aerobic systems to get going.

Short-term responses - thresholds

The concept of a **threshold** applies to the time at which one particular system of ATP regeneration takes over from another as the major regenerator of ATP during flat out exercise - marked as T in figure 21.7.

Short-term responses - thresholds

- For example, **ATP muscle stores** are depleted **within 2 seconds**, and towards the end of this period the ATP-PC system has risen enough to be able to provide the ATP necessary for the exercise.
- **Peak anaerobic power** is attained within the first 5 seconds of flat-out exercise, but depletion of PC occurs between 7 and 9 seconds.
- At this point, the lactic acid system has risen enough to be able to provide the ATP required for the next 40 seconds or so.

Hence the **threshold** between **ATP-PC and lactic acid** systems occurs between 7 and 9 seconds after the start of an exercise period.

A **second threshold point** occurs at about 50 seconds and is between the lactic acid and aerobic systems reflecting a switch of ATP resynthesis from a predominantly **anaerobic mode** to a predominantly **aerobic mode**.

Long-term training effects - thresholds

It is found that thresholds are **delayed** by training, so that the trained individual has a greater capacity for ATP-PC, has a greater lactic acid toleration, and more efficient ATP regeneration than the untrained person.

Recovery

There is improved oxygen recovery as a result of long-term aerobic training because of **better muscle capillarisation**. If an efficient cool-down is used, **lactic acid removal** is improved, hence there is a reduction in **DOMS** (delayed onset muscle soreness).

OBLA (Onset of Blood Lactate Accumulation)

As **work intensity** increases, **lactic acid** starts to **accumulate** above resting values. At a certain point (called the **OBLA** point) this produces muscle fatigue and pain, since the resultant low pH (high acidity) inhibits enzyme action and cross-bridge formation. This means in turn that muscle action is inhibited and **physical performance deteriorates**.

OBLA can be expressed as a percentage of $\dot{V}O_{2max}$ as shown in figure 21.8.

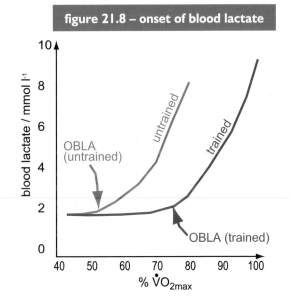

figure 21.8 – onset of blood lactate

This point governs the **lactic-aerobic threshold**.

- In the graph (figure 21.8), as exercise intensity increases and $\dot{V}O_2$ increases, **untrained people** have blood lactate which increases sharply at about 50% of $\dot{V}O_{2max}$.
- But **trained athletes** can exercise up to 70% of $\dot{V}O_{2max}$ before lactate concentration in the blood increases markedly.
- Hence **trained athletes** begin **OBLA at higher work intensities** - especially since trained athletes have higher values of $\dot{V}O_{2max}$ than untrained people in the first place.
- All this means that the **lactic-aerobic threshold** moves to **higher values of $\dot{V}O_{2max}$**.

Other factors affecting the proportions of energy systems

- The **level of fitness** (whether adaptations to training have included enhancement of relevant enzymes - which would for example postpone levels of lactate accumulation).
- The **availability of O_2 and food fuels**. For example, a high CHO diet would assist replenishment of glycogen stores which would then be available for glycolysis.

The recovery process

Bodily processes do not immediately return to resting levels after exercise ceases. The time taken for this to occur is called the **recovery period**. The recovery period is dependent on the intensity and duration of the exercise.

Excess post-exercise oxygen consumption (EPOC)

After every strenuous exercise (figure 21.9), there are **four** tasks that need to be completed before the exhausted muscle can operate at full efficiency again:

- **Replacement of ATP and phosphocreatine** (fast replenishment component).
- **Removal of lactic acid** (slow replenishment component).
- **Replenishment of myoglobin** with oxygen.
- **Replacement of glycogen**.

The first three require oxygen in substantial quantities, hence the need for rapid breathing and high pulse rate to carry oxygen to the muscle cells.

figure 21.9 – factors contributing to EPOC

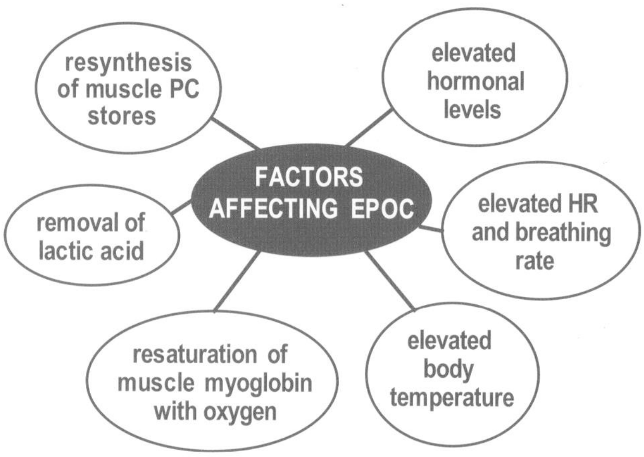

resynthesis of muscle PC stores

elevated hormonal levels

FACTORS AFFECTING EPOC

removal of lactic acid

elevated HR and breathing rate

resaturation of muscle myoglobin with oxygen

elevated body temperature

The need for oxygen

The need for oxygen to rapidly replace ATP and remove lactic acid is known as the oxygen debt. The more modern term for oxygen debt is **excess post-exercise oxygen consumption** (EPOC) or oxygen recovery. This represents the elevation of the metabolic rate above resting values which occurs after exercise during the recovery period.

EPOC is the excess O_2 consumed following exercise. This excess O_2 is needed to provide the energy required to resynthesise ATP used, and remove lactic acid created during previous exercise. EPOC has **two** components (figure 21.10):

- **Alactic or alactacid**.
- **Lactic or lactacid**.

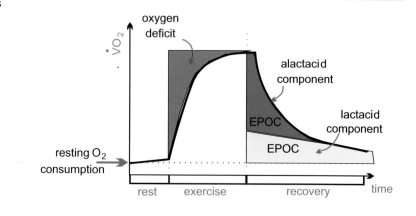

figure 21.10 – oxygen consumption during exercise and recovery

The **oxygen deficit** is the difference between the oxygen required during exercise and the oxygen actually consumed during the activity. The graph in figure 21.10 shows the relationship between oxygen consumption and the time before, during and after exercise.

The alactacid component

This component involves the **conversion of ADP back into PC and ATP**, and is known as **restoration of muscle phosphagen**. This is a very rapid process (120 seconds to full restoration - see figure 21.11) and is of size 2 to 3.5 litres of O_2.

Phosphagen recovery

Phosphagen recovery (figure 21.11) is achieved via **three** mechanisms:

- There is **aerobic** conversion of carbohydrates into CO_2 and H_2O to resynthesise ATP from ADP and P_i.
- Some of the ATP is immediately utilised **to create PC** using the coupled reaction: **ATP + C → ADP + PC**.
- A small amount of ATP is **resynthesised via glycogen,** producing small amounts of lactic acid.

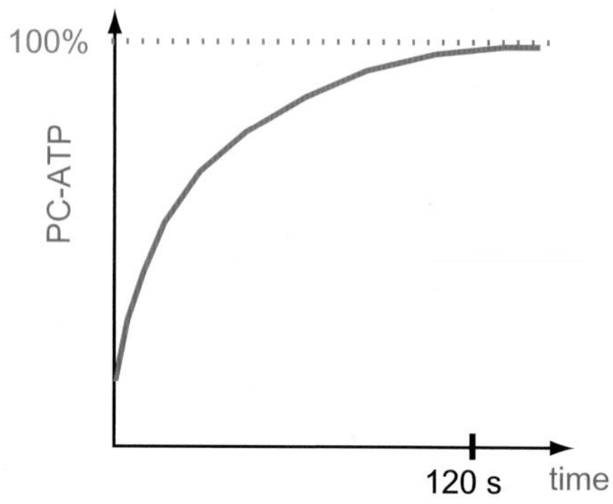

Continuous oxygen recovery

During the **post-exercise period**, oxygen recovery is continuous.

This is because:

- Muscle myoglobin recovers.
- Temperature falls.
- Hormone levels fall.

figure 21.11 – phosphagen recovery

100%

PC-ATP

120 s   time

During the **recovery period**, temperature and hormone levels are higher than normal (although falling), which:

- Keeps metabolic rate high.
- Keeps respiratory rate high.
- Keeps heart rate high.
- Requires more oxygen than normal.

Hence EPOC increases.

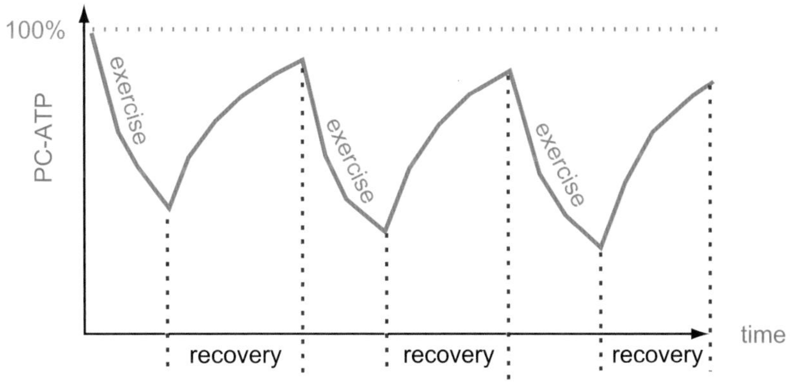

The implications for interval training

- If there is only a short interval between bouts of exercise, the level of phosphagen stores gradually reduces (see figure 21.12) thereby reducing the energy available for the later bouts.
- This stresses the ATP and PC storage and forces the muscle cells to adapt by storing more of these quantities.
- Also, cells will adapt by improving their ability to provide O_2, and hence increase the possible size of the alactic component.
- Anaerobic interval training studies have shown that 30 second bouts of exercise increase the activity of **glycolytic enzymes**, such as phosphorylase, phosphofructokinase and lactate dehydrogenase, from around 10% to 25%.
- This increase in **glycolytic capacity** will allow the muscle to develop greater tension for a longer period of time as the muscle tissue increases its **tolerance to lactate**.

See further information on long-term adaptations on page 141 onwards.

figure 21.12 – phosphagen recovery during interval training

figure 21.13 – lactacid recovery

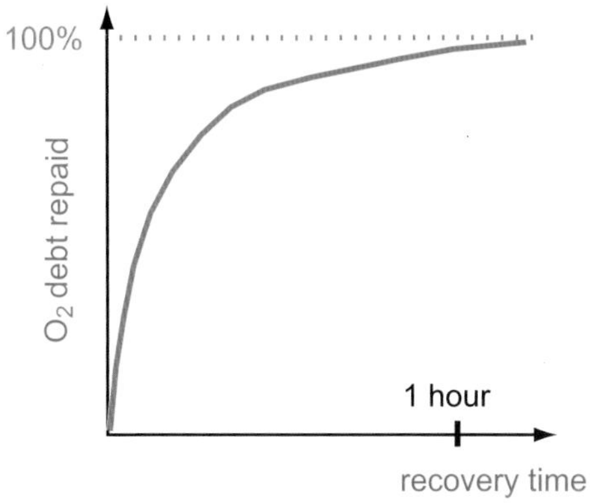

Lactacid oxygen recovery

High intensity exercise up to about 60 seconds creates **lactic acid**, and **oxygen is needed** to remove this lactic acid. This process begins to restore muscle and liver glycogen, and is relatively slow with **full recovery** taking up to 1 hour (figure 21.13).

Relatively large amounts of lactic acid (15 to 20 times the resting value of 1 to 2 mmol litre^{-1}) are produced during high intensity exercise, which is removed according to the proportions listed in table 21.2.

Removal of the lactic acid

Table 21.2 – **removal of the lactic acid**

oxidation into CO_2 + H_2O	65%
conversion into glycogen then stored in muscle and liver (Cori cycle)	20%
conversion into protein	10%
conversion into glucose	5%

The lactate shuttle

During the recovery process after intense exercise, a small proportion of the lactic acid produced is recycled back into glucose in the muscle cell. This is the reverse process to glycolysis and requires energy from ATP breakdown.

Buffering

A **blood buffer** is a chemical substance which resists abrupt changes in hydrogen ion (H^+) concentration. For example, when H^+ concentration increases as a result of intense exercise, H^+ reacts with oxyhaemoglobin (buffer) to form haemoglobinic acid. These ions are released when H^+ concentration falls. So this is a temporary solution to rapid changes in acidity or alkalinity which would otherwise cause rapid fatigue symptoms.

Cool-down following exercise

Cool-down (the process of continuing low level exercise immediately after the end of a high intensity exercise bout) **continues to provide oxygen** to skeletal muscle. This therefore **enhances oxidation of lactic acid** and ensures that less lactic acid remains in tissue. Hence there is less muscle soreness (**less DOMS**).

Figure 21.14 shows how blood lactate falls after exercise, and that when an active cool-down is undertaken less lactate remains in muscle tissue.

figure 21.14 – blood lactate concentration after exercise

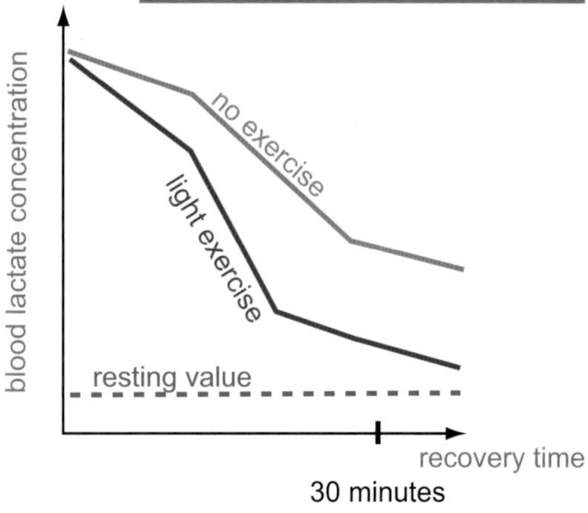

Restoration of muscle glycogen stores

• During short duration high intensity exercise, restoration of glycogen takes up to 2 hours, and after prolonged low intensity aerobic exercise, restoration can take days.

• A **high carbohydrate diet** speeds up the glycogen recovery process, and there is a need for the athlete to restore stores as soon as possible after activity, with for example, a high CHO loaded drink immediately following exercise.

Restoration of myoglobin

Muscle myoglobin (an iron protein molecule located in skeletal muscle similar to haemoglobin) serves as a storage site for O_2, and has a temporary but greater affinity for O_2 than haemoglobin. Hence it acts as a **carrier of O_2** from HbO_2 (in blood) to mitochondria (in a muscle cell). Myoglobin is reoxygenated within 2 minutes.

Restoration of muscle myoglobin is important for recovery from high intensity exercise.

Practice questions

1) Define energy, and briefly describe how energy is released from food in the body.   5 marks

2) a) Identify the only form of usable energy in the body.   1 mark

   b) What is meant by an exothermic reaction? Illustrate this definition with an example.   2 marks

   c) What is meant by an endothermic reaction? Illustrate this definition with an example.   2 marks

3) a) An elite cyclist wants to discover her maximum output when sprinting. A load of 85 newtons is applied to the wheel of a cycle ergometer. The cyclist then sprints for 10 seconds and records a distance travelled of 200m. Assuming that no other force is acting on the cycle, calculate the power output of the cyclist. Show each stage of your calculation.   4 marks

   b) Name the predominant energy system that would be utilised during this activity and describe how ATP is re-created within this system.   4 marks

4) a) An elite swimmer performs a flat-out 100 metre freestyle swim in 50 seconds. Describe how most of the ATP is regenerated during the swim.   4 marks

   b) Sketch a graph, which shows the use of the appropriate energy systems against time during the swim.   4 marks

5) a) Taking part in a triathlon involves swimming, cycling and running. Briefly describe how the aerobic energy system within the cell mitochondria supports this endurance event.   6 marks

   b) Construct a graph, which illustrates the food fuel usage against time during a triathlon race lasting 2 hours.
                                                                                                                  2 marks

6) Compare the relative efficiency of ATP production via the aerobic and anaerobic routes. Explain your answer.   3 marks

7) The diagram in figure 21.15 is an energy continuum in relation to a variety of sports activities.
   a) Explain the concept 'the energy continuum'. 2 marks
   b) At each end of the continuum examples of sporting activities have been omitted. Give one example of a sporting activity that is predominantly anaerobic and one example of a sporting activity that is predominantly aerobic. 2 marks
   c) Suggest two factors that need to be considered in evaluating sports activities on the basis of their relative position on the energy continuum. 2 marks
   d) Explain, using specific examples, why a game of hockey has aerobic and anaerobic components. 4 marks

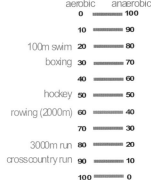

figure 21.15 – variation in contribution of energy system

8) a) State where and in what conditions lactic acid is commonly found in relatively large amounts. 2 marks
   b) There are several ways by which lactic acid can be removed from active muscles. Identify the major pathway for the removal of lactic acid and the organs and tissues involved. 4 marks
   c) How does light exercise influence lactate removal? 3 marks

9) Explain why cool-down is important within an exercise regime. 4 marks

10) Figure 21.16 shows oxygen uptake of an elite games player undertaking exercise followed by a recovery period.
   a) Using the appropriate letters, identify the oxygen deficit and Excess Post Oxygen Consumption (EPOC). 3 marks

   b) Why does the elite player incur an oxygen deficit during exercise? 2 marks

   c) Excess Post Oxygen Consumption (EPOC) is considered to have two components. State two aims of the first component and explain how this component is achieved. 4 marks

   d) Describe the process of ATP production that restores the oxygen debt or EPOC. 6 marks

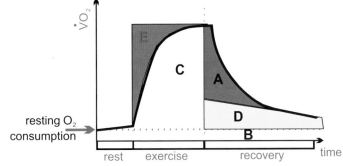

figure 21.16 – oxygen consumption during exercise and recovery

11) An elite games player performs an interval training session during which the rate of muscle phosphagen levels during the recovery period was recorded. The results from this training session are given in table 21.3.

   a) Using the results in table 21.3, plot a graph of recovery time against the percentage of muscle phosphagen restored. 3 marks

   b) What resting value would you recommend for a full recovery, and what would be the effect of restarting the exercise after 30 seconds? 2 marks

   c) Part of the recovery mechanism after anaerobic exercise involves myoglobin. Explain the function of myoglobin during the recovery process. 3 marks

Table 21.3 – muscle phosphagen during recovery

recovery time (s)	muscle phosphagen restored (%)
10	10
30	50
60	75
90	87
120	93
150	97
180	99
210	101
240	102

12) How could information on oxygen debt recovery be of use to an athlete and coach in designing training sessions? 6 marks

13) Physical activity by far provides the greatest demand for energy. Discuss how the intensity and duration of the exercise period and the relative contributions of the body's means for energy transfer affect performance. In your answer mention availability of O_2, food fuels used, energy threshold points, enzyme control and how the fitness of the participant affect performance. 20 marks

CHAPTER 22 – AEROBIC CAPACITY

Oxygen uptake - $\dot{V}O_2$

Aerobic capacity is the ability to do physical work which is dependent on the **aerobic mechanism** of ATP regeneration and hence energy supply. The amount of oxygen consumed per unit of time (usually 1 minute) is expressed as $\dot{V}O_2$, and the mean value of $\dot{V}O_2$ at rest = 0.2 to 0.3 litres min^{-1}.

- $\dot{V}O_2$ increases proportionally to work intensity (see figure 22.1) up to a maximum value - called $\dot{V}O_{2max}$.

- $\dot{V}O_{2max}$ represents the maximum amount of oxygen that can be taken in, transported and consumed by working muscle per minute. Aerobic capacity, aerobic power and maximal oxygen uptake are all terms used interchangeably with $\dot{V}O_{2max}$.

- Because individuals' energy requirements vary with body size, $\dot{V}O_{2max}$ is generally expressed relative to body mass in millilitres of oxygen per kilogram of body weight (ml kg^{-1}min^{-1}). This allows a more accurate comparison of different sized individuals.

- You can see from figure 22.1 that $\dot{V}O_{2max}$ is bigger for trained athletes. This is an adaptation produced by aerobic training, which means that the athlete can work harder for longer.

- $\dot{V}O_{2max}$ is therefore a key component of aerobic endurance and is called **aerobic capacity (or aerobic power or maximum oxygen uptake)**, and so represents an accurate indicator of an athlete's fitness.

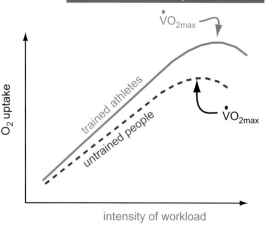

figure 22.1 – oxygen uptake as exercise intensity increases

Values for oxygen uptake - $\dot{V}O_2$

$\dot{V}O_{2max}$ mean values are:

males (20 yo)	= 3.5 litres min^{-1}	
	= 40 ml kg^{-1} min^{-1} (for average male body mass 87.5 kg)	
females (20 yo)	= 2.3 litres min^{-1}	
	= 35 ml kg^{-1} min^{-1} (for mean female body mass 66 kg)	
endurance athletes	= 4 to 6 litres min^{-1}	
	= 60 to 90 ml kg^{-1} min^{-1} (for mean body mass 66 kg)	

Table 22.1 – **factors affecting $\dot{V}O_{2max}$**

factor	effect
genetics	accounts for 25% to 50% of the variance in $\dot{V}O_{2max}$ values, for example, the proportions of muscle fibre types are genetically determined, and this could account for specialisms of individuals such as whether a person becomes good at marathon running or weight lifting
physiology	the limitations of the cardiovascular and pulmonary systems vary, for example, the percentage of slow twitch muscle fibres, heart and lung size, number of red blood cells and mitochondria and the ability of muscle cells to extract oxygen are all physiological factors that will enhance or limit $\dot{V}O_{2max}$
gender	$\dot{V}O_{2max}$ values decrease in females from late teens onwards, probably because of the tradition of less physical activity for women - highly conditioned female endurance athletes have $\dot{V}O_{2max}$ values around 10% lower than those of highly conditioned male endurance athletes
age	$\dot{V}O_{2max}$ reduces at about 10% per decade during ageing for sedentary people - and $\dot{V}O_{2max}$ reduces less for active sportspeople as they age
training	aerobic training can cause $\dot{V}O_{2max}$ values to be improved by 10-20% (figure 22.1), for example, in an untrained population $\dot{V}O_{2max}$ values peak between 10-19 years whereas for athletes $\dot{V}O_{2max}$ values peak between 18-32 years, the differences in $\dot{V}O_{2max}$ mean values in trained athletes is due to the specificity of training
lifestyle	habits such as smoking and a poor diet adversely affect $\dot{V}O_{2max}$ values
body composition	$\dot{V}O_{2max}$ decreases as the percentage of body fat decreases
altitude	$\dot{V}O_{2max}$ decreases in proportion to the decrease in atmospheric pressure

STUDENT NOTE

For details of long-term training adaptations that have a direct impact on $\dot{V}O_{2max}$ values, refer to page 58 of 'AS Revise PE for OCR' ISBN: 978 1 901424 52 2.
You should be able to describe and evaluate $\dot{V}O_{2max}$ tests.

$\dot{V}O_{2max}$ tests as a measure of aerobic endurance

- A $\dot{V}O_{2max}$ test assesses the maximum amount of oxygen that a person can consume per minute during a progressive exercise test to exhaustion.
- $\dot{V}O_{2max}$ is assessed directly when using closed-circuit spirometry (refer to table 22.2 below).
- Simple **predicted $\dot{V}O_{2max}$** tests are used as indicators of aerobic fitness or stamina, and include the Physical work capacity test (PWC170), the Cooper run/walk test, the Multi-stage shuttle run test, and the Queen's College step test (table 22.2).
- Elite marathon athletes run at optimal percentages of their $\dot{V}O_{2max}$ in order to achieve World class performances.

Table 22.2 – **examples of $\dot{V}O_{2max}$ tests**

test/fitness component	description	advantages	disadvantages
PWC-170 test/ aerobic fitness	two 6 minute cycle ergometer rides at predicted heart rates, used to extrapolate power output	popular and inexpensive cycle ergometer test	predicted test by extrapolation, fitness levels influence interpretation of results
Queen's College step test/ predicted $\dot{V}O_{2max}$	3 minutes of stepping at a set cadence, $\dot{V}O_{2max}$ predicted from HR recovery	easy to administer, cheap equipment	length of leg levers affects results, depends on stepping technique and rhythm, only produces a predicted $\dot{V}O_{2max}$
Closed circuit spirometry/ actual $\dot{V}O_{2max}$	a progressive test to exhaustion (treadmill, rowing machine or bike) lasting between 8 and 10 minutes, using a gas analyser O_2 uptake is calculated from measures of oxygen and carbon dioxide in the expired air, $\dot{V}O_{2max}$ value is determined at or near test completion	high reliability and validity offers different modes of exercise	performer has to work to a state of exhaustion, needs specialist testing laboratory equipment therefore inaccessible to non-elite performers

The importance of aerobic capacity to endurance performers is that it is useful as an indicator showing athletes' maximal physiological capacity. Repeated tests would show the effects of endurance training on $\dot{V}O_{2max}$.

STUDENT NOTE

Refer to page 150 for details of different types of training used to develop aerobc capacity.

The use of target heart rates as an intensity guide

A **target heart rate** is a specific heart rate (HR) to be achieved and maintained during exercise.
If aerobic adaptations are to occur, training must take place at a HR above the aerobic threshold.
This theory is based on the fact that $\dot{V}O_2$ is proportional to heart rate.

Aerobic training zone
This is shown on the graph in figure 22.2.
It shows a range of HR values at which aerobic training should occur.
This will enable adaptations to occur which improve $\dot{V}O_{2max}$.

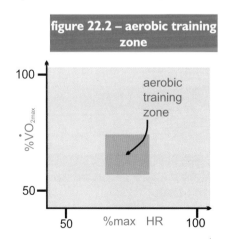

figure 22.2 – aerobic training zone

Table 22.3 – **classification of exercise intensity based on 20 to 60 minutes of endurance activity, comparing heart rate maximum, Karvonen's maximum heart rate reserve**

classification of intensity	relative intensity by HR_{max}	relative intensity by VO_{2max} or HR_{max} reserve - the Karvonen method
very light	<35%	<30%
light	35 - 59%	30 - 49%
moderate	60 - 79%	50 - 74%
heavy	80 - 89%	75 - 84%
very heavy	>89%	>84%

(From Table 19.3 Wilmore, Costill, Kenney 'Physiology of Exercise 4e', 2008, Human Kinetics)

Heart rate maximum (HR_{max}) method

If it is required to operate at 60% of maximum heart rate then the following example shows how to work out the heart rate at which training should occur:

$$\text{Maximum HR } (HR_{max}) = 220 - age$$
$$age = 20$$
$$\text{Therefore, } HR_{max} = 220 - 20 \quad = \textbf{200 bpm}$$

$$\textbf{aerobic threshold HR} = \textbf{0.6 x } HR_{max}$$
$$\textbf{Therefore aerobic threshold HR} = 0.6 \times 200 \quad = \textbf{120 bpm}$$

Target heart rate (HR estimation) Karvonen method

The difference between this method and the HR maximum method is that in the **Karvonen method**, the target HR will depend on the fitness of the athlete.

The following calculation shows the maximum HR at which aerobic exercise can be undertaken if it is required to operate at 60% maximum - according to Karvonen, called the **aerobic threshold heart rate**.

Aerobic threshold (Karvonen) HR $= HR_{rest} + \textbf{0.6}(HR_{max} - HR_{rest})$

The following example shows how this is used:

$$\text{Again, maximum HR } (HR_{max}) = 220 - age$$
$$age = 20$$
$$\text{Therefore, } HR_{max} = 220 - 20 \quad = \textbf{200 bpm}$$

The heart rate at rest is measured at:
$$HR_{rest} = 70 \text{ bpm}$$

$$\text{So } \textbf{the aerobic threshold HR} = 70 + 0.6(200 - 70)$$
$$= 70 + 0.6 \times 130 = 70 + 78$$
$$= \textbf{148 bpm}$$

Aerobic energy system and food fuel usage

Table 22.4 – **relationship between aerobic intensity and food fuel used**

% aerobic intensity	fuel food used
50 - 60%	fats
60 - 70%	glycogen and fats
70 - 80%	glycogen

The use of the aerobic system of ATP regeneration will promote aerobic capacity, regardless of the level of intensity.

But the more intense the training, the more work that can be done before the anaerobic system has to be used. The **intensity** and **duration** of training will determine which **food fuel** is used. Endurance athletes tend to train at an intensity close to the OBLA, which therefore requires a high CHO food intake.

Adaptations produced by aerobic training

The **aims of training** are to improve performance, skill, game ability, and motor and physical fitness. As mentioned above, **adaptation** refers to **long-term changes** (figure 22.3) produced in the human body which are caused by training overload.

Cardiovascular systems

The cardiovascular system becomes more efficient as the heart becomes bigger and stronger and pumps more blood per pulse. More **haemoglobin** is available in blood for oxygen transport, and the capillary system in a trained muscle bed is utilised better and developed more.

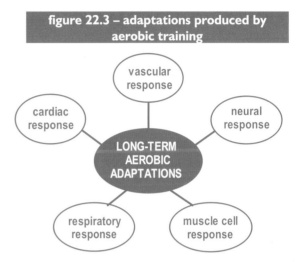

figure 22.3 – adaptations produced by aerobic training

Cardiac response to aerobic exercise

- The heart becomes bigger and stronger (mainly the left ventricle) as a result of prolonged aerobic exercise (figure 22.4), creating **increased ventricular muscle mass** and **stronger elastic recoil** of the myocardium. This is **cardiac hypertrophy**.

- The increased strength of the cardiac muscle causes a more forceful contraction during ventricular systole.

- Therefore stroke volume increases and HR decreases (this is called **bradycardia**), which provides more oxygen per pulse.

- Blood volume increases with training which in turn increases the size of the left ventricular chamber. This means that more blood volume enters the left ventricle per beat (increased **pre-load**) increasing the stretch of the ventricular walls by the Frank-Starling mechanism.

- Reduced systemic vascular resistance (**decreased afterload**) also contributes to the increase in volume of blood pumped from the left ventricle per beat.

- The net effect is up to 20% bigger stroke volume and greater oxygen delivery to muscles.

- Heart rate during recovery decreases more rapidly after training.

- Cardiac output at maximal levels of exercise increases considerably and is in a response to an increase in $\dot{V}O_{2max}$. This is because the two components of the cardiac output, namely stroke volume and heart rate, balance each other out and there is an increase in a-$\bar{v}O_{2diff}$ reflecting greater oxygen extraction by the active tissues.

- Cardiac output at rest (or at submaximal exercise) remains unchanged or decreases slightly after endurance training. Hence there is a **decrease in resting heart rate** (HR) and an **increase in HR during maximal workloads**.

- **Blood vessels in the heart evolve** to reduce the blood flow to the heart because the heart muscle itself is more efficient.

figure 22.4 – long-term responses of the heart

trained heart		untrained heart
120 ml	stroke volume	100 ml
60 bpm	resting heart rate	75 bpm
200 bpm	maximum heart rate	180 bpm

Vascular response to aerobic exercise

The increase in blood flow to muscle is one of the most important factors supporting increased aerobic endurance capacity and performance. This increase is attributable to:

- An **improved capillary system**, there is better dilation of existing capillaries due to increase in blood volume, and there is increased capillarisation of trained muscle.

- **Diversion of a larger portion of cardiac output** to the active muscle, known as an enhanced vascular shunt. Hence increased vasodilation of blood vessels (such as arterioles) and precapillary sphincters to working muscle.

- **Increase in blood volume** is attributed to an increase in plasma volume and number of red blood cells. The increase in plasma volume would result in a reduction in fluid friction drag as the blood flows through blood vessels, which would improve circulation and oxygen availability.

- **Increased elasticity and thickness of smooth muscle** of arterial walls result from extended aerobic exercise which makes arterial walls tougher and therefore less likely to stretch under pressure.

- Hence blood pressure is maintained (which therefore continues to force blood through the capillary network).

Vascular response to aerobic exercise

- Systolic and diastolic **blood pressure decreases** during rest and submaximal exercise. This is because there is a training-induced reduction in sympathetic nervous system hormones. This response decreases peripheral vascular resistance to blood flow, causing blood pressure to drop.

The **net effect** is for the body to develop a more effective blood distribution system both at rest and during exercise.

Respiratory adaptations to aerobic exercise

The respiratory system undergoes the following adaptations to endurance training to maximise its efficiency:

- Pulmonary systems become more efficient, because the musculature of the torso **becomes stronger** and more efficient.
- **Lung volumes increase slightly**, hence greater volumes of air can be breathed per breath (known as tidal volume or TV), and per minute (known as minute ventilation or $\dot{V}E$), hence increased gaseous exchange and $\dot{V}O_{2max}$.
- There is an **increase in vital capacity** at the expense of residual volume, hence a decrease in breathing rate at submaximal workloads.
- **Maximal pulmonary ventilation** is substantially increased following a period of endurance-based training – compare 100 to 120 dm^3min^{-1} for untrained sedentary subjects with in excess of 200 dm^3min^{-1} for highly trained endurance athletes.
- Two factors can account for an increase in maximal pulmonary ventilation. These are **increased tidal volume** (TV) and **increased respiratory frequency** (f) during maximal exercise.
- There is **increased capillarisation of alveoli**, and more alveoli are utilised, hence increased gaseous exchange and $\dot{V}O_{2max}$.
- There is an increase in **pulmonary blood flow** (due to increase in stroke volume) and **plasma volume**. This increase in pulmonary driving pressure causes a bigger distortion in red blood cells as they pass through the alveolar capillaries. Hence greater O_2 transfer.

Muscle cell adaptations to aerobic exercise

- Extended **aerobic exercise** causes **more myoglobin** and more and **bigger mitochondria** to be created in muscle cells, which improves the oxygen delivery and energy creation within a cell.
- There will also be **increased oxidative enzymes** (such as pyruvate dehydrogenase) produced within muscle cell mitochondria. Hence there will be increased activity of Kreb's cycle and the electron transport chain to restore ATP in muscle cells.
- Increase in stores and utilisation of **fat**, and increase in stores of **glycogen** in muscle, will enable more fuel to be available for aerobic work.
- **Glycogen sparing** is a muscle cell response within the specific muscle cells of the person who has undertaken sustained aerobic training.
- An adaptation is produced where fats are used earlier on in exercise inside the muscle cells being trained, thus conserving glycogen stores (respiratory factors indicate greater use of fats).
- The chart in figure 21.6 (on page 132 above) shows a higher proportion of fats utilised by the trained person, thereby releasing CHO for higher intensity work. This reduces the respiratory exchange ratio (**RER** is a method used in determining which metabolic fuel is predominantly in use during exercise. It is calculated by analysing oxygen consumption and carbon dioxide production).
- There is an **increase in a-$\bar{v}O_{2diff}$**. This is due to a more effective distribution of arterial blood away from inactive tissue to active tissue and an increased ability of active muscle to extract more oxygen.
- A lower mixed venous oxygen content contributes towards the increase in $\dot{V}O_{2max}$ in trained athletes.
- **Extended aerobic training** will initiate conversion of type 11b to type 11a fibres, along with a small increase in the percentage of type 1 fibres. Hence even better aerobic performance.

How to plan an aerobic training programme

- **Assess** your aerobic fitness level, for example do the NCF multistage fitness test and find out your predicted $\dot{V}O_{2max}$.
- Determine your aerobic **fitness goals**, such as to improve cardiovascular performance or sport performance.
- Consider your **time constraints** - time of day/days available/times per day.
- Look at your **exercise preference** - could be general or sport specific.
- Consider the **type of training** (continuous or interval) you need to do.
- Consider what **facilities** are available to you such as a gym, track, pool in town, or paths, lanes in the country.
- Apply relevant **training principles** such as progression, overload, duration, frequency, intensity and variance.
- Place basic elements within a session such as warm-up, work-out and cool-down.

Table 22.5 – **example training programme for an elite male 800m runner**

day	time of day	training
day 1	am evening	30 min medium paced run continuous 30 min medium paced run continuous
day 2	am pm	30 min easy paced run continuous 3 sets of (2 x 400m (55s) 2 x 200m (26s)) interval 20 min recovery between sets
day 3	am	45 min medium paced run continuous

day 4	am
	pm
		30 min easy paced run continuous
		2 x 30m, 40m, 50m, 60m walk back recovery interval session 2 sets of 3 x 200m (25s)
		    5min recovery
		    15 min recovery between sets

day 5	rest	
day 6	pm	competition
day 7	am	long medium paced run, 60 min continuous

Practice questions

1) a) Define the term $\dot{V}O_{2max}$ and describe two main factors which limit $\dot{V}O_{2max}$. **3 marks**

   b) Describe a field test used to estimate a person's $\dot{V}O_{2max}$. **3 marks**

2) a) Figure 22.5 shows variation in $\dot{V}O_{2max}$ between three different sports. Suggest reasons for variations in $\dot{V}O_{2max}$ between these three sports. **3 marks**

   b) Explain the potential physiological advantages for endurance athletes having a high $\dot{V}O_{2max}$. **2 marks**

   c) What other factors contribute to an individual's $\dot{V}O_{2max}$? **3 marks**

3) $\dot{V}O_{2max}$ is the best indicator of cardiovascular endurance capacity and increases substantially in response to long-term endurance training. Define the term $\dot{V}O_{2max}$ and identify its units of measurement. Through what mechanisms does this improvement occur? **8 marks**

4) a) Identify **two** valid and reliable submaximal tests that measure endurance or stamina. Why are submaximal tests often favoured over maximal tests? **4 marks**

   b) Explain why fitness testing is necessary for both the coach and the athlete? **3 marks**

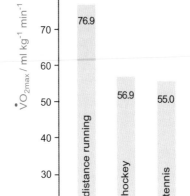
figure 22.5 – $\dot{V}O_{2max}$ for different sports

5) Using practical examples from the cardiovascular systems explain the difference between a short-term response and a long-term adaptation to exercise. **4 marks**

6) Identify the long-term adaptations an elite performer would expect to occur to the structure and the functioning of the cardiovascular system, as a result of an intense aerobic training programme. **12 marks**

7) Jodie Swallow is a top class female British Triathlete, and has a resting heart rate of 36 beats per minute. Give reasons why such an athlete might have a low resting heart rate. **4 marks**

8) Describe and account for some of the long-term effects of regular aerobic training methods on respiratory volumes.

6 marks

9) Describe four changes that occur in muscle cells as a result of an endurance-based training programme. 4 marks

10) Your PE group has been asked to devise a running training schedule for an elite 1500m runner. Using your knowledge of both intermittent and continuous training methods show how you could use this information to produce both aerobic and anaerobic adaptations.
Justify the content of your training programme for an elite 1500m runner, with regard to the expected respiratory adaptations. 20 marks

11) Describe a method of monitoring exercise intensity and give an advantage and disadvantage for the method you have selected. 5 marks

12) A group of students wish to create an aerobic weight training programme. Suggest how they could calculate working intensities that would give them optimal strength endurance gains. Illustrate your answer with examples. 8 marks

13) Continuous training is one of the least used methods of training by top performers. Identify the main characteristics of continuous training and suggest how this can benefit a performer. 4 marks

14) Fartlek training is a type of training that is used to develop aerobic capacity. What does the term Fartlek mean? Answer by outlining the training principles used to create a typical Fartlek training session. 3 marks

CHAPTER 23 – STRENGTH

Strength

Strength (figure 23.1) is defined as 'the maximum force exerted by a specific muscle or muscle groups during a single maximal muscle contraction (1RM)'.

figure 23.1 – strength

- **Static strength** is exerted without change of muscle length, for example holding a weight at arms length, or pushing hard in a stationary rugby scrum thus creating an **isometric muscle contraction**.

- **Dynamic** or **explosive strength** is the maximal strength exerted during a movement or exercise in which muscle length changes. Most sports use this type of maximal strength. This is the sort of strength weight lifters use in competition when performing an Olympic lift (figure 23.2), and is the most usual in sports situations such as throwing and sprinting. Most games or activities require flat out movements such as sprinting and therefore require dynamic strength. A sub-category of dynamic strength is **elastic or plyometric strength** or the ability to apply as large a force as possible using an **eccentric** contraction (in which the active muscles get longer) **followed** by a **concentric** contraction (in which the active muscles get shorter). For example, rebound jumping and high jump take-off.

- Strength can be assessed with the use of **dynamometers** (hand grip or back lift dynamometer) or a one repetition maximum (1RM) test.

figure 23.2 – dynamic strength requires maximum strength

Strength endurance

Strength endurance (sometimes called muscular endurance) can be defined as '**the ability of a muscle or muscle groups to sustain repeated contractions over time sufficient enough to cause muscular fatigue**'.

- Muscular endurance relies on the ability of the body to produce energy under aerobic and anaerobic conditions.

- This type of exercise stresses slow twitch fibres and fast twitch fibres type IIa, both muscle fibre types are fatigue resistant.

- Simple tests that evaluate local muscular endurance include the multi-stage abdominal test and maximum chin test i.e. the total number of chin-ups completed to exhaustion or within one minute.

Factors affecting strength

- Strength exercises stress **fast twitch fibres type IIb** which are able to generate high forces rapidly. Long-term, this type of exercise results in **muscle hypertrophy** (enlargement of individual muscle fibres).
- **Muscle fibre type** is inherited, and strength is affected by fibre type distribution. For example, sprinters tend to have a majority of fast twitch type II, and endurance athletes tend to have a majority of slow twitch type I.
- **Type of muscle contraction**, because **eccentric** work exceeds the isometric maximum by about 30%. This is due to the ability of the neuromuscular system to mobilise a greater number of motor units when under the greater stress of an eccentric movement under tension. During this type of contraction, a large force acts to brake and control the movement.
- **Muscle cross sectional area**, in which people with larger muscles tend to be stronger! **Females** in general have muscles with smaller cross section than males, hence a smaller muscle mass. Peak power is less for females by about 20%.
- **Muscle mass differences** between individuals is a large factor.
- **Regression** or **detraining** is a factor which will affect strength as little as 5 days after training stops. The amount and rate of regression depends on the length of time training has occurred.

Table 23.1 – **types of muscle contraction as a factor affecting strength**

type of contraction	strength gain over range of motion	least possibility of muscle soreness	skill improvement
isokinetic	excellent	excellent	excellent
isometric	poor	good	poor
isotonic	good	poor	good

Specialised training

This section considers several specialised training methods used by sports performers as summarised in figure 23.3.

figure 23.3 – specialised strength training methods

Intermittent or interval training

This type of training is characterised by periods of **alternating exercise** and **rest**, providing a very versatile training method that enables the individual to perform considerably more work and with greater physiological benefits.
Variables include:

- **Duration** of the exercise period.
- **Intensity** of the exercise period.
- Number of **repetitions** within a set.
- Number of **sets** within a session.
- Duration of the rest intervals (rest relief) or **recovery**.

The exercise **type** and **loading**, number of **repetitions** and **sets**, and length of **rest relief** govern the **adaptive response** produced, thus enabling the individual to select the required intensity of work to stress the relevant energy system:

- **ATP-PC intervals** are characterised by high intensity effort (80-100% of maximum effort) lasting between 3-10 seconds and no more than 2 minutes recovery. Increases ATP-PC stores.
- **Lactic acid intervals** are characterised by medium to high intensity effort (60-80% of maximum effort) lasting between 15-90 seconds with variable recovery depending on exercise duration. Increases blood buffering capacity or increased lactate tolerance.
- **Aerobic intervals** are characterised by low intensity effort (below 50% of maximum effort) lasting beyond 20 minutes with short recovery. Increases aerobic capacity or VO_{2max}.
- See table 23.4 on page 148 for examples of interval training.

Weight training

Weight training is a form of interval training and can be used to develop or stress several components of fitness such as strength and strength endurance depending on the resistance, number of repetitions, sets and rest relief.

Exercises are normally classed in four groups:

- **Shoulders and arms**: bench press, pull downs, curls.
- **Trunk and back**: back hyperextensions, sit ups.
- **Legs**: squats, leg press, calf raises.
- **All-body exercises**: power clean, snatch, dead lift.
- See table 23.4 on page 148 for details of how to include these exercises in a session.

Circuit training

A type of interval training that provides all-round body fitness, characterised by a number of exercises or stations performed in succession so that different body parts are exercised successively. The training is normally organised to work for a set time period at each station. See table 23.4 on page 148 for details of how to include these exercises in a session.

Plyometric training

- **Plyometrics**, also known as **stretch-shortening cycle** exercise, is a form of **resistance** training involving **eccentric-to-concentric** actions at 100% intensity, performed quickly so that the muscle stretches prior to the concentric contraction.
- Plyometrics uses the **stretch reflex** to facilitate the recruitment of motor units within the active muscle tissue.
- Muscles and tendons contain specialised **proprioceptors**, such as **muscle spindles** and **Golgi tendon organs** sensitive to stretch, tension and pressure.
- **Muscle spindles** respond to any stretch of a muscle, and through the reflex response they initiate a stronger muscle action to counteract this stretch. This response inhibits the overstretching of muscle fibres.
- Stimulated **Golgi tendon organs** cause relaxation of muscle tissue.

In figure 23.4, two athletes are throwing a medicine ball back and forth. The catch phase of this movement is eccentric for the trunk musculature and the shoulders, with the throw movement being concentric in the same muscle groups. Normally this exercise is done too slowly to activate the stretch reflex, but a rapid rebound movement could have the desired effect.

figure 23.4 – catch and throw as eccentric then concentric exercise – similar to plyometrics

In figure 23.5, the athlete is performing two-footed jumping (bunny jumps), which would have to be performed quickly to activate the stretch reflex in time with the concentric phase of the jump.

figure 23.5 – bounding and jumping can be plyometric

- The **adaptations** produced by these types of training are almost exclusively **anaerobic**, with muscle elastic strength and hypertrophy as the primary aim.
- Plyometrics additionally involve neuro-muscular adaptations such as the **recruitment** of additional **fast twitch** motor units and **improved co-ordination** of fast twitch motor units as the eccentric effect is utilised.

- For the training to be **most effective**, the greatest force is applied when the **concentric phase** of a movement **coincides** with the **stretch reflex response** occurring at the limit of eccentric stretch.

STUDENT NOTE

Muscle soreness (DOMS) often occurs following plyometric training. This is because of associated damage to muscle tissue and cell membranes (micro tears) and inflammatory reactions within the muscles.

Adaptations produced by anaerobic training

Changes to the body caused by anaerobic training are listed in figure 23.6 overleaf.

Connective tissue response

In response to anaerobic training there will be:

- Increase in thickness and strength of **tendons**.
- Increased flexibility of **ligaments**.
- Thickening and improved **elasticity of cartilage**.
- Improved capability of cartilaginous tissue to absorb and expel synovial fluid (McCutchen's weeping lubrication theory), hence improved **cushioning** against impact within a joint.
- Strengthening of **bone tissue** due to increased depositing of calcium, therefore reduced risk of injury.

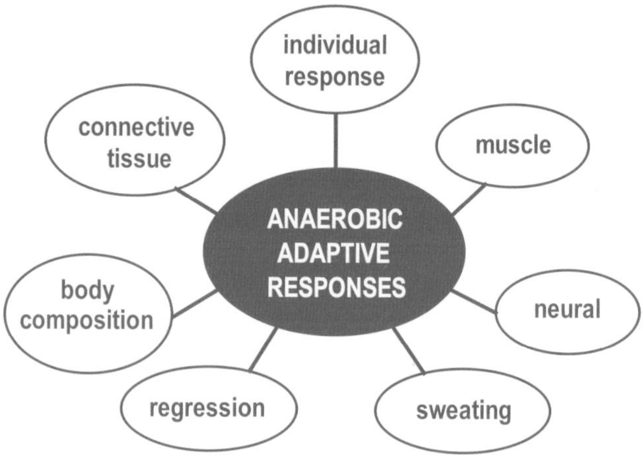

Individual response

Adaptive response to anaerobic training depends on the individual:

- Fitness.
- Cultural differences.
- Gender.
- Psychological factors.
- Maturation.

figure 23.6 – adaptations produced by anaerobic training

Sweating as an adaptation to training

As training continues, **heat energy** is produced as a **side product of the metabolic process**, and the need to lose this energy (and avoid heat stroke or hyperthermia) becomes greater. So the sportsperson develops an improved ability to sweat, hence with more efficient heat loss.

Regression

It is a well established principle of training that when training stops, adaptive responses cease. The longer the training the more stable the adaptation produced by the training - the longer the adaptation remains in the person's body and (for example) his or her strength remains high.

Muscle cell adaptations

Table 23.2 – **adaptations produced by anaerobic exercise**

adaptations to muscle cells produced by anaerobic exercise
fast twitch muscle **hypertrophy** - increase in size by increased cross sectional area of a muscle
increase in the number of **myofibrils** within each muscle cell
increase in the **sarcoplasmic** volume within each cell
increase in the size and strength of the contractile proteins, **actin and myosin**, leading to increase in the mass of fast twitch fibres
increase in the number of fast twitch muscle fibres (**hyperplasia**), which means that the proportion of type II muscle fibre increases and the proportion of type I decreases
increase in muscle **cell stores** of substances such as ATP, PC, and glycogen, and increase in anaerobic enzymes such as creatine kinase (CK), PFK, GPP, and LDH, which makes the muscle stronger and more powerful
improved toleration of **lactate** in fast twitch fibres, and improved ability to remove lactate from muscle cell into blood - which enhances lactate thresholds and **reduces OBLA**
increased rate of response of **CNS** (Central Nervous System), **recruitment** of additional **fast twitch** fibre motor units, improved co-ordination of fast twitch fibre motor units
toughening of **proprioceptors** so that more force is required to stimulate inhibitory signals, an improved agonist/antagonist response
reduction of **delayed onset muscle soreness (DOMS)**
reciprocal innervation, in which **antagonist action is reduced** without conscious effort as a sportsperson performs a powerful movement (using agonists as prime movers) this leads to a small **increase in strength** of the performer in learned and **specific** movements

Improved lactate handling enhances alactic/lactate and lactate/aerobic thresholds, and causes a delay in the onset of blood lactate accumulation (**OBLA**). These processes enable an improved capacity of alactic (ATP-PC) and lactic acid systems to resynthesise ATP, and hence to deliver energy more rapidly. Also there would be increases in maximum possible peak power, and the ability to maintain maximal power output for longer. There would be a decrease in delayed onset muscle soreness (**DOMS**), particularly following eccentric training.

The adaptations in which more muscle fibres are recruited within an activity will better utilise fast twitch muscle fibres at their existing level before hypertrophy occurs. Initial measured strength gains are almost exclusively via this process.

figure 23.7 – a female bodybuilder with muscle hypertrophy

STUDENT NOTE

The adaptive response depends on an individual's fitness, cultural norms, gender, psychological preparedness and state of maturation. Given that anaerobic training will have the above effects, the outcomes will vary between individuals. Particularly, female athletes will acquire muscle hypertrophy if exposed to high intensity anaerobic exercise (figure 23.7).

figure 23.8 – body composition changes due to training

can he 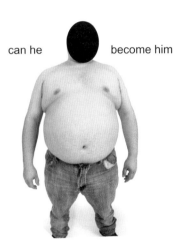 become him  with anaerobic training?

Body composition changes due to strength training

Anaerobic training can result in:
- Loss or increase in total body mass (depending on the training regime used and whether male or female).
- **Loss of fat mass**.
- Losses in relative fat (see figure 23.8).
- Gains in fat free mass (FFM).

Females gain much less in FFM than males due to hormonal differences:
- The presence of **testosterone** in males causes an androgenic effect (the building of muscle mass in males).

The **change** of body mass depends on total energy expenditure.

A strength training programme

- **Assess** your strength levels using the 1RM method for specific exercises.
- Determine your **strength goals**, such as leg strength for cycling or shoulder strength for swimming.
- Consider your **time constraints** - time of day/days available/times per day.
- Look at your **exercise preference** - could be general or sport specific.
- Consider the **type of training** (free weights, multigym, plyometrics) you need to do.
- Consider what **facilities** are available to you such as a gym, or availability of medicine balls or free weights at home.
- Apply relevant **training principles** such as progression, overload, duration, frequency, intensity and variance.
- Place basic elements within a session such as warm-up, work-out and cool-down.

Table 23.3 – **weight training programme for novice jumper**

sessions	programme
day 1	bench press, power clean, 6 sets of 6 at 70% (of 1RM) to 6 sets of 4 at 90% at week 5
day 3	trunk exercises (6 exercises) 6 sets of 20 plyometrics (5 exercises), 6 sets of 10 (jumps), height of jumps increasing over 5 weeks
day 5	full squat, power snatch, 6 sets of 5 at 65% to 6 sets of 3 at 95% at week 5

Table 23.4 – **training methods examples, advantages and disadvantages**

training method	examples	advantages	disadvantages
continuous training	**alternative activities:** 30 km bike ride 3 km run 30 minute swim	trains cardiovascular and muscular endurance, needs no specialist equipment, highly suitable for fat burning metabolism/weight loss, time efficient can be sport-specific, can be assessed using methods such as the exercising heart rate less chance of injury because of lower intensity workloads	can lead to tedium may not be sport-specific, for example usefulness for fencers?
fartlek	**continuous activity:** 10 minutes jogging 6 x 20 seconds fast striding with 60 seconds walk recovery 5 minutes jogging 2 uphill runs, jog down recovery 5 minutes jogging	beneficial to games players where the demands of the game are constantly changing develops both aerobic and anaerobic capacities	
intermittent or interval training	**endurance interval training for a 5000m runner:** **session 1:** 4 x 1500m @ 80% pace with 5 min rest relief (recovery period) **session 2:** 20 x 400m in 65 seconds (s) with 20 s rest relief **session 3:** 3 x (8 x 200m) with 30s rest relief between reps and 5min rest relief between sets	versatile training method since it can be used in almost any activity (sport specific) effective in establishing levels of required fitness for both anaerobic and aerobic activities individual able to perform more work during session due to rest periods or intervals between sets	can lead to over-training and chronic injury (chronic repetitive trauma), because of the repetitive nature and higher training intensity takes more time to complete session because of rest periods
weight training **free weights or multigym**	**example:** athlete selects 2 exercises from each group, (shoulders & arms/trunk & back/legs/all body) working at 85% of 1RM 4 sets of 5 repetitions 2 minutes recovery/ rest relief between sets this session stresses the ATP-PC energy system & so will enhance the PC muscle stores and create **muscle hypertrophy**	can be sport-specific trains cardiovascular, muscular strength and strength endurance easy to measure improvements from previous sessions **multigym** provides a safe training machine with easily adjustable resistance, good for inexperienced trainers, no need to worry about technique refinement	needs access to equipment issues of safety using equipment can cause chronic injuries through repetitive impact **multigym** usually provides restricted joint range depending on size of performer very expensive
circuit training	**8 station circuit:** each circuit performed 3 times: star jumps, rope climb, v-sit-ups, alternate dumbbell press, shuttle runs, chinnies, step ups, bench dips performer works for 60 seconds at each station on 1st circuit, 30 seconds at each station on 2nd circuit and 15 seconds at each station on final circuit	can be sport specific trains cardiovascular, muscular strength and strength endurance enables a large number of participants to train together easy to measure improvements from previous sessions - for example counting the number of repetitions achieved in the time period time efficient	needs access to equipment can cause chronic injuries through repetitive impact
plyometrics	**jumping example:** depth jumping from a box and rebounding quickly from impact point, 2 foot bounds over a flight of hurdles, bounding exercises 3-5 sets of 3-10 repetitions with medium recovery (1-3 minutes)	maximises muscular development by improving power/elastic strength can be very sport specific, for example in explosive take-off as when jumping and bounding in events such as triple jumping	because of the repetitive nature, can cause chronic repetitive trauma injuries such as Achilles tendinosis, patellar tendinosis and shin splints because of vigorous nature of exercise, can cause acute injuries such as sudden ruptures of muscle, tendons and ligaments particularly to vulnerable knee and ankle joints (such as a sprained ankle)
mobility training	**dedicated session after intense specific training session:** choose 10 exercises covering all joints/body areas 4 sets of 10 seconds hold at each exercise	helps prevent potential injury sport specific mobility training can improve performance, for example extreme spinal flexibility is needed by elite high jumpers when performing the flight phase of the Fosbury flop, or elite gymnasts performing floor or beam moves	can lead to hyper-flexibility and reduce effectiveness of muscle strength extreme range of motion isn't necessary in many sports activities - how flexible must long distance runners be? since they don't raise their knees very high or extend their hips very far!

Practice questions

1) a) Define the fitness components of strength, static strength and strength endurance. How does each component relate to athletic performance? **6 marks**

   b) Identify and describe a valid and reliable test that measures either strength or strength endurance. **3 marks**

2) Individuals respond to a given training programme in different ways and to different extents. Identify some of the factors that affect strength. **6 marks**

3) Discuss the various forms of interval training programmes a sports performer may use within their training programme. Identify the advantages and disadvantages of each type of interval training that you have selected and indicate the sport or event most likely to benefit from each one. **20 marks**

4) a) The graph in figure 23.9 illustrates neural and hypertrophic adaptations that have occurred in skeletal muscle tissue following 60 weeks of strength training. Explain why early increases in strength are more associated with neural adaptations, but later long-term gains are almost solely the result of muscle hypertrophy. **6 marks**

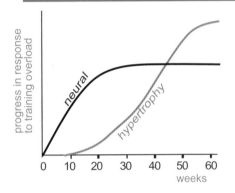

figure 23.9 – anaerobic adaptations to high intensity exercise

   b) What effect would a strength-training programme have on anaerobic capacity and muscle fatigue? **4 marks**

   c) How could these strength gains be used in the planning of a strength-training schedule for an elite power performer? **3 marks**

5) Study table 23.5 which outlines some interval training regimes for the training of different fitness components in a track athlete.

   a) Briefly explain the meaning and purpose of the term 'set' in interval training. **4 marks**

   b) What important information is missing from these outline interval training regimes? **3 marks**

   c) Select two of the regimes in the table and briefly explain how their particular fitness components respond to such training. **8 marks**

Table 23.5 – **interval training regime**

component	training regime
alactic anaerobic	3 x (10 x 50m)
lactic anaerobic	2 x (3 x 400m)
aerobic	1 x (3 x 1000m)

6) a) Plyometric training is a type of power training, which involves performing exercises with maximum power and speed. Describe the main concepts of plyometric training, illustrating your answer with an example of an exercise. Identify the type of sports performer who would most benefit from this training method. **6 marks**

   b) Discuss the advantages and disadvantages of plyometric training. **4 marks**

   c) Why does muscle soreness (DOMS) often occur following a plyometric training session and how could muscle soreness be reduced? **4 marks**

7) a) Describe an appropriate interval training session for a specific component of fitness in a named sport. **3 marks**

   b) Discuss the advantages of using interval training in both aerobic and anaerobic training programmes. **3 marks**

CHAPTER 24 – FLEXIBILITY and BODY COMPOSITION

Flexibility

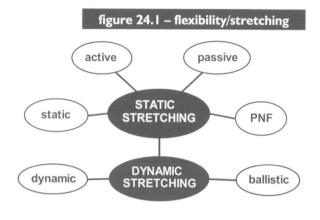

figure 24.1 – flexibility/stretching

Flexibility – stretching

- The **aim** of flexibility training is to improve (or maintain) the **range of motion** over which muscles can act and joints can operate. In simple language this can be expressed as how far you can reach, bend and turn.

- **Joint flexibility** depends on the distensibility of the joint capsule, adequate warm-up, muscle viscosity and the compliance of ligaments and tendons.

- **Gender**, **ageing** and **body composition** affect flexibility, females are generally more flexible, older people are less flexible, and obese people tend to be less flexible (mostly because the extra mass gets in the way!).

- Flexibility is improved by stressing all these components. The effect produced is based on the **stress-overload** principle by forcing the contractile tissues such as muscle tissue to operate at full stretch.

- Mobility work is best done at the end of an anaerobic training session, during cool-down. This is because the muscular system is usually more relaxed at this time, with muscle temperatures slightly higher than during the warm-up.

figure 24.2 – hold this static stretch

Types of stretching and flexibility exercises

There are **two** main types of stretching (figure 24.1):

- **Static**.
- **Dynamic**.

Static stretching

Static stretching refers to stretching exercises that are performed **without movement**. In other words, the individual gets into a stretch position and **holds** the stretch for a specific amount of time.

Static stretching is performed by placing the body in a position **whereby the muscle to be stretched is under tension**. At this point the position is held to allow the muscle to lengthen. This is a very safe and effective form of stretching with a limited threat of injury. See figure 24.2 as an example of a static stretch.

figure 24.3 – active stretch

Active stretching

Active stretching is **slow stretching** in which flexibility is achieved **without assistance**. This form of stretching involves using only the strength of the opposing muscles (antagonist) to generate a held stretch (held for 10-15 seconds) within the agonist. The contraction of the opposing muscles helps to relax the stretched muscles. See figure 24.3 as an example of an active stretch. Active stretching is a very effective form of conditioning.

figure 24.4 – passive stretch

Passive stretching

Passive stretching is similar to static stretching, however a **partner** or **apparatus** can be used to help further stretch the muscles or joints. Figure 24.4 is an example of a passive stretch in which the floor is assisting the position.

Dynamic stretching

Dynamic stretching refers to stretching exercises that are performed with **movement** and are classified depending on the vigorousness of the bounce. Dynamic stretching uses a **controlled**, **soft bounce** or **swinging movement**, that moves a particular body part to the limit of its range of movement and is a preferred method over ballistic stretching.

Ballistic stretching

figure 24.5 – ballistic stretch

- **Ballistic stretching** involves **aggressive**, **dynamic** or **rapid**, **bouncing** or **swinging** movements during which the contraction of the agonist forces the antagonist to relax. Ballistic stretching fails to allow the stretched muscle time to adapt to the stretched position and instead may cause the muscle to tighten up by repeatedly triggering the stretch reflex.

- Ballistic stretching should be **used towards the end of a warm-up** because the muscle temperatures are slightly higher than at the start of the warm-up phase.

- Ballistic stretching is considered to be an outdated form of stretching because of its vigorous nature and risk of muscle tear injury. Activities such as trampolining rely on ballistic stretching during routine work such as a ten-bounce routine. Figure 24.5 shows a side-to-side swinging movement aimed at stretching the lower trunk muscles.

STUDENT NOTE

Note that the **aim** of stretching training is to initiate anaerobic adaptive changes which involve the neuromuscular system, particularly reciprocal innervation (in which the antagonist action at a joint is inhibited), and **toughening of proprioceptors** so that more force is required to stimulate inhibitory signals. **Sensory organs**, such as Golgi tendons and muscle spindles (within the muscle belly), will become **less sensitive** which would allow **large muscle forces** to develop in a given muscle as a joint is stretched to its limit, which in an untrained person could cause injury.

STUDENT NOTE

figure 24.6 – PNF

The force of the contraction should be relevant to the condition of the muscle. For example, if the muscle has been injured, do not apply a maximum contraction.

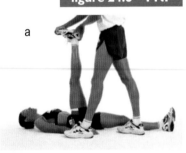

a

Proprioceptive Neuromuscular Facilitation (PNF)

PNF is a progression on passive stretching, whereby after a stretch is held, the muscle is contracted **isometrically** for **between 6-10 seconds**. It then **relaxes** and is **contracted** again, usually going further the second time. This is known as the **CRAC** method (Contract-Relax-Antagonist-Contract).

This method is best described in **three** stages:

Stage 1:
- The athlete and partner assume the position for the stretch (figure 24.6a), then the partner extends the body limb until the muscle is stretched and tension is felt.

Stage 2:
- The athlete then contracts the stretched muscle isometrically for 5-6 seconds and the partner must inhibit all movement (figure 24.6b).

b

Stage 3:
- The muscle group is relaxed, then immediately and cautiously pushed past its normal range of movement (figure 24.6c) for about 6 seconds.

Allow 30 seconds recovery before repeating the procedure 2-4 times.

The aim of PNF is to **toughen** up or inhibit proprioceptors (such as **muscle spindles and Golgi tendons**) in the relaxation of muscle tissue.

This is a **long-term** adaptation.

c

Evaluating flexibility

To assess the flexibility of an individual, measurements can be made, for example, the red arrow in figure 24.7a.

The goniometer

A goniometer is a device containing a 180° protractor for measuring the maximum angle turned through by the bones at a joint, which is then a measure of the flexibility of the joint. The centre of a goniometer is positioned at the axis of rotation of the joint, and the arms of the goniometer (figure 24.7b) are aligned with the long axis of the two bones which articulate at the joint.

figure 24.7 – flexibility measurements

a   sit and reach test

b   goniometer measuring shoulder mobility

Physiological adaptations caused by flexibility training

- Limited stretching of soft tissues such as **ligaments** and **tendons** will cause an increase in resting or residual length.

- Stretching o**f skeletal muscle tissue** causes an **inhibition** of the stretch reflex within the particular muscle.
- As muscle spindles lengthen, the stretch reflex limits flexibility, therefore this inhibition would improve flexibility.

Training programmes for flexibility

- **Assess** your flexibility using the sit and reach test for example.
- Determine your **flexibility goals**, such as hip mobility for a gymnast.
- Consider your **time constraints** - time of day/days available/times per day.
- Look at your **exercise preference** - could be general or sport specific.
- Consider the **type of training** (static, passive, ballistic or active) you need to do.
- Consider what **facilities** are available to you such as a gym, or availability of a carpet at home!
- Apply relevant **training principles** such as progression, overload, duration, frequency, intensity and variance.
- Place basic elements within a session such as warm-up, work-out and cool-down.

Table 24.1 – **flexibility training programme for a novice athlete**

sessions	programme
day 1	during cool-down, static stretching (6 exercises), 6 repetitions at each exercise, hold end point for 6 seconds, 15 second rest between repetitions
day 3	during warm-up, ballistic stretching (6 exercises) 6 sets of 20 performed in a circuit
day 5	separate session, active stretching or PNF (10 exercises), 6 repetitions at each exercise, hold end point for 6 seconds, 15 second rest between repetitions for PNF, hold end point for 6 seconds, relax, then force past end point for a further 3 seconds

Body composition

Body composition has two basic components (figure 24.8):

- **Body fat** or accumulated adipose tissue.
- **Lean body mass** or the fat-free mass (FFM), including the mass of other tissues such as muscle, bone and skin.

Measurement of the **proportion of body fat is** one of the measures of physical fitness. There are many methods that are used to assess body composition.

figure 24.8 – body composition

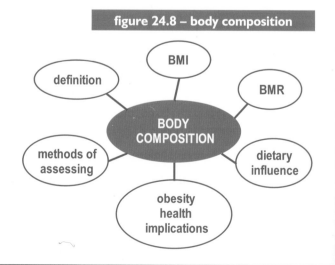

BMI

definition

BMR

BODY COMPOSITION

methods of assessing

dietary influence

obesity health implications

Body composition assessment

Table 24.2 – **methods of assessing body composition**

test	description	advantages	disadvantages
skinfold	skinfold is taken at 3 sites on the body using calipers % body fat read off Jackson Pollock Nomogram	easy test to administer, can get a gender and age related value for % body fat	measurements may not be taken at the correct anatomical site correct pinching of skin needs teaching
BIA	**bioelectrical impedance analysis**: sends a low safe electrical current through the body relies on fat having more resistance (impedance) than muscle tissue % body fat read off depending on gender, height, athletic status	very easy to administer to get a predicted value of % body fat	result depends on the moisture of the skin
underwater weighing	performer is weighed in air, then reweighed completely immersed in water while fully breathed out difference between the two measurements is related to % body fat	relies on the fact that fat is less dense than muscle tissue	person gets wet, and requires a large container within which the subject can be completely immersed
body scanner body-pod	the body scanner and body-pod gives a direct reading of % body composition	direct method with very accurate results	very expensive and only available at a central laboratory slight radiation risk with scanner

Body mass index (BMI)

Body mass index is now the most widely used clinical standard to estimate obesity. To determine a person's BMI, body weight in kilograms is divided by the square of the body height in metres. For example, a person weighing 104 kg and 1.83m tall would have a BMI $= \dfrac{104}{1.83^2} = \dfrac{104\,kg}{3.35\,m^2} = 31\,kg/m^2$

BMI values are divided into five categories: underweight, normal weight, overweight, obese and morbidly obese.

Table 24.3 – **BMI classification and disease risk**

BMI	classification	disease risk
<19	underweight	normal
19-25	normal	normal
26-29	overweight	increased
30-39	obese	high
>40	morbidly obese	extreme

This classification system is a major contribution to our understanding of the true prevalence of overweight and obese conditions, and in predicting percent body fat in a typical category. As in the calculation above almost all people with a BMI of 30 or higher are obese.

Its **weakness** is the fact that it ignores the factor of body-frame size and it is prone to errors in lean athletes such as power athletes and in older persons.

Metabolic rates, energy output

Basal metabolic rate (BMR)

The **BMR** is the **least rate of energy usage** needed to carry out **basic body functions**, and would be measured while lying down after 8 hours sleep or 12 hours fasting.

Typical values for men and women at 20 years of age are:

BMR$_{male}$ = **100 kJ kg^{-1} per day**   **BMR**$_{female}$ = **90 kJ kg^{-1} per day**
BMR$_{male}$ = **0.069 kJ kg^{-1} min^{-1}**   **BMR**$_{female}$ = **0.063 kJ kg^{-1} min^{-1}**

Instead of BMR, most researchers now use the term **resting metabolic rate** (RMR) because most measurements follow the same conditions required for measuring BMR. Hence BMR and RMR values are essentially the same. RMR values are measured 3 to 4 hours following a light meal.

Basal metabolic rate

Establishing basal values provides the important energy baseline for constructing a sound programme of weight control by use of diet, exercise or the effective combination of both.

The total energy expended during a day is determined by the influence of 3 factors:

- **Resting metabolic rate** (RMR) that includes basal and sleeping conditions plus the added cost of arousal estimated between 60 to 75% of daily energy expenditure. It typically ranges from 4,600 to 10,500 kJ per day.

- **Thermogenic influence** of food consumed which accounts for the extra energy needed for digestion, absorption and transport of the nutrients to body cells, and represents 10% of the energy (in kJ) in food consumed. Also known as the **specific dynamic action** (SDA).

- **Energy expended** during and in recovery from physical activity above the resting state.

Therefore:

a person's **total metabolic rate (TMR) = all energy requirements for activity + RMR + SDA**

Table 24.4 – **metabolic rate contribution by different activities**

activity	energy expenditure (kJ kg^{-1} min^{-1}) over BMR
sitting at rest	0.10
walking	0.26
jogging and swimming (moderate)	0.6
cycling (moderate)	0.46
vigorous exercise	1.09

When daily activity is added the value of TMR rises from 7,140 to 13,020 kJ per day depending on the intensity and duration of the activity.

A typical example for a female athlete of mass 56 kg is set out in table 24.5 below.

Table 24.5 – **total daily energy calculation**

activity	duration of activity (minutes)	energy expenditure (kJ kg^{-1} min^{-1}) over BMR	total energy (kJ) for body mass
sitting at rest	480	0.10	2688
walking	230	0.26	3349
swimming	30	0.6	1008

+RMR	5080
+SDA	1213
total MR	13338

Metabolic equivalent task (MET) system

Exercise intensity can also be measured on the basis of the **MET system** in which it is assumed that the amount of oxygen the body consumes is directly proportional to the energy expended per kilogramme per minute.

The resting metabolic rate (as in sitting at rest) is referred as 1.0 MET. So an activity that is rated as a 2 MET activity (such as slow walking) would require double the resting metabolic rate or 7 millilitres of oxygen per kilogramme per minute (7 ml O_2 kg^{-1} min^{-1}). Moderate jogging or swimming requires 15 METs, and very vigorous exercise could be as much as 30 METs. Hence activity intensities can be classified by their oxygen requirements as multiples of the resting metabolic rate.

Although the MET system is a useful guideline for training, it fails to account for changes in environmental conditions or changes in physical conditioning.

Energy intake

STUDENT NOTE

You need to be able to estimate and critically evaluate your own diet by counting energy intake. This can be achieved by recording details of all food and drink taken in during a 24-hour period. List the food eaten and the amounts. The energy values can be calculated using standardised food energy tables.

To critically evaluate your diet, compare your energy intake with your energy output.

Ideally if you are hoping to maintain your current body weight and keep it constant you should have a **neutral energy balance**:

energy input = energy output

In addition you may wish to consider what you are eating and compare your daily food selection with the recommended proportions of the different food groups illustrated in figure 24.10, the food pyramid.

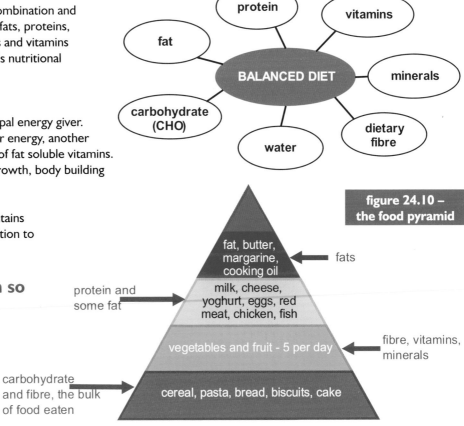

figure 24.9 – balanced diet

A balanced diet

A **balanced diet** (figure 24.9) is the combination and proportions of carbohydrates (CHO), fats, proteins, roughage, water and essential minerals and vitamins which best provide for a sportsperson's nutritional requirements.

A **balanced diet** should contain:

- **60% carbohydrate** as the principal energy giver.
- **20-25% fats** used as a storage for energy, another source of energy and as a carrier of fat soluble vitamins.
- **10-15% proteins** essential for growth, body building and repair.

It is important to have a diet that maintains appropriate weight and body composition to maximise physical performance.

figure 24.10 – the food pyramid

Why is body composition so important?

The following table 24.6 shows how the body fat content for people of various age groups depends on whether they are fit or not. The data takes us up to 40 years of age.

Table 24.6 – **example data of relative body fat values for untrained and trained males and females**

	relative body fat (%)			
	untrained		trained	
age group	**females**	**males**	**females**	**males**
15-19	20-24	13-16	12-20	7-13
20-29	22-25	15-20	10-18	6-12
30-39	24-30	18-26	12-20	8-14

STUDENT NOTE

The **average body fat** for **untrained females** is about 8% higher than untrained males. However, **trained females** are exceptionally lean and their relative body fat values are **well below** those values for untrained males. Therefore **females** can **reduce fat stores** well below what is considered normal for their age.

Untrained males and females have increased body fat when they get older, whereas trained people (both sexes) remain lean.

Optimal body mass

The achievement of optimal body mass will require manipulation of the **energy balance**. When energy input and output are balanced (**energy input = energy output**), a person's body mass will be stable, with no tendency to add to or subtract from stored adipose tissue.

It is important to have a diet that maintains appropriate mass and body composition to maximise physical performance.

Controlling excess body mass

The only method of controlling (reducing) excess body mass is to shift the energy relationship so that energy output exceeds energy intake, known as a **negative energy balance** and expressed as:

$$energy\ output > energy\ intake$$

Causes and health implications of obesity

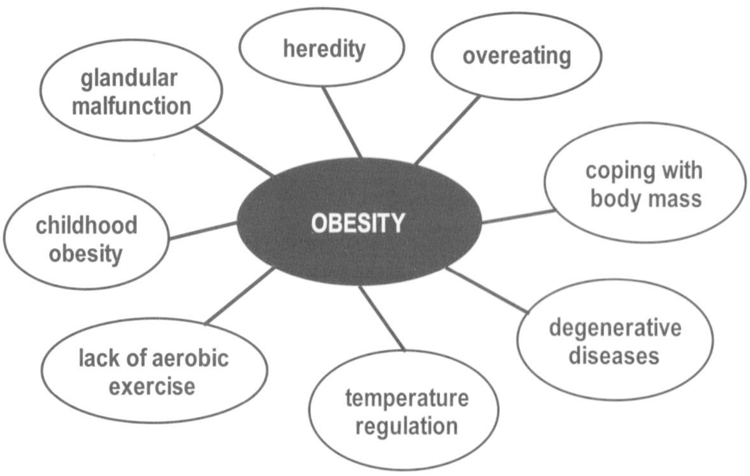

- The major cause of obesity (figure 24.11) for most people is a **positive energy balance**, i.e. energy intake is greater than energy output. This means **overeating**.
- Excess carbohydrate (CHO) is stored as **glycogen**. When glycogen stores are filled, CHO together with excess fat intake, are converted to fatty acids and glycerol, and then stored as triglycerides or fat in adipose tissue.

- These **fat stores** are situated around major organs such as the heart and stomach, underneath the skin, and in skeletal muscle.

- **Overindulgence in food** is also associated with psychological, social and cultural factors. For example, the overeater may eat in an attempt to relieve anxieties.

- **Heredity,** you inherit your body type from your parents i.e. lean, muscular or fat.

- **Glandular malfunction**, a small percentage of obese people suffer from a glandular malfunction, which results in a hormonal imbalance in the body and tends to create adipose tissue abnormally.

- **Childhood obesity**. It has been shown that childhood obesity is strongly linked to adult obesity, which means that the fat child grows into a fat adult! This is because the development of fat cells begins during the first 2 years of life, and numbers of fat cells in young overfed children may proliferate to five times the normal number of cells.
- So, as the child grows, she/he may have thousands of extra fat cells just waiting to fill with fat. In the adult the number of fat cells remains constant but the cells increase in size as weight is gained. Once this weight is gained it will be maintained unless a negative energy balance is achieved.

- **Lack of aerobic exercise**. There is strong evidence to suggest that overweight children and adults are far less active (figure 24.12) than their thinner counterparts. Obesity has the long-term effect of limiting the mobility of joints, thus restricting the person's ability to co-ordinate movement. It also places an additional strain on the cardiovascular and respiratory systems, as described earlier.

- **Endurance and speed** are impaired as a result of weight gain.

- A combination of physical and **psychological** factors (such as **poor self-esteem**, **learned helplessness** caused by repeated failure at sporting activities and unwillingness to expose the body to the scrutiny of others) often **inhibit** the person from participating in sport and leisure activities.

figure 24.11 – causes and health implications of obesity

heredity

overeating

glandular malfunction

coping with body mass

OBESITY

childhood obesity

degenerative diseases

lack of aerobic exercise

temperature regulation

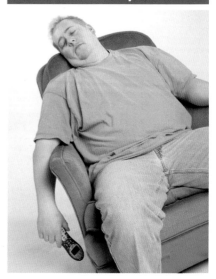

figure 24.12 – obesity and inactivity

Serious health implications

Obesity increases the risk of certain chronic degenerative diseases such as:

- Coronary artery disease.
- High blood pressure or hypertension.
- Coronary and cerebral thrombosis.
- Elevated blood lipids or atherosclerosis.
- Mature diabetes.
- Metabolic syndrome.
- Respiratory problems.
- Joint overload and limited flexibility such as backache and damage to joint structures and associated osteoarthritis (refer to AS Revise PE for OCR ISBN 978 1 901424 52 2 page 31).

Also obesity can worsen pre-existing health conditions and diseases, as well as creating adverse psychological reactions and reducing the urge to be physically active.

Obesity and physical activity

Obese people have difficulty in **regulating heat loss** and hence **body temperature**.

This is because the excess **adipose tissue** layer under the skin, and a **decrease in sweat gland density** make it much harder for the vascular system to remove waste heat energy.

These factors result in **heart overload** and **increased respiratory** functioning, to keep pace with the increases in total metabolic functioning.

> **STUDENT NOTE**
>
> **Adipose tissue** acts as an insulating barrier to heat conduction from the body core to the skin, where it would be radiated off to the surroundings or lost by convection and evaporation.
> Therefore, when exercising, an obese person would become unduly hot and uncomfortable, and require extra cooling methods such as ice packs or cold drinks.
>
> Conversely, the same layer helps keep obese people warm in winter!

Short and long-term effects of aerobic exercise

- **Exercise reduces obesity** by burning off excess fat during and after activity when the body's metabolic rate remains elevated.
- For example, an increase of energy output of approximately 5000 kJ per day through exercise, will burn off 1 kg of body fat in 1 week.

- The result of such an **excess of energy output** through exercise, against input via food, is a steady progressive long-term weight loss.

- **Cardiac workload** (hence risk of CHD - coronary heart disease) is less with a lower body mass. The capability to move around (walk, run and climb) is therefore better with a lower body mass. This is because a person's strength to weight ratio increases, as he or she becomes lighter.

- Exercise relieves symptoms of **osteoarthritis** as flexibility of joints improves.

Refer to page 139 above for more specific long-term aerobic adaptations.

Practice questions

1) a) Stretching is a key element in any warm-up. Using an example, identify two other elements of a warm-up and explain how they help to prepare an athlete. 4 marks

   b) Describe three different methods of stretching and state a sport that would benefit most from each type. 6 marks

   c) Identify two physiological adaptations to skeletal tissue following a three-month flexibility training programme. 2 marks

2) a) Give two advantages of using static stretching within a flexibility programme. 2 marks

   b) Identify two structural limitations to muscle flexibility. 2 marks

3) You have been asked to prepare a flexibility training programme for a group of A-level Physical Education students who wish to improve their flexibility for their chosen individual activity.

   a) Identify key factors that would need to be considered during the planning of the programme.   4 marks

   b) Outline the content of a basic programme that aims to achieve an increase in flexibility for these students.   4 marks

4) What is meant by the term body composition? There are several field techniques for estimating body composition. Describe and evaluate the use of skinfold fat thickness measurements, identifying one strength and one weakness of this technique.
                                                                                                                       6 marks

5) a) What is meant by the expression 'an ideal body weight'. List two ways in which it can be determined?   3 marks

   b) Define body mass index (BMI). How does this concept assist in the understanding of the changing patterns of body composition?   3 marks

6) a) What is a balanced diet and suggest the proportion of carbohydrates, fats and proteins a 17 year old person should eat in order to maintain a physically active lifestyle?   4 marks

   b) Briefly describe an outline for a week's exercise programme that would be maintain a physically active lifestyle for a 17 year old student. In your answer identify the major fitness components to be stressed.   8 marks

7) What do you understand by 'healthy eating' and how can this concept be applied to dieting?   4 marks

8) Identify some of the health implications of being obese.   4 marks

9) How can exercise be used as a means of weight control?   4 marks

10) What are the causes and physical effects of obesity on health, based on energy considerations? How can an obese person reduce body mass and best monitor their progress to achieve this aim?   20 marks

CHAPTER 25 – APPLICATION of the PRINCIPLES of TRAINING

Principles of training

The **aims** and **objectives** of training are to improve performance, skill, game ability and motor and physical fitness. Repeated days of training can be considered as positive stress because training improves one's capacity for energy production, tolerance of physical stress and exercise performance. A well-designed training programme follows a set of guidelines called '**principles of training**' (figure 25.1).

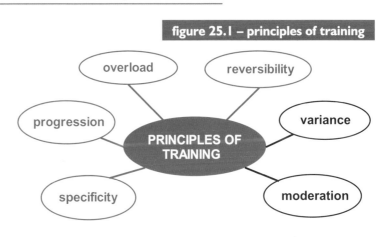

figure 25.1 – principles of training

Specificity

Specificity is defined as '**the relevance of the choice of exercise to the activity to be improved**'.

Choices to be made involve energy demands, strength, power, endurance and skill. This notion is thought to be very important for high performance in a chosen sport. For example, the shot put event requires speed and power developed by stressing the ATP-PC anaerobic energy system. So, in order to put the shot successfully, the shot putter needs to work on explosive muscular power in training. Hence the training programme must **stress** the **physiological systems** that are critical for optimal performance in the given sport in order to achieve the required specific training adaptations. Similarly, the marathon runner requires endurance which must be obtained by stressing the aerobic energy system. Hence his or her training programme must be largely based on lengthy endurance-based runs.

Overload

Overload is defined as '**training activities that are harder, more intense and/or lengthier than the normal physical activity undertaken by an individual**'.

Overload (figure 25.2) can be achieved by increasing the frequency, intensity or duration of the activity. These terms are also referred to using the acronym '**FITT principles**' described below. Overload places physiological systems under **stress** and the human body responds by becoming more capable of coping with this stress. This training principle applies to muscular endurance as well as to strength and power training.

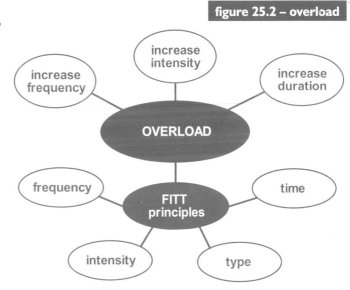

figure 25.2 – overload

The major variables used for increasing or decreasing intensity are:

• Sets.

• Repetitions.

• Resistance.

• Rest relief or recovery period.

For example, an athlete performs bench press: 5 sets of 6 repetitions at 85% of 1RM (one repetition maximum as described above on page 143), and 2 minutes recovery between sets. This exercise would stress the anaerobic fast twitch muscle fibres type IIb of the muscles: anterior deltoid, pectoralis major and triceps brachii.

FITT principles of training

F (frequency) = how often do we train? How often we train will determine the physiological adaptations achieved. For example, the elite professional sportsperson may be required to train twice a day and thereby achieve optimal physiological adaptations and improvements in performance. On the other hand, a person who just wants to stay fit by attending three aerobic classes a week at their local leisure centre, may notice minor physiological changes such as easier breathing and less tendency to be out of breath when digging the garden.

I (intensity) = how hard do we train? For the elite athlete, training intensity will vary depending on the training emphasis in relation to the periodised year. **Periodisation** is a concept centred around a cyclical load design principle, see page 161 opposite.

Intensity of training can be measured scientifically using lactate testing or calculating the respiratory exchange ratio. Field methods of measurement include Karvonen's training heart rate (see page 138 above), weights lifted, or the heart rate maximum method (see page 138 above).

T (type) = what type of training do we do? Type of training relates to the principle of specificity above. Types of training include:

*   Continuous.
*   Intermittent.
*   Circuit.
*   Weights.
*   Plyometrics.
*   Mobility.

(see page 144 onwards for explanations of these types of training)

T (time) = how long do we train for or what is the duration of the activity?
The intensity of training and exercise type often determines the duration of the activity. For example an aerobic or weight-reducing training programme should last for a minimum 30 minutes because of the time it takes for fat burning metabolism to commence. A plyometric workout may only last for 10 minutes before fatigue sets in, whereas an ultra-distance runner may be unlimited by time during a long-distance run.

figure 25.3 – athlete wins a marathon

figure 25.4 – recreational cyclist on a 40 min ride

Progression

Progression is defined as '**a state of moving onwards, which implies an increase in training load as time goes on**'.

The principle of progression involves the gradual application of the overload principle. You should note that progression could occur without overload, but if overload does not happen, then you cannot obtain the necessary adaptations to body systems such as the muscular system, which would cause improvement in (for example) endurance or strength. The key point about progression is that the sportsperson should be performing at a higher level after the training period than before.

Moderation

Successful training programmes will include **moderation**, which implies that note is taken of the sportsperson's state of physical health, and when signs of deteriorating performance are detected, training loads will be reduced and recovery times increased until feelings of tiredness are reduced.

Reversibility

Reversibility is also known as **regression** and is defined as '**when training loads are reduced or removed completely, the state of fitness or performance returns to a normal untrained state**'. This is often summed up as '**use it or lose it**'.

This principle explains why performance deteriorates when training stops or intensity of training is reduced. With reversibility, physiological systems revert or **regress** to their normal untrained state eventually. This will not happen immediately, but research has shown that the process begins within 5 days of ceasing training. Interestingly, it is found that adaptations established by longer periods of training remain for longer after training stops, than those produced by a short period of training.

Variance

Changing activities in training with the specific aim of reducing tedium is called **variance**, and is a crucial feature of a successful training programme.

Training exercises, drills, or games which are the same (with the same outcomes and feelings) week in and week out, will eventually result in a lowering of motivation as the feelings of mastery of the activity are reduced. In other words, the person becomes used to the outcomes of the activity and his or her drive to continue with the same activity reduces. This can be overcome by setting goals for sessions which vary (even though the activity itself may be the same), or completely changing the activity while retaining the same goals (for example goals to improve strength or endurance).

STUDENT NOTE

Warm-up and cool-down are usually considered as essential elements of a training programme, and they are discussed in detail on page 28 of 'AS Revise PE for OCR' ISBN: 978 1 901424 52 2.

Periodisation

Periodisation is a method of training which varies training intensity cyclically, organised in periods and cycles of training. Such cycles of training take place long-term, over time spans of months and years.

Each period within a training plan will have a specific aim or objective within the overall training plan, for example:
- **Period 1** may be aimed at basic conditioning.
- **Period 2** may be aimed at strength development.
- **Period 3** may be aimed at speed development.

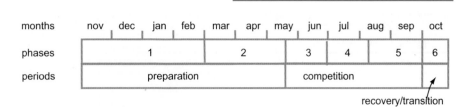

figure 25.5 – a single periodised year

The time intervals within this training method can be defined as follows:
- A **period** is a basic year subdivision between 1 and 6 months.
- A **macrocycle** is a phase lasting between 4 and 26 weeks.
- A **mesocycle** is a phase lasting 2 to 4 weeks which would be part of a macrocycle.
- A **microcycle** is a phase lasting 1 week or less, and is the basic repetitive cycle of activities.

- Sometimes **daily cycles** of up to 3 sessions may be required for elite performers.

Figure 25.5 shows how periods and cycles can be laid out for a whole year. Note that an elite athlete may need a four or five year periodised programme to peak for an Olympic Games.

Planning a periodised training programme
- You will need to utilise the principles of training, decide on general activities, and then decide on specific activities.
- You will need to break down activities into relevance to different energy systems and ensure that this fits the energy system profile for your sport.
- You will next decide on time allocations (**duration**), and decide on the volume of work in a session (**intensity**).

- See figure 25.6 for an example breakdown of training intensity over the days of a microcycle (in this case 7 days long, one week).
- Note that elite athletes who don't need to plan round the working week (most people would have to fit in with school, college or work), often use 5, 6 or 8 day micro cycles to fit in with the time needed to recover from intense training.

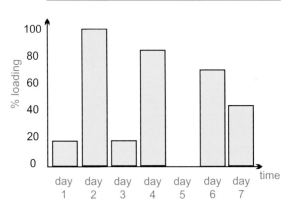

figure 25.6 – variation in training intensity during a microcycle

Planning a periodised training programme
* Decide on how many times in the microcycle you would like to train (**frequency**).
* Set out sets and repetitions within an activity (**repetition**).
* Ensure that **warm-up** and **cool-down** are included.
* Make notes on **progression** for future microcycles.
* Ensure that appropriate rest and **rest relief** is indicated.

Planning mesocycles
* You need to establish your **maximum training intensity** using fitness tests - this is your initial **100%** training intensity.
* Then decide on a **starting point** below this (for example, 80%).
* Then plan a **progressive intensity** mesocycle taking you up to 100% in say 4 weeks (figure 25.7).
* Next plan the subsequent 4-week **cycle** taking you up to 110%.
* With subsequent 4-week cycles taking you up to your planned goal for the year.

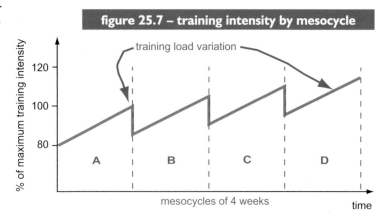

figure 25.7 – training intensity by mesocycle

Alternative methods of periodisation
* The example in figure 25.5 previously is a single periodised year (just one competitive period). The same sort of arrangements can be made for two competitive periods - called a **double periodised year**.

* Figure 25.8 shows the possible layout for a **double periodised** year, the blue vertical line shows the end of the first competitive period.
* At this point the second half of the year (period) begins and the process of structure towards the

figure 25.8 – a double periodised year

months	nov	dec	jan	feb	mar	apr	may	jun	jul	aug	sep	oct
phases	1	2		3	4	5		6		7	8	9
periods	preparation			trans	comp	preparation				trans	comp	

trans = transition   comp = competition   recovery

second competitive period starts. Research has shown that this sort of programme can initiate greater progress in various indicators of fitness (strength, speed, endurance).

Tapering and peaking
* The periodisation method of training enables the coach to vary training intensity and quantity, so that a performer can **peak** for a major games such as the Olympics.
* This peaking usually involves **tapering**, which means that training intensity gradually reduces over a period of up to 14 days beforehand, which enables the athlete to be fresh and full of energy for the big event.

Peaking is partly psychological. How a performer feels about him or herself, and how confidence is flowing, are often as important as the state of fitness or strength.

See page 150 above for details of various training programmes.

Planning a personal health and fitness programme

Planning training
* **Assess** fitness levels using standard fitness tests.
* Determine **fitness goals** such as to improve cardiovascular performance or strength.
* Consider **time constraints**, such as time of day, days available, times per day.
* Look at **exercise preference**, out jogging or in the gym, swimming or playing a game of badminton or squash?
* What **facilities** are available? Gym, track, pool in town, or paths, lanes in the country?
* Apply **training principles**, progression, overload, duration, frequency, intensity, variance and periodisation.
* Place basic elements within a session with warm-up, work-out, cool-down.

A mesocycle example

Table 25.1 – **example exercise programme for general fitness**

day	activity	major fitness component
day 1	45 min run at 60% HR$_{max}$ 15 min stretching	cardiorespiratory endurance flexibility, balance, working major muscle groups
day 2	badminton game 50 min	speed, agility, co-ordination
day 3	30 min weights circuit at local gym light weights, repetition 6-12 1 set at each of eight different exercises	muscular endurance, co-ordination, agility
day 4	rest	
day 5	30 min fartlek 15 min flexibility, active + passive	power, speed, endurance flexibility, balance
day 6	30 min aerobic class	cardiorespiratory endurance
day 7	rest	

Practice questions

1) Explain why you would use the principles of training when developing a training programme to improve the fitness of 16+ physical education students. **8 marks**

2) Periodisation is a training concept that explains the variation in training volume and intensity over a specific period of time. Outline the basic structure of a single periodised year and illustrate how a coach is able to use this structure when planning a training programme for an athletics group. **20 marks**

3) You have been asked to prepare a personal health and fitness programme for a 16 year old student.
   a) Identify key factors that would need to be considered during the planning of the programme. **4 marks**

   b) Provide an example of a 7 day training programme that would be part of a long-term schedule. In your answer identify the major fitness components stressed in each session. **10 marks**

CHAPTER 26 – PERFORMANCE ENHANCEMENT

Ergogenic aids

Sports supplements as ergogenic aids

An **ergogenic aid** is **any substance or method which enhances performance**. This includes any method used in training which has this effect including training equipment and nutrition as well as doping and supplementation.

Ergogenic aids fall into two main categories, **legal** and **illegal**. Figure 26.1 summarises legal sports supplements or methods identified in your syllabus.

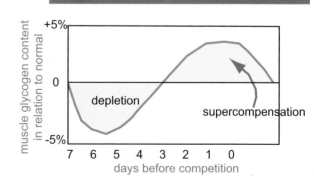

figure 26.1 – sports supplements

caffeine
creatine
sports drinks
SPORTS SUPPLEMENTS
carbo-loading
protein supplements

Carbo-loading

figure 26.2 – carboloading

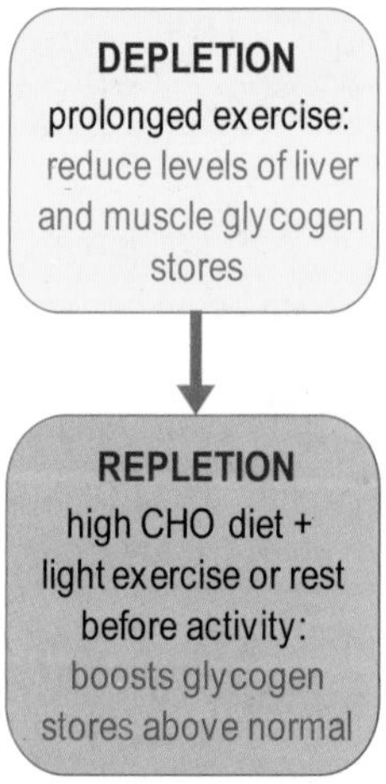

DEPLETION
prolonged exercise: reduce levels of liver and muscle glycogen stores

↓

REPLETION
high CHO diet + light exercise or rest before activity: boosts glycogen stores above normal

Carbo-loading aims to raise muscle glycogen stores above their normal resting levels prior to endurance competitions with over 90 minutes continuous activity. This process is suitable for activities with low anaerobic and high aerobic components.

Figure 26.2 outlines the **depletion-repletion** model upon which carbo-loading is based. It is suitable for any activities lasting longer than 15-20 minutes. Note that a two-day high CHO diet beforehand provides the best CHO boost for an endurance event.

Carbo-loading - glycogen supercompensation

The graph in figure 26.3 shows how the muscle glycogen level returns to above normal values when the **depletion-repletion** process is undertaken as outlined in the previous paragraph. In effect the body reacts to a loss of glycogen by vigorously replacing it to a level above normal. This is a normal reaction to **biological stress**.

figure 26.3 – glycogen supercompensation

muscle glycogen content in relation to normal

+5%

0

-5%

depletion

supercompensation

7 6 5 4 3 2 1 0

days before competition

Pre-competition nutrition

Should consist of:
*   Fluids for hydration.
*   Light complex CHO such as pasta or wholemeal bread at least 3 hours before activity.
*   Fruit (banana) contains complex CHO.
*   Small amounts of glucose.

The effect is to provide the slow release of blood glucose and reduce hunger sensations.

Post-competition or training nutrition

Should consist of:
*   **Hypertonic** sports drink immediately after exercise has finished.
*   This begins **replenishment of blood glucose** and **glycogen** stores.
*   A **high CHO** meal within 15 minutes of exercise ending (or as soon as possible) continues glycogen replenishment.

The importance of high glycogen content in muscle before a marathon race

The graph in figure 26.4 shows that a runner's time would increase by around 10 minutes in a 2 hour run if muscle glycogen started at 50% of its maximum possible. The effect of reduced muscle glycogen begins to be felt at the 1 hour mark. Hence the importance of glycogen loading to endurance sportspeople.

Nutritional dietary manipulation during training

The graph in figure 26.5 shows the influence of dietary carbohydrate on **muscle glycogen** stores. In this training situation, repeated daily exercise of 2 hours is followed by either a high CHO or low CHO diet.

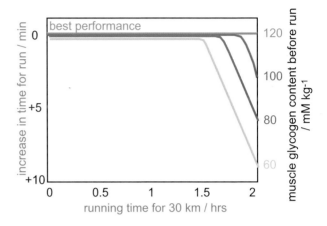

figure 26.4 – effect of glycogen store on endurance running times

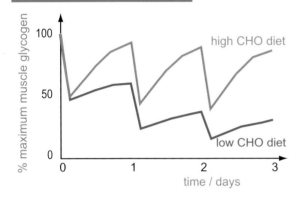

figure 26.5 – the athlete's diet

STUDENT NOTE

Note the difference that high CHO makes to the energy available to the sportsperson, and a major possible reason for exhaustion for those 'on a diet'!

figure 26.6 – Paula Radcliffe will be taking in water throughout a marathon

Water and electrolyte balance

Fluid intake has almost become an obsession with modern sportsmen and women. Modern athletes frequently use isotonic sports drinks, such as Isostar and Red Bull, just prior to competition to maintain rehydration and alertness respectively.

Exercise is thirsty work. Fluid loss during exercise depends on the intensity and duration of the exercise, temperature and humidity, body size and fitness levels. The **longer** and more **intense** the exercise period, for example in a long distance race, the more the need to drink before, during and after the event.

Bearing in mind that water comprises 60% of total body mass, it is important that **water balance** is maintained during exercise. **Water balance** depends on electrolyte balance and vice versa. For optimal performance, the body's water and electrolyte contents should remain relatively constant.

At rest, water loss occurs mainly via the **kidneys** (as urine) along with **excess electrolytes** - sodium and chloride.

Hydration

Water intake will depend on climate and body mass. The modern fashion of carrying water bottles for ready consumption reflects modern concerns about water balance.

During exercise urine production declines as electrolyte loss occurs primarily alongside water loss through sweating. The need to replace body fluid is greater than the need to replace electrolytes, because sweat is very dilute (electrolyte concentration in sweat is much lower than in urine).

Loss of water

- Also, the loss of water raises the osmotic pressure in body fluids because the electrolytes become more concentrated in these body fluids.

- The thirst mechanism does not exactly match the body's hydration state, so more fluid should be consumed than thirst dictates.

- Only by **replenishing water** content can the electrolytes return to normal concentrations.

In extreme exercise situations, for example during a marathon (figure 26.6), 6 to 10% of body water content is lost, hence the need for water intake during exercise. This means that during 1 hour's exercise an average person could expect to lose around 1 litre of fluid, and even more in hot conditions. This could represent as much as 2 litres an hour in warm or humid conditions.

Dehydration and loss of performance

Excessive loss of fluid impairs performance as blood plasma volume decreases and body temperature rises. The graph in figure 26.7 shows how heart rate is affected by **fluid intake** during prolonged exercise. Heart rate rise without fluid intake is explained earlier, but the graph also shows how heart rate is kept constant - if suitable water is taken during the exercise.

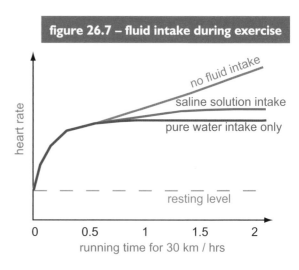

figure 26.7 – fluid intake during exercise

The potential benefits of sports drinks

Sports drinks are designed to supplement energy, fluid and protein needs of the athlete.

When taken during exercise the carbohydrate concentration of a sport drink should not exceed 7% to maximise both sugar and fluid intake and absorption. This is known as an **isotonic** sport drink because the dilute level of glucose is the same level of concentration as in the blood. An isotonic sport drink is an important source of energy during exercise and reduces the risk of dehydration.

During recovery, **hypertonic** drinks contain much higher levels of glucose - up to 20%. This highly concentrated drink is used to replenish depleted glycogen stores and should be drunk as soon as the exercise period has been completed.

Caffeine

- Caffeine **stimulates** the central nervous system thereby reducing reaction times.
- Caffeine acts as a **diuretic**, which can lead to dehydration and heat related conditions.
- Caffeine used to be illegal in large quantities, but the rules changed in 2002, when drinking large amounts of coffee became **legal** again!
- Caffeine is also used as a substance to promote **fat metabolism** and hence to reduce adipose tissue in the elite sportsperson.
- Consuming caffeine before prolonged exercise increases fat metabolism thus **sparing precious glycogen reserves** for later.

- Caffeine produces a state of **nervousness**, and can disrupt normal sleeping patterns therefore contributing to fatigue.
- Abrupt ceasing of caffeine intake can lead to severe headaches.

Alcohol

Alcohol is a relaxant in quite small quantities. It is absorbed into the body as an alternative to water therefore causes dehydration. Quite small quantities of alcohol can cause a drastic loss of performance.
Alcohol is a **legal** ergogenic aid - but anyone using it as such must be aware of the consequences!

Creatine supplementation

Creatine is a substance found in skeletal muscle and which is stored as **phosphocreatine** (PC). Creatine supplementation (usually together with large amounts of CHO) increases PC levels to enhance the ATP-PC system of ATP resynthesis, thereby delaying the alactic/lactic threshold (see page 130 and 131 above). This is a **legal ergogenic aid**.

Creatine supplementation

Sportspeople use creatine in a way which will help improve anaerobic power and lengthen the time over which they can apply maximal power. It is not a muscle development 'drug', and eating lots of raw white meat (as in fish) would have the same effect. This is because white muscle cells (those not containing lots of myoglobin, which is red in colour and is present in large quantities in slow twitch muscle cells) are predominantly fast twitch in nature and contain creatine in relatively large quantities.

Power athletes, such as weight lifters, sprinters, field events athletes, and gymnasts, use in their competitive event a little bit of the ATP-PC system and mostly ATP storage. But almost all the training will be serviced by the ATP-PC system, and therefore creatine supplementation will help the training process.

Creatine supplementation can cause muscle cramps and can be responsible for athlete weight gain.

Protein supplementation

Many athletes regularly consume sports drinks that are designed to supplement the energy, fluid and protein needs of the athlete.
Protein supplements, such as whey protein, are used to increase total protein content of an athletic diet. Sportspeople need more protein than the untrained person to enable muscle hypertrophy and muscle repair following hard training. This particularly applies to sports requiring large muscle mass, as in weight lifting and gymnastics.

Most protein supplements are **legal**, but can cause liver and kidney damage if taken to excess.

Illegal ergogenic aids

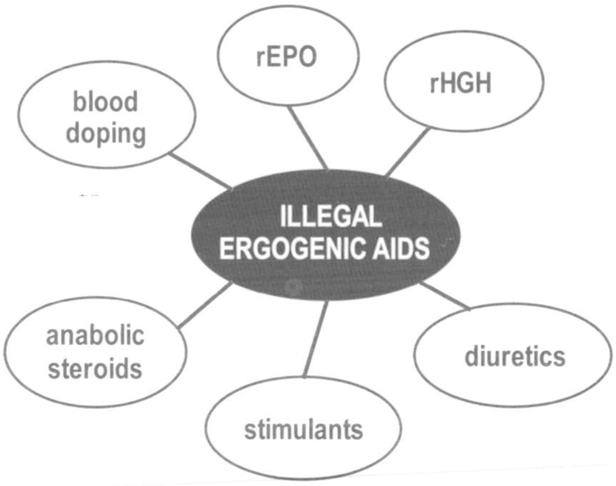

Figure 26.8 summarises the categories of illegal ergogenic aids used by sportspeople, as identified in the syllabus.

figure 26.8 – illegal ergogenic aids

WADA

The **World Anti-Doping Agency (WADA)** is the World body set up in 1998 tasked with enforcing the international regulations on doping or drug taking. WADA aims to bring together governments, the IOC, International Governing Bodies and National Governing Bodies (NGBs) to sort out the difficulties posed by athletes performing on the international stage. This issue was brought to a head at the Athens Olympics 2004, when two of the host nation's best athletes went missing just before the games and a compulsory drug test. These athletes faked a road accident and sought hospitalisation falsely in order to avoid taking the test. The same athletes had a record of going missing from international training venues just before the IAAF drug testers arrived - and even being found registered under false names in hotels so that their **whereabouts** could not be definitely fixed.

WADA has introduced the '**Athlete passport**' which contains an on-going collection of an individual's urine and blood profiles which have so far been collected and tested during the international athlete's performance lifespan. Samples are stored and then made available for retro-testing when appropriate. It is projected that future profile collection could include endocrine information. For futher information go to: www.wada-ama.org/en/dynamic.ch2?pageCategory.id=870

Modern developments

The latest and most insidious attempt by the cheaters is to use **gene doping** to enhance performance. Gene doping is defined by WADA as '**the non-therapeutic use of cells, genes, genetic elements, or of the modulation of gene expression, having the capacity to improve athletic performance**'.

For example, **Insulin-like growth factor 1** (IGF-1) is a protein that is important in promoting the growth of skeletal muscle. Injected into an athlete, a harmless virus, such as IGF-1, could carry a performance-enhancing gene and splice it into a muscle cell to increase muscle mass and achieve increased muscle hypertrophy.

Protein chemicals may be indistinguishable from their natural counterparts. In such cases, nothing unusual would enter the bloodstream so officials would detect nothing in a blood or urine test.

PERFORMANCE ENHANCEMENT

Table 26.1– **the categories of illegal substances used in top level sport today**

type of substance	known ergogenic effects	known health risks
stimulants example: amphetamines	increase alertness, reduce fatigue, increase competitiveness and hostility	can drive competitor beyond safe boundaries can cause lasting tissue and organ damage as well as masking injury are addictive, known to cause death

rHGH
recombinant human growth
hormone cloned through
genetic engineering
	mimics body's naturally occurring hormone
	    HGH produced by the pituitary gland
	    which increases protein synthesis and lean
	    muscle mass
	stimulates bone growth
	increases blood glucose levels
	enhances healing after musculo-skeletal
	    injuries
	used by power athletes such as sprinters,
	    weight lifters, American football players
		muscle joint weaknesses
		acromegaly (giantism) causes bone thickening
		    of hands, feet and jaws
		enlargement of internal organs
		causes glucose intolerance, diabetes,
		    hypertension and heart disease

anabolic steroids
related to naturally occurring
hormone testosterone
example: THG
tetrahydrogestrinone
stanazolol
	increases synthesis of protein within cells
	increases fat free mass, strength and power
	    for aggressive sports such as American
	    football or wrestling
	reduces recovery time between sessions
	increases muscle strength and bulk,
	    promotes aggressiveness
		excessive aggressive behaviour outside the
		    activity
		testicular atrophy in men
		masculinisation in women
		liver damage
		cardiovascular diseases
		causes acne
		causes pituitary failure

blood doping
refers to **any means** by which
a person's total volume of red
blood cells can be increased
often achieved by transfusion
of red blood cells previously
withdrawn from the recipient
	temporarily increases red blood cell count
	    (polycythemia) and hence O_2 carriers,
	    hence increases $\dot{V}O_{2max}$ and energy
	    delivery to enhance aerobic performance
		problem of mismatching can lead to
		    transfusion reaction or allergic reaction
		also runs the risk of hepatitis or HIV pathogen

rEPO
recombinant erythropoietin
cloned through genetic
engineering **is a form of
blood doping**
	mimics body's naturally occurring hormone
	    EPO that stimulates red blood cell
	    production to increase oxygen transport
	    and therefore increases aerobic capacity,
	    hence aids recovery in endurance based
	    activities such as long distance cycling
	    (Tour-de-France) and marathon running
		major risk of thrombosis (blood clot) and
		    heart failure due to increase in blood
		    viscosity
		reduces resting heart rate to dangerously low
		    level during sleep
		
		taking rEPO reduces production of naturally
		    occurring hormone EPO

diuretics
example: bumetanide
	reduce weight quickly
	used by gymnast and combat sports where
	    there are bodyweight categories
	reduce concentration of substances by
	    diluting urine (hence increasing urine
	    flow), also used as a masking agent to
	    dilute concentration of illegal substances
	    in urine
		loss of water leads to dehydration and heat
		    loss impairment
		loss of water-soluble vitamins leads to
		    impaired performances

Other methods of performance enhancement

Cooling aids

Cold therapies (**cryotherapy**) are popular ergogenic aids for cooling core body temperatures. They reduce the effect of delayed onset of muscle soreness (DOMS) and are well established in the treatment of acute sports injuries.

The value of **cold therapy** lies in its ability to decrease cellular metabolism, reduce inflammation, swelling and pain, and promote vasoconstriction. Cold packs do this by absorbing heat from the injury. The more heat absorbed, the faster the pain relief and healing. There are a variety of cooling aids available ranging from ice jackets, wet ice packs, ice gels and chemical packs.

Ice/cooling jackets
Cooling jackets (packed with ice or chemical coolants) are used to attempt to reduce the core temperatures of sports participants in very hot conditions. For example, the Australian rowing eight in the Atlanta Olympic Games 1996 as shown in figure 26.9.

figure 26.9 – use of ice jackets in a competitive situation

Wet-ice packs
Water is a much better conductor of heat energy than air or plastic. By being wet, the wet-ice pack allows for greater heat energy transfer out of the body compared to gel or chemical packs. For example, tennis players use wet-ice packed towels during match intervals in long hot matches.

figure 26.10 – are ice baths fun?

Ice baths
Ice baths (figure 26.10) use the fact that **chilling** the affected area can **reduce local inflammation**. Athletes use total immersion ice baths or cryogenic chambers to implement this therapy. The use of ice baths is very popular during the recovery phase of a training session as it assists in the removal of lactic acid (DOMS) and aids the healing process of damaged tissue.

Precautions should be taken because prolonged application (immersion) at very low temperatures could initiate frostbite!

Ice therapy and injury
The use of **cold therapy** in acute sports injuries as well as in rehabilitation of the injured athlete and injury prevention has become a generally accepted treatment method. Various cooling methods that are adjustable and compress the injured area are recommended.

Research has shown that the impact of injury is substantially reduced by the use of cold therapies. The sooner the cold therapy is used following injury, the more effective the therapy. The use of ice packs, ice towels, ice massage, frozen gel packs and ice baths are just a few examples of cold therapies that are used in acute sports injury treatments.

Resistance training with the use of mechanical specialist equipment

Resistance training equipment such as weight training **machines** or pulley machines (with stacks or hydraulics), are designed to add extra resistance to the performer through a range of motion. Many of these devices are designed to mimic the sports movement, which make the movement **specific** to the sport and so provide an alternative method of training.

Resistance aids form an integral part of land-based training drills for elite athletes such as swimmers, rowers and canoeists, as well as providing specialist equipment for individual athletes and team players.

A comprehensive range of specialised resistance training equipment is available such as pulleys, speed chutes, strength tubes and sledges.

The swim ergometer

Operates on a pulley system and **simulates swimming actions** on land. This pulley provides the tools necessary to develop aerobic endurance and anaerobic power for swimming without getting wet. An example of a type of swimbench is the expensive Vasa ergometer which is equipped with an electronic monitor that provides instant feedback on performance, including time, distance, pace, stroke rate, force, and power in watts. It features variable wind resistance that can be adjusted.

The rowing ergometer

The Concept II ergo rower is a specialist resistance training machine that has been used for this type of sport in the training and preparation of athletes for many years. More recently, indoor rowing has grown from a tool for off-the-water training for the serious rower to a sport in its own right.

Latex tubing

A cheaper alternative is for the athlete to use extendable latex tubes, which consist of tubes made of rubber with varying degrees of thickness and strength. This type of resistance training is known as **stretchcord resistance training** and the idea is to pull on the tube for the selected movement pattern.

Parachutes

Otherwise known as **speed chutes**, this type of resistance training device is towed behind a running athlete to provide resistance to forward motion. It is designed to improve maximal speed, start acceleration and speed endurance, and is used in a variety of sports where speed is an essential physical fitness component.

Towing sledges

A **towing sledge** is a training device, which includes a powder coated steel sledge and belt attached to a shoulder harness as shown in figure 26.11. The user is required to add weights to the sledge to vary the training load or intensity

figure 26.11 – sledge resistance

Sledge resistance training is thought to improve speed, acceleration and leg strength. However some studies have shown that during flat-out work there is an immediate extension of the knee joint at the beginning of the support phase on the ground. This means that a concentric contraction is applied early thereby eliminating the important eccentric contraction phase of the initial ground contact. This may be a significant disadvantage in the context of improving the sprinter's ability at maximum speed.

These examples of resistance aids can help reduce the tedium of training by adding variance to the training regime.

Practice questions

1) a) How does dehydration affect heart rate, body temperature and exercise performance? 3 marks

   b) How is body water balance maintained during prolonged aerobic exercise? 3 marks

   c) What are the potential benefits of using sports drinks? 3 marks

2) Give a brief outline and comment upon the following techniques, which may be employed in the belief that they will enhance sport performance: the use of recombinant human growth hormone (rHGH), gene doping, creatine supplementation and caffeine. In your answer highlight the potential risks known to be associated with the use of each of these techniques. 20 marks

3) Cryotherapy methods are used as aids to recovery and rehabilitation for the elite performer. Briefly describe how an ice bath can assist in this process. 3 marks

4) Briefly describe an illegal ergogenic aid that would be of benefit to an endurance athlete. How would the use of this aid help performance, what are the health risks and how is the aid detected? 7 marks

5) Discuss the use of legal ergogenic aids in their role of improving physical performance. In your answer explain the positive and negative effects of each aid you have chosen to write about. 20 marks

INDEX

INDEX